NEW VOICES: SELF-ADVOCACY BY PEOPLE WITH DISABILITIES

New Voices

Self-Advocacy by People with Disabilities

Gunnar Dybwad
Hank Bersani Jr.
Editors

Foreword by David Braddock
Introduction by Bob Williams

Brookline Books

ISBN 1-57129-004-4

Cover design, book design and typography by Erica Schultz.
Printed in Canada by Best Book Manufacturing/Imprimerie Gagné, Louiseville, Québec.

Library of Congress Cataloging-in-Publication Data
New voices : self-advocacy by people with disabilities / Gunnar
    Dybwad, Hank Bersani, Jr., editors.
         p.   cm.
    Includes bibliographical references and index.
    ISBN 1-57129-004-4 (pbk.)
    1. Mentally handicapped–Political activity.   2. Social advocacy.
I. Dybwad, Gunnar. II. Bersani, Hank A.
HV3004N45   1996
362..3–dc20   95-50279
                                        CIP

Published by
BROOKLINE BOOKS
P.O. Box 1047, Cambridge, Massachusetts 02238-1047

Contents

Foreword

David Braddock

DAVID BRADDOCK, PH.D., is Professor of Human Development and Director of the Institute on Disability and Human Development at the University of Illinois at Chicago. He was formerly President of the American Association on Mental Retardation (AAMR).

New Voices is a compelling story of courage, character, and leadership. It tells how, against immense odds, a handful of pioneers profoundly changed the field of intellectual disability around the world. In 1974, there were only 16 self-advocacy groups in the United States. Today, there are 743 groups active in 48 states. At least 20 states have statewide organizations, and last year a nationwide organization, Self-Advocates Becoming Empowered, was officially incorporated. I would estimate the number of active participants in formal self-advocacy groups in the United States to be in excess of 17,000 persons. Thousands more are participating around the world. A critical mass of membership has been established. A new and vital social and political force has been created. It will get stronger and stronger over the next generation, and a more appropriate and collaborative balance of power will evolve among professionals, consumers (self-advocates), and families.

This book will be a classic because the origins of the movement have never before been thoroughly described under one cover by self-advocates themselves. With contributions from leaders in Australia, Canada, Great Britain, New Zealand, Scandinavia, and the United States, the worldwide character of the movement is captured for the first time. It is exciting to read of the struggles and triumphs of Barbara Goode in Canada, Nancy Ward in Nebraska, Valerie Schaff in Oregon, Åke Johansson in Sweden, and many other self-advocacy leaders. Their successes remind professionals like myself that expectations play a big role in influencing personal achievement, and that IQ and the concept of mental age are of extremely limited utility in measuring human potential.

Self-advocacy challenges professionals to examine our propensity to control persons with intellectual disabilities. Our role—as clinicians, educators, advocates, and support workers—is most properly to facilitate the self-determination of persons with intellectual disabilities. It is not our role to substitute *our* sense of their needs for *their* sense of their needs and aspirations. An implicit assumption must be made that every person with an intellectual disability has the capacity to speak for himself or herself. Only by nurturing this capacity, however limited in scope it may be, can the true potential of an individual human being be realized.

Today, a new paradigm of support, participation, and inclusion of individuals with disabilities is replacing the old way of segregation and exclusion. Families of persons with intellectual limitations spearheaded adoption of the new paradigm, with significant assistance from enlightened professionals like Gunnar Dybwad and Hank Bersani Jr., the esteemed co-editors of this book. The self-advocacy movement has emerged from the new support paradigm primarily because the recent freedoms earned by people with intellectual disabilities to live, work, and create in the community has developed their self-esteem and personal competence beyond what most people imagined possible only a generation ago.

Professor Gunnar Dybwad, however, has a grand imagination. He has been telling professionals and families for 50 years to listen to what people with intellectual disabilities themselves have to say. He's also been repeatedly reminding us professionals that, in order to *hear* self-advocates' quiet and dignified voices, we must first stop talking so loudly. Then we must open our minds to the possibilities.

I am pleased that the American Association on Mental Retardation (AAMR) has recently been making progress in this regard. Change comes slowly to the world's oldest and largest interdisciplinary organization of professionals in the developmental disabilities field. But come it does. In 1988, the Association dropped the term "mental deficiency" from its name. This action was a commendable effort to try to reduce the stigma and pain caused by the "deficiency" label among consumers and families. Last year, for the first time in the Association's 120-year history, self-advocates began joining the Association and participating on the Board of Directors. Can it be very long before enough self-advocates join AAMR and bring about another name change? The "MR word" has become so painful for self-advocates that it is time for AAMR to adopt a more contemporary descriptor in its name, such as "intellectual disability" or "developmental disability." The movement to change AAMR's name this time will be led by the self-advocates!

AAMR has, to its credit, redefined the field conceptually by publishing its new *Manual on Terminology and Classification*. The signal contribution of this publication is the elucidation of the support paradigm. Thus, the 1992 *Manual* focuses not on a person's IQ, but rather on the kinds and intensity of support an individual needs to improve his or her quality of life. This multidimensional emphasis on environmental interaction instead of on a global numeric representation of "intelligence" is an important advance in the field.

New Voices documents an especially important advance in the field of intellectual disability. By recording the international evolution of self-advocacy from its inception in Sweden to the present day, Dybwad and Bersani present a milestone publication that will be consulted for years to come. I believe that Åke Johansson captures the voice of self-advocacy in Chapter Four when he speaks about the "positive consciousness" of being intellectually disabled. Positive consciousness of disability requires a confrontation with and acceptance of the presence of a disability in oneself. Confrontation and acceptance is difficult, yet at the same time it is existentially liberating. Positive consciousness allowed Åke to, as he puts it, "accept responsibility for myself... and to feel solidarity with other mentally handicapped people."

Åke's realization is no less profound than the existential insight of Sartre and Camus. In an age dominated by scientific rationalization and empiricism, Åke has grasped the meaning of his disability. He recognizes that merely what one *knows* is not very important. One must also *act*. With positive consciousness, Åke knows and he acts through his self-advocacy. Perhaps the Stanford-Binet could be revised to provide 50 bonus points for such brilliance!

The voice of self-advocacy has arrived, and it is here to stay. Read *New Voices* and listen to the crescendo of self-advocates rising up around the world.

— David Braddock, Ph.D.

November 1995
Chicago, Illinois

Preface

As in any volume of this size and scope, we as editors were forced to make some decisions in the production of this book. We trust that readers will understand our decisions.

A word about language: We support the use of "people first" language, and strive to represent people in positive manners. However, in several portions of this text, we refer to historical documents and old organizations. In this instances, we have preserved the terms that were in use at those points in history. We do not endorse these old labels, but we feel it is important to report the historical usage accurately.

Professional jargon and preferred terms vary from country to country. In collaborating with some 24 authors from 7 different nations, we have worked to preserve the diversity of these nations and authors by retaining certain terms as they are used in each country. We have attempted to clarify the usage for other readers by explaining how such terms relate to others used outside that nation.

We believe that readers of this book may find special interest in the words of self-advocates themselves, as opposed to those of us who are friends, advisors, and university researchers. For this reason, Section II of the book features the perspectives of self-advocates. In addition, throughout the text, the words of self-advocates appear **in a different typeface** to assist the reader. We have offered only minor editorial changes to the text written by self-advocates, and have not attempted to rewrite their words.

— Gunnar Dybwad
— Hank Bersani Jr.

November 1995
Wellesley Hills, Massachusetts
Salem, Oregon

Introduction

BOB WILLIAMS is currently Commissioner on Administration of Developmental Disabilities for the United States Department of Education. Selections from his 1989 book, In A Struggling Voice: Selected Poems of Robert Williams *(Washington, DC: Author), are reprinted throughout this volume.*

One of the most compelling needs and limitations we share as human beings is trying to label that which we do not fully understand. The labels "mentally retarded" and "self-advocate" are examples of this.

On the surface, both terms seem accurate and innocent enough. But look again, and I believe you will see that these labels — like all others — are at best stab-in-the-dark explanations of real and perceived differences in learning styles, abilities, life experiences and expectations.

It is only when we grapple with, throw off, and begin to erase our *own* mark of Cain that we begin to define ourselves, our prospects, and our possibilities completely anew. Not just in our own hearts and minds, but eventually in the hearts and minds of others: family, friends, and complete strangers.

This collection of oral histories and critical essays, so carefully compiled and edited by Gunnar Dybwad and Hank Bersani, represents an important crossroads on this journey. For, like signposts along the way, each turning page makes one thing increasingly clear: *The voices of those who tell their stories, and that of their shared struggle, are not new.*

What *is* new is our increased capacity to listen and to recognize that these voices for freedom and justice in the world are not unlike our own.

— Bob Williams

November 1995
Washington, D.C.

Section I

The Historical Setting

SPEAKING FOR OURSELVES

Chorus: We are speaking for ourselves
        Speaking for ourselves
        No one else can do as well
        Speaking for ourselves

Once I was afraid to speak
I was lonely, I was weak
With a voice so very small
That I had no voice at all

Chorus

Then I found a friend like me
And another made us three
And we laughed and then we cried
And then this is what we tried

Chorus

We've been called by many names
We've been made to feel ashamed
We've been locked behind a door
But we'll come outside once more

Chorus
Repeat Chorus

— *Karl Williams*
(see p. 30)

1

Setting the Stage Historically

Gunnar Dybwad

So much of the self-advocacy movement today is a reflection of the last 60 years of change. Here, Professor GUNNAR DYBWAD offers a unique personal insight into this history, and sets the stage for the rest of the book.

In 1930, Stanley P. Davies published a book entitled *Social Control of the Mentally Deficient*, the first comprehensive American text on that subject. In this work, Dr. Davies represented the then-prevailing view that strict social control and, where needed, indefinite confinement of people with mental deficiencies were required to protect society.

Sixty years later, a group of individuals from across the United States who had been labelled in their childhood as people with mental retardation met in Estes Park, Colorado, for the First North American People First Conference. There they appointed a national steering committee to plan a unifying organization, eventually to become known and incorporated as Self-Advocates Becoming Empowered.

In 1959, at about the halfway point of this sixty-year period, Stanley P. Davies published a radical revision of his original text, significantly retitled *The Mentally Retarded in Society* — a title which at that time reflected more his own changed, far more positive views than it did the actual conditions still prevailing throughout the country.

This chapter sketches the major developments which led from the years of social control, institutional confinement, segregation, repression and exclusion to the present self-assertiveness, empowerment, and organizational drive of those who reject the labels by which they were once known and now proudly consider themselves People First. The details of this organizational effort are reported in Chapter 17. As a point of reference, I want to cite here the definition of self-advocacy adopted in September 1991 by the Second Annual North American People First Conference in Nashville. Rejecting any reference to the depised "scientific" terminology of *mental retardation* or *mental handicap*, the group defined its cause as follows:

> Self-Advocacy is about independent groups of people with disabilities working together for justice by helping each other take charge of their lives and fight discrimination. It teaches us how to make decisions and choices that affect our lives so we can be more independent. It teaches us about our rights, but along with learning about our rights, we learn about our responsibilities. The way we learn about advocating for ourselves is supporting each other and helping each other gain confidence in themselves to speak out for what they believe in.

The Context

The late 1940s and early 1950s brought a strong revitalization in the fields of mental retardation and mental illness. The literature in the field, as well as research and practice, showed an interesting dichotomy. Mental illness was seen as an *adult* experience, while mental retardation was seen as a *childhood* problem, albeit one that extended way beyond the normal childhood years. Thus, the Canadian Film Board produced a mental retardation documentary entitled *Eternal Children*; Pearl Buck wrote a book about her daughter with the title *The Child Who Never Grew* (Buck, 1950). Numerous accounts in both the professional and popular literature related how both men and women confined in institutions were clothed and treated like young children. This misapprehension was greatly reinforced by the misunderstanding of what was so unfortunately referred to as an individual's *mental age* (MA): namely, that a person with a chronological age of twenty-two and a mental age of six would *"be"* – i.e., would act and react like – a child six years old. While to some degree this misconception of the "childlike" person with mental retardation lasts into the present, a distinct change began to be evident in the 1960s.

On the theoretical side, there was the seminal contribution of Henry Cobb, head of the Department of Psychology, University of South Dakota, who in October of 1960 presented a paper entitled "The Self-Concept of the Mentally Retarded" to the New England Institute of Mental Retardation. Dr. Cobb's paper was subsequently published in *The Rehabilitation Record* (Cobb, 1961). Equally significant, but unfortunately little known, was a New York State Interdepartmental Health Resources Board research report by Gerhard Saenger, *The Adjustment of Severely Retarded Adults in the Community*. This report was based on a large sample of children who had attended so-called low-IQ classes in New York City and whose subsequent adjustment as adults in the community was far more favorable than was generally anticipated in those days.

There was, in fact, considerable evidence gathering in the early 1960s contradicting the formulations of earlier decades concerning people with mental retardation. A brief sampling:

- Sarason and Gladwin (1958) cited evidence from studies at the Vineland State School that IQ scores among residents kept rising into their late 20's, belying the earlier dicta that scores on the Stanford-Binet would ceiling at 14 years — or (in a later version) at 16 years, or (still later) at 18 years.
- Ruby Kennedy (1948) reported that a large proportion of her sample of persons from special educational classes for the mentally retarded were gainfully employed in mainstreamed jobs after leaving school in Connecticut. A follow-up study ten years later (1960) indicated that many of these workers had progressed to higher-skilled jobs during this period.
- In recognition of these and many other such findings from varied sources, the President's Panel on Mental Retardation issued a booklet (1966) entitled *The Six Hour Retarded Child*, which recognized that many students were classified as retarded based on their performance in school, not in level of function in their community and family. Mercer and Lewis' SOMPA test (1977) sought to distinguish these students who were falsely identified as mentally retarded.

Two 1960 conferences contributed substantially to the recognition of the adult person with mental retardation. The first was the 35th Spring Conference of the Woods School, held in cooperation with the Massachusetts Special Commission on Retarded Children in Boston and entitled *Outlook for the Adult Retarded*. In a presentation on "Developing Patterns for Aid to the Aging Retarded and their Families," attention was called to the fact that the lengthening lifespan of persons with mental retardation was raising the eventual problem of a proper domicile in the community for such people. To highlight the inappropriateness of existing institutional facilities, the question was phrased, "Who shall be the innkeeper?" (Dybwad, 1960a).

The second national conference of significance in this context was the 1960 Golden Anniversary White House Conference on Children and Youth, where for the first time a specific question was raised about the legal status of the mentally retarded child and adult, particularly with reference to the degree of legal protection required as related to the degree of mental handicap. "A large number of retarded, by far the majority, are capable of moving about in the community, attending school, being employed or participating in formally organized or informal activities, yet by virtue of their being considered mentally retarded are considered not to have the minimum endowment for an independent life" (Dybwad, 1960b).

While it took many years for the Board and the general membership of the National Association for Retarded Children actually to drop the word *children*, it was already at the Tenth Anniversary Conference in 1960 that the concept of the

"eternal child" was challenged by raising the questions, "Are we retarding the retarded? Are we holding back their potential growth and maturation by limiting
their program to our narrow expectations?" (Dybwad, 1960c). And at the 1961
NARC conference, this point was put into even more specific form:

> Particularly as we deal increasingly with the adult retarded, the use of
> the words *educable retarded* and *trainable retarded* become more and more
> damaging, if not pernicious, because it simply labels the mentally re-
> tarded person for life on the basis of what we earlier judged his adjust-
> ment to be to a particular school situation. Surely most of you are aware
> that these were terms specifically selected to deal with a technical educa-
> tional situation — to what kind of school group a particular schoolchild
> should be assigned. It gives rise to concern if this kind of school classi-
> fication is now used in a broad general application to retardates of all
> ages, because if we have learned anything in the field of rehabilitation of
> the adult retarded, it is that we by no means can take school perfor-
> mance as a sure predictor of later vocational performance.
>
> It should be obvious that lack of attention to basic terminology makes
> it very difficult for us to communicate. One of our biggest problems
> right now is to establish communication between the field in which we
> first began most of our activities — that of schooling of the mentally
> retarded — and the newly developing field of programming for the adult
> retarded. (Dybwad, 1962)

In 1961 as well, the *American Journal of Public Health* carried an article entitled
"Rehabilitation for the Adult Retarded," which emphasized the same general theme
as follows:

> ...The community at large and public officials in the states have heard
> so much of the mentally retarded having the mentality of children — of
> well-meaning but so misleading labels as "eternal children" or "the un-
> finished child" — that there remains considerable hesitancy to recognize
> the retarded as adults, let alone as adults capable of sustained produc-
> tive effort (Dybwad, 1961).

Significantly, the article was preceded by this comment of the editor: "Rehabilitation of the retarded individual, especially of the adult, is a relatively new, yet important concern in community health work. For this reason, this presentation is especially welcome and is clearly of interest to public health workers" (Dybwad, 1961).
    Considering the general negative opinion in the professional community to-
ward persons with mental retardation — especially the general belief that they lack
insight and judgment — an article entitled "Sterilized Mental Defectives Look at

Eugenic Sterilization" (Sabagh & Edgerton, 1962), is significant because it reports verbatim the opinions of formerly institutionalized men and women regarding this operation. Unfortunately, since it was published in *Eugenics Quarterly*, it did not have a wide readership among people working in the field of mental retardation.

Noteworthy also is an article by Tobias and Cortazzo in the May 1963 *Training School Bulletin*, "Training Severely Retarded Adults for Greater Independence in Community Living," which definitely reflects recognition that the earlier view of the person with mental retardation as "childlike" and incapable of engaging in adult activities and relationships can no longer be justified.

In 1965, the Division of Mental Retardation in the Social and Rehabilitation Service of the U.S. Department of Health, Education and Welfare began planning a new program giving high school and college students a vacation experience in working with children and young adults with mental retardation. The project was subsequently titled SWEAT (Student Work Experience And Training). Eventually a large variety of such programs was established and funded in a number of states, all of them with one common theme: to have young volunteers interact in constructive ways with children and young adults with mental retardation. (United States Department of Health, Education and Welfare, 1967)

One such project was started in 1965 by the executive director of the Dallas [Texas] ARC, who organized a group of young people to be known as TARs (Teens Aid Retarded). The program quickly spread to other communities in Texas and to other states. In October of 1967, the National Association for Retarded Children sponsored the first National Youth Conference on Mental Retardation in Portland, Oregon, and the second in October 1968 in Detroit, Michigan. Following that conference, a new national organization was created with the name Youth-NARC. National guidelines were adopted by the Youth-NARC steering committee and subsequently approved by the NARC board. The first point listed on the statement of purpose was, "To serve as a friend of mentally retarded persons... to help the retarded learn to live in, work in, and attempt to better his world" (National Association for Retarded Children [NARC], 1968).

At the third National Youth Conference on Mental Retardation, sponsored by Youth-NARC October 9-12, 1969, in Miami, astonishing progress was in evidence. A panel of young adults with mental retardation discussed their personal reaction to programs offered them. This kind of active participation, a new departure to be sure, was undoubtedly a response in part to the *Youth-NARC Orientation Handbook*, issued that same year, which had the following suggestions relative to working with adults:

> Talk to him. Listen to him. Find out what he thinks, how he feels, what he wants to do.
>
> Help him to be part of the bigger world. Arrange recreation activities

for the adults alone, rather than including them in programs for the youngsters. Teach him to bowl or skate or fish and encourage him to plan suitable leisure time activities for himself.

Help him to understand what is expected of him in public places, how to pay a restaurant bill, wait his turn at a bowling alley, behave at parties. Help him to learn the bus route from his home to his job or to the workshop. Encourage him to do everything he can for himself.

(NARC, 1969)

It was reported at that time that more than 70,000 people between the ages of 13 and 25 were involved in Youth-NARC projects.

On the international scene, a Symposium of Volunteers in October 1971 — arranged by the International League of Societies for the Mentally Handicapped (ILSMH) and co-sponsored by the President's Committee on Mental Retardation, NARC and the DHEW Social and Rehabilitation Services — had a panel session on the youth volunteer composed of Ray Beechey (President, Youth Across Canada with the Mentally Retarded), Inger Claeson (Youth Volunteer with FUB, the Swedish parent association), and Mary Lou Nappi (Pennsylvania Youth Association for Retarded Children). While their main focus was on training for youth volunteers, one point put forth was: "The retarded themselves may be trained in leadership. Seminars are organized which develop the skills of social interaction with the non-retarded" (PCMR, 1972). In spite of the large numbers of participants and the obvious significance of the nationwide and international activity, it appears to have been largely forgotten. Yet there is no doubt that it contributed substantially to the eventual developments in the self-advocacy field.

When the President's Panel on Mental Retardation submitted its report "A Proposed Program for National Action to Combat Mental Retardation" in 1962, it contained no specific reference to the individual rights of persons with mental retardation. However, this was decisively remedied in 1967 when the International League of Societies for the Mentally Handicapped convened a symposium in Stockholm on *Legislative Aspects of Mental Retardation*. The symposium was composed of prominent experts from seven European countries and the U.S. The published *Conclusions* (International League of Societies for the Mentally Handicapped [ILSMH], 1967) included a section on Individual Rights with the following introductory paragraph:

The symposium considered that no examination of the legislative aspects of the problem of mental retardation would be complete without general consideration being given to the basic rights of the mentally retarded, not only from the standpoint of their collective rights and those of their families, but also from that of the individual rights of the retarded person as a human being.

There followed an enumeration of rights such as the right to choose a place to live, to engage in leisure-time activities, to preserve the physical and psychological integrity of this person, to vote, to marry, to have children, and to be given a fair trial for any alleged offense. This was followed by several sections dealing with the implementation of these rights.

When these conclusions of the Stockholm symposium were reported to the ILSMH's Fourth International Congress in Jerusalem in October of 1968, it was decided to appoint a committee to transpose those recommendations into a Declaration of General and Special Rights of the Mentally Retarded. This was done — but some of the more conservative members of this committee decided to leave out the references to marriage and childbearing. Obviously this was not yet acceptable to the more conservative of the parents. (ILSMH, 1968)

The Declaration was otherwise received very favorably, and the League's member association in France was so well impressed that they went to the French delegation to the United Nations and suggested that this Declaration be submitted to the United Nations. Thus it was introduced to and approved by, in turn, the Social Development Committee at the United Nations, the U.N. Economic and Social Council, and the League's General Assembly, which adopted it on the 21st of January, 1972, without a dissenting vote. There was one important editorial change recommended by the U.N. staff, of great significance in this context: the title was changed to "Declaration on the Rights of Mentally Retarded *Persons*," a most fitting addition considering the message the Declaration was trying to convey (United Nations, 1971).

Questions are often raised as to the significance of United Nations declarations, in terms of the actual legal situation in the various countries. It deserves to be mentioned, therefore, that in *Wyatt v. Stickney* (1972), Judge Johnson of the Federal District Court in central Alabama referred specifically to this U.N. Declaration to underline his finding that significant changes had occurred in the field of mental retardation which called into question the prevailing practices in state institutions.

At this point, consideration must be given to a decisive influence originating in Sweden. At the first Congress of the International Association for the Scientific Study of Mental Deficiency (IASSMD), held in 1967 in Montpelier, France, Bengt Nirje — Executive Director of FUB, the Swedish association of parents of children with mental handicaps — presented a report of the work he had done with a group of adolescents with mental retardation. The group had gone from Sweden on a vacation trip to Italy and had done remarkably well in managing the challenges of traveling in a foreign country. It was in this presentation that Nirje related for the first time how "In Scandinavia we usually say that the aim is to give the mentally retarded an existence as close to the normal one as possible — in their daily life and in the regular community" (Nirje, 1967). Two years later, in 1969, at the eleventh World Congress of the International Society of Rehabilitation of the Disabled meeting in Dublin, Ireland, Bengt Nirje presented the paper "Toward Independence," in which he reported that the Swedish Parents' Association had instituted a weekend course in parliamentary procedure techniques for sixteen mentally retarded young adults.

He reported that the year before, the Swedish Parents' Association had arranged a national conference of young adults active in some of their clubs. This gave the young adults an opportunity to discuss among themselves, and bring out their own views on, activities and matters which concerned them: leisure-time activities, vocational training, employment and wages of the sheltered workshops, and vacation questions (Nirje, 1969). Nirje's presentation was met with considerable interest by the international audience, and subsequently was credited with leading to similar meetings of adults with mental retardation in other countries.

England was the first country to follow through with a conference sponsored by the Spastics Society and organized by the Campaign for the Mentally Handicapped in July of 1972. The proceedings, published under the title *Our Life: A Conference Report* (Shearer, 1972), were the first such documentation.

Canada had its first conference in British Columbia in 1973. Several people from Oregon attended and in turn, in 1974, organized their own meeting with participation from the neighboring state of Washington. In following up on this first conference, people there decided to create an organization, and they adopted the name People First. In 1978, G. Allan Roeher addressed the Annual Conference of the Canadian Association for the Mentally Retarded with words that are of particular relevance today:

> There is no clear alternative to the volunteer in some human service areas. Only the experienced parent can help the new parent, in a way no other can — and this leads to Pilot Parent programs and the growth of new leadership. Only the unpaid volunteer can be a true citizen advocate, and the growth of Citizen Advocacy programs provided another source of new leadership potential. Only a dedicated teen volunteer can mobilize the brothers and sisters and friends of mentally retarded people — and challenge them. Only young people can truly relate to our young mentally retarded citizens. Only mentally retarded people can organize themselves in *People First* organizations...."

Matters developed somewhat differently in Massachusetts, where there was a very active program of Youth-NARC. A proposal was submitted to the Oettinger Foundation for a grant to initiate a project, sponsored by Youth-NARC, that would facilitate a self-advocacy conference and follow-up services by a consultant. The grant was received in 1973, and the first statewide conference was held in 1974.

A project of a quite different nature developed in Nebraska, the brainchild of a man who had spent many years in the state institution for persons with mental retardation. His name was Raymond Loomis, and his goal was to organize a project that would create greater visibility and opportunities for persons with mental retardation. He had no doubt about the importance of the ENCOR program of community services that had been developed in Omaha, and so, considering that to be Project I, he decided to call his own creation Project II. His introductory statement includes these sentences:

> We believe people should be treated like human beings — with kindness and love....
>
> We also believe that all the people should be moved out of Beatrice [the state institution] into their own communities. We believe that all people, no matter how handicapped they are, can live in their own communities. We think that the money that is being spent right now to keep people in Beatrice should be spent to bring them back here.
>
> We are Project II, a group who believes that we are people first and our handicaps come second.... We know that people can be served humanely in their own communities. We urge the people of Nebraska to support these programs. We intend to keep fighting for our goals. In the next few months, we will be speaking to community organizations and on talk shows. We will also be talking to our state senators about our experiences and our concerns. (Loomis, 1975)

Project II proved to be very effective in developing community programs, leisure-time activities, and a program of active "problem solving" workshops.

1977 saw the publication of a self-advocacy curriculum developed by the Wisconsin Association for Retarded Citizens and the Wisconsin Coalition for Advocacy, signifying that agencies in the field now recognized the great potential of that new activity (Hellgren & Norseman, 1977). The following year, the Office for Developmental Disabilities in Washington issued an RFP (Request For Proposals) for a project to organize People First groups across the nation. People First of Oregon submitted an application, feeling assured that as the oldest, most experienced group in the country, they had a good chance to be awarded the grant. They were very indignant when it was eventually announced that the grant had been awarded to the Bureau of Child Research at the University of Kansas, Lawrence. When People First of Oregon protested the decision, the federal agency pointed out that the University wrote a good proposal, with "credible," "realistic" methodology, which indicated that it would be able to carry out the purposes of the grant within reasonable time limits. Clearly, the problem was that the federal agency used a traditional yardstick appropriate for established social agencies — but lacked the vision to recognize the need for different criteria in order to judge the pioneering proposal of a group of self-advocates.

The strong legislative and policy developments of the 1960s and 1970s led to a new chorus of voices for self-advocacy in the 1980s. It started with the June 1980

World Congress of Rehabilitation International in Winnipeg, Manitoba. On the first day of the conference, a large number of participants with disabilities protested that the Congress, in spite of their earlier demands, had continued to neglect the needs and representation of the disabled community. This protest resulted not only in changes to the structure of Rehabilitation International, but also in the establishment of a new worldwide organization known as Disabled People International (DPI), a strong new international presence in self-advocacy (Driedger, 1989).

There is no question that Canada's delegation to that Congress contributed materially to this successful protest action. And Canada scored again the following year, in 1981, when self-advocates from the People First movement established themselves as a definite factor in the field of public policy. At issue, once again, was sterilization, based on a mother's concern that her adolescent daughter with an intellectual disability might become pregnant by her boyfriend. The authority to petition for and to arrange sterilization of a person with a disability became a judicially disputed issue which eventually came before the Canadian Supreme Court.

When it was suggested that the Canadian Association for Community Living assume a public position and offer testimony in court in opposition to the proposed sterilization, the Board hesitated to do so. Several years earlier, the Association had dropped the words "mentally retarded" from its name at the insistence of its Consumer Advisory Board, composed of persons with intellectual handicaps. So when People First of Canada became aware of the Association's hesitancy to face the issue of sterilization, they asked their legal advisor to arrange for them to be heard in court. This was done, and so another milestone was reached: People First, an association of persons formerly judged to be incompetent "eternal children," was now accepted and given a voice as *amicus curiae*, "friend of the court," in Canada's highest tribunal.

In 1982, the International League of Societies for Persons with Mental Handicaps had its 8th World Congress in Nairobi, Kenya. For the first time, the program accommodated self-advocates by allowing them to assume full responsibility for the morning plenary session on the fourth day. A panel of eight participants from Germany, France, the U.S., Sweden, and Gaza made presentations and subsequently (with the help of an interpreter) fielded questions directed at them from the international audience of seven hundred people. The session was chaired by Kevin Tracy, who had developed this skill through several years of chairing meetings of self-advocates for the Texas Association for Retarded Citizens. The international audience was amazed how sensibly their questions were answered by the panel — some even with a nice sense of humor. On the last day of the congress, John Randolph, a man from New Jersey who had spent decades in a closed institution, was chosen by the self-advocates to present some recommendations to the League's General Assembly (see box, next page).

Two years later, at the invitation of People First of Washington, the first international self-advocacy leadership conference was held in Tacoma, Washington, with

RECOMMENDATIONS

Thank you Mr. President for the opportunity to present the recommendations of our group of persons with mental handicap. We think it was a good Congress, and at the next Congress, we would like to meet again.

We recommend that more countries participate in our program, and that one day, before the regular program begins, we would meet to get organized and to get to know each other.

We see ourselves as equal partners and would like to be on the regular program committee too. More people with mental handicaps should be invited to serve on committees and to take part in discussions.

We would like everyone to speak slowly so that we can understand. Sometimes the speeches are too long and too technical.

The topic of our program each day should be the topic to be discussed the next day by the Congress. It is important that we be called adults, and that we be treated like everyone else.

We will need money if we are to be effective. Our national associations should sponsor people with mental handicap to come to the Congress. Each national and local association should have persons with mental handicap on their board.

The League should help each country promote groups like "People First" in their country. All Congresses of the League should be held in buildings where people in wheelchairs can move freely.

Next Congress, we would like to meet again to explain what it means to be mentally handicapped and what it does not mean.

I thank you.

(ILSMH, 1982)

participants from Australia, Canada, England, New Zealand, and the United States. The conference's theme well described the proceedings: "Speaking Up and Speaking Out" (People First of Washington, 1984). The group decided to meet again in four years, and indeed, the second international self-advocacy leadership conference met in September 1989 in London, England. Major themes at that conference were labeling, employment, housing, and most of all, leadership.

These international developments in self-advocacy were underlined in a book written jointly by Paul Williams of England and Bonnie Shoultz of the United States. Entitled *We Can Speak For Ourselves*, it contained a comprehensive review of self-advocacy developments up to that time (Williams & Shoultz, 1983). The authors' message was loud and clear and, indeed, was reflected in the name of Pennsylvania's statewide self-advocacy group, Speaking For Ourselves.

Meanwhile, the influence of the parent groups was not waning. New developments in the provision of services stressing individual approaches created new and significant roles for parents. Indeed, this was described as the "rediscovery of the family" (Dybwad, 1982).

In 1984, People First of California published a manual with the challenging title *Surviving in the System: Mental Retardation and the Retarding Environment* – a significant but definitely unintended reference to the aforementioned 1960 NARC presentation "Are We Retarding The Retarded?" The sophistication of the manual's title was matched by the group's decision to have the draft of its manual put into proper English form by a person skilled in writing, but not acquainted with the field of mental retardation or any organizations related to it. Altogether, the aggressive tone of the manual contrasts significantly with the *Self-Advocacy Work Book* produced by the Technical Assistance for Self-Advocacy Project at the University of Kansas, together with an *Advisor's Guide Book* – carefully and professionally done, but for that reason less representative of the groups for whom it was written.

By this time, in the mid-1980s, hundreds of groups of self-advocates were meeting in the USA on a local, regional, or state level. Two gatherings deserve a special mention. They took place in Princeton, New Jersey, in 1986 and in Stamford, Connecticut, in 1987, with a very special arrangement: half of the participants were "self-advocates" (people with developmental disabilities), and half were "advocates," or people without apparent disabilities (including heads of state programs and agencies). The special feature of these two conferences was that each self-advocate roomed with an advocate, creating an unusual atmosphere of closeness and communication. The self-advocates' new spirit of independence and self-assertiveness was mixed with a nice sense of humor and a bit of sarcasm; these came into full view at the 1986 conference when many of them sported large lapel buttons saying **Mildly Normal, Moderately Normal, Severely Normal,** or **Profoundly Normal.**

It was at this same conference that Bernard Carabello – well known for his significant role in exposing the horrors of Willowbrook (Rothman & Rothman, 1984) – pointed to a puzzling question by asking, **"How long do I have to be a** *self-advocate* **before I can become an** *advocate?"*

Very clearly, the self-advocacy movement was gaining strength and self-confidence. The most cogent demonstration of this came in 1988, when the residents of the Southbury Training School in Connecticut, in open disagreement with the parents who wanted to keep the institution open indefinitely, called a press conference without the knowledge of the institution's administration. To the assembled reporters they gave a strong and unequivocal message: *We want out!* Their well-planned effort to gain public attention was rewarded by ample press coverage both locally and nationally.

The 1990s

The decade of the '90s has brought a strong consolidation of the self-advocacy movement both nationally and internationally. In the fall of 1990, four hundred people from thirty-eight states and two Canadian provinces met in Estes Park, Colorado, at the first North American People First Conference. It quickly became obvious that in the minds of many of the participants coming from all around the country, there was a desire to create a national organization. For this purpose, they established a pattern of five regions, with two delegates from each region creating a national steering committee. (Actually, only four of the regions were ready to vote; the Pacific region felt they were not yet sufficiently coordinated to take that step.) The Steering Committee was charged with working out the details for a national organization and bringing a report to the second annual North American People First Conference, scheduled for the fall of 1991 in Nashville, Tennessee. That conference attracted more than eight hundred self-advocates from across the United States and Canada.

This was the first time that such a large group of self-advocates had met in a metropolitan hotel with a program that provided for simultaneous sessions, discussion groups, and regional meetings. Nevertheless, the conference ran so smoothly that on the last day, at the end of the luncheon, the *maitre d'* had all his staff come up on the stage and, as a group, express thanks for having had the privilege of serving this conference. During the conference it had been decided to follow the usual national pattern of having nine regions, so the Steering Committee was now composed of eighteen regional representatives. The Steering Committee that had been appointed at the Colorado meeting the year before had prepared ten recommendations as guidelines for the establishment of a national organization.

In 1992, international concerns came to the fore in a seminar on self-advocacy in Vancouver, British Columbia, sponsored jointly by the International League of Societies for Persons with Mental Handicaps, the Canadian Association for Community Living, and People First of Canada. Self-advocates were present from Canada, the Netherlands, Sweden, Mexico, and Argentina. Later, in October 1992, Barb Goode of Canada had the unusual distinction of addressing the General Assembly of the United Nations as a representative of the International League, which as an accredited "NGO," or Non-Governmental Organization, had the privilege on that occasion to take the floor.

The year 1992 also produced a new manual with the provocative title *No More BS! A Realistic Survival Guide for Disability Rights Activists*, produced by People First of Washington and advertised as "straight shooting! myth bashing, tell-it-like-it-is, real life!" The strident tone of the book was indicative of the growing self-confidence within the self-advocacy movement in its determination to free itself from long-established prejudices, discriminatory practices, and paternalism (Medgyesi, 1992).

1993 brought the third International Self-Advocacy Conference to Toronto, Ontario. Thirteen hundred people from some thirty countries around the globe were in attendance, including a large group from Japan who brought their own interpreters. The Program Committee introduced some significant innovations, such as brief ten-minute keynote speeches followed by lengthy discussions, a reversal of what is usually the case. For the considerable number of self-advocates who were attending their first large conference, the committee had arranged numerous small discussion groups, limited to twelve self-advocates with no outsiders allowed, in small rooms to facilitate active involvement by all present. On the other hand, buffet lunches and formal dinners were served to thirteen hundred participants in the large ballroom without a hitch. Again, as eleven years earlier in Nairobi, it was astonishing how well participants were able to communicate with each other in spite of the language barriers.

Also in 1993, the International League of Societies for Persons with Mental Handicap – now known as Inclusion International – established a Committee on Self-Advocacy comprised of self-advocates from several countries and chaired by Barb Goode of Canada (see Chapter 3). They produced a significant publication entitled *The Beliefs, Values, and Principles of Self-Advocacy* (ILSMH, 1995) which in clear, simple language sets forth the essence of the "People First" Movement:

Beliefs and Values
- Being a person first
- Being able to make our own decisions
- Believing in my value as a person
- Having other people believe in you as a person

Principles
- Empowerment
- Equal opportunity
- Learning and living together
- Non-labelling

These are the Beliefs, Values and Principles of the Self-Advocacy Committee of the International League of Societies for Persons with Mental Handicap. We would like all members of the ILSMH to understand that we want them to be adopted so that we can continue to help others and advocate for our rights.

Always aware of its major mission – teaching their fellows – the Committee added these explanations:

Beliefs and Values: Things of the heart you believe in.
Principles: Guidelines that we follow in making decisions.

(ILMSH, 1995)

The Third National Self-Advocacy Conference (no longer styled as "North American") met in 1993 in Alexandria, Virginia, with the title *Self-Advocacy: Voices for Choices*. Later that year, with a grant from the Joseph P. Kennedy Jr. Foundation, the new national organization — now known as Self-Advocates Becoming Empowered — issued a publication with the title *Taking Place: Standing Up and Speaking Out About Living in Our Communities*. The final section is entitled "What Would We Like to See Happen In Our Communities By The Year 2000 That Are Not Happening Now." Among them were:

- Supported employment and real jobs for everyone... no more sheltered workshops!
- A service system where the money follows the person and where the person gets what they say they need (not others say they need).
- To have professionals get their act together by the year 2000 so they actually be supportive. (Self-Advocates Becoming Empowered, 1993)

1994 also brought a literary event, the publication of *Count Us In: Growing Up with Down Syndrome* by Jason Kingsley and Mitchell Levitz, two more "Voices for Choices."

Self-Advocates Becoming Empowered is now duly incorporated in Louisiana, with bylaws that were passed in April of 1994. At their meeting in January of 1995, the Steering Committee elected three national advisors for three-year terms. This demonstrated how speedily the self-advocacy movement was proceeding in its organizational efforts. The ground had been broken only a few years earlier when forward-looking parent associations established consumer advisory boards to provide self-advocates with some degree of participation and consultation. And now the recipients of that generosity turned the tables and, on their part, officially arranged for participation and consultation by a small group of outsiders.

In Conclusion

In the first half of this 20th century, strange contradictory views of persons with mental retardation were in evidence. One view saw them as objects of pity, "holy innocents," "angels unaware," and children who never grew. On the other hand, professionals from the social sciences and government officials were apt to see them as a potential criminal element, sexually dangerous, and incapable of contributing to society.

The second half of the century saw decisive change. From its sporadic, tentative beginnings in the 1970s, self-advocacy in the 1990s has become a policy-forming reality in public and private efforts to deal with the challenges posed by persons with intellectual limitations. Furthermore, it has brought forth a well-organized, internationally connected movement that provides an ever-growing voice to what was, until the recent past, a universally rejected minority among a nation's minorities. Indeed, on September 26, 1995, Judge Jon Phipps McGella of the U.S. District Court for the Western District of Tennessee issued a ruling certifying – over the protest of the Tennessee authorities – that People First of Tennessee was qualified to represent the residents of the Arlington Developmental Center in suing for the closure of that state institution.

Thus, people with intellectual impairments have – *in my lifetime* – gone from "feebleminded patients" to empowered agents of social change. They work to make the world better not just for themselves, but for the rest of us as well.

References

Buck, P.S. (1950). *The child who never grew.* New York: John Day Co.

Cobb, H. (1961). Self-concept of the mentally retarded. *Rehabilitation Record, 2*(3).

Davies, S.P. (1930). *Social control of the mentally deficient.* New York: Crowell.

Davies, S.P. (1959). *The mentally retarded in society.* New York: Columbia University Press.

Driedger, D. (1989). *The last civil rights movement.* New York: St. Martin's Press.

Dybwad, G. (1960a). Developing patterns for aid to the aging retarded and their families. In *Proceedings of the 1960 Woods Schools Conference,* Langhorne, PA: The Woods Schools.

Dybwad, G. (1960b). Trends and issues in mental retardation. In *Children and Youth in the 1960s.* Washington, DC: Golden Anniversary White House Conference on Children and Youth.

Dybwad, G. (1960c). Are we retarding the retarded? In *Challenges in mental retardation.* New York: Columbia University Press.

Dybwad, G. (1961). Rehabilitation of the adult retardate. *American Journal of Public Health,* 51: 998-1004.

Dybwad, G. (1962). *Old worlds and new challenges.* New York: National Association for Retarded Children.

Dybwad, G. (1982). The rediscovery of the family. *Mental Retardation* (Canada), *32*(1), 18-36.

Hellgren, B., & Norseman, A. (1977). *Life, liberty and the pursuit of happiness: A self-advocacy curriculum.* Madison, WI: Wisconsin Association for Developmental Disabilities.

International League of Societies for the Men- tally Handicapped [ILSMH] (1967). *Legislative aspects of mental retardation: Conclusions, Stockholm symposium.* Brussels: Author.

International League of Societies for the Mentally Handicapped [ILSMH] (1968). *From charity to rights: Fourth international congress - Jerusalem 1968.* Brussels: Author.

International League of Societies for Persons with Mental Handicaps [ILSMH] (1995). *The beliefs, values, and principles of self-advocacy.* Cambridge, MA: Brookline Books.

Kennedy, R.J.R. (1948). *The social adjustment of morons in a Connecticut city.* Hartford, CT: Mansfield-Southbury Training Schools (Social Service Department).

Kennedy, R.J.R. (1960). *A follow-up appraisal of the post-school status of the educable mentally retarded.* Connecticut State Department of Health.

Kingsley, J., & Levitz, M. (1994). *Count us in: Growing up with Down syndrome.* New York: Harcourt Brace & Co.

Loomis, R. (1975). Project II statement. In P. Williams & B. Shoultz, *We can speak for ourselves.* Cambridge, MA: Brookline Books (1983).

Medgyesi, V. (1992). *No more BS! A realistic survival guide for disability rights activists.* Clarkston, WA: People First of Washington.

Mercer, J.R., & Lewis, T.F. (1977). SOMPA. Psychological Corporation.

National Association for Retarded Children (1968). *State and local unit guidelines for Youth-NARC.* New York: Author.

National Association for Retarded Children (1969). *Youth-NARC orientation handbook.* New

York: Author.

Nirje, B. (1967). Integrational Swedish programs in social training. In *The adolescent retardate*. Jerusalem: Akim.

Nirje, B. (1969). *Toward independence*. Paper presented at the 11th World Congress on Rehabilitation, Dublin.

People First of Washington (1984). *Speaking up and speaking out: An international self-advocacy movement*. Tacoma, WA: Author.

President's Committee on Mental Retardation (1972). Report of international symposium on volunteers. Washington, DC: DHEW Publication No. (05)72-41

President's Panel on Mental Retardation (1962). *A proposed program for national action to combat mental retardation*. Washington, DC: Author.

President's Panel on Mental Retardation (1966). *The six hour retarded child*. Superintendent of Documents.

Rothman, D.J., & Rothman, S.M. (1984). *The Willowbrook war*. New York: Harper & Row.

Sabagh, G., & Edgerton, R.B. (1962). Sterilized mental defectives look at eugenic sterilization. *Eugenics Quarterly, 9*(4), 213-222.

Saenger, G. (1959). *The adjustment of severely retarded adults in the community*. Albany, NY: New York State Interdepartmental Health Resources Board.

Sarason, S.B., & Gladwin, T. (1958). Psychological and cultural problems in mental subnormality. In Masland, Sarason & Gladwin, *Mental subnormality*. New York: Basic Books.

Self-Advocates Becoming Empowered (1993). *Taking place: Standing up and speaking out about living in our communities*. Author.

Shearer, A. (1972). *Our life: A conference report*. London: Campaign for the Mentally Handicapped.

Tobias & Cortazzo (1963). Training severely retarded adults for greater independence in community living. *Training School Bulletin*, May.

United Nations (1971). General Assembly, Resolution 2856 (XXVI). Adopted 12-20-1971.

United States Department of Health, Education and Welfare (1967). *We are concerned: Three youth programs for the mentally retarded*. Washington, DC: Superintendent of Documents.

Williams, P., & Shoultz, B. (1983). *We can speak for ourselves: Self-advocacy by mentally handicapped people*. Cambridge, MA: Brookline Books.

Wyatt v. Stickney (1972). 344F. Supp. 387 (MD Alabama, 1972).

2

Self-Advocates On The Move

A Journalist's View

Robert Perske

ROBERT PERSKE is a journalist and freelance author who is well known for his work about people labeled as "mentally retarded." Although Bob maintains a rigorous writing schedule for his own books, he graciously agreed to share with us some of his reflections from his life working and advocating alongside self-advocates.

Trying to define the self-advocacy movement is like trying to hold back a river with one's hand. It just keeps moving.

Such a movement by persons with developmental disabilities was unthinkable three decades ago. Then, in the late 1960s, in defiance of all professional standards, small pockets of persons with disabilities began organizing and trying to speak for themselves. Their first attempts were ragged, but they kept trying. Today these persons represent themselves with a sophistication and confidence that amaze us all. No one even tries to project what these groups will be doing in ten years!

Even so, some professionals are driven (or funded) to create charts showing the sequential steps one takes to become a self-advocate. Others engage in projects to define self-advocacy and to measure its progress. The movement, however, just keeps flowing over every educated attempt to corner it and classify it.

So how does one even begin to understand this rapidly changing, always-flowering thing called self-advocacy? By watching it — simply *watching* it.

What follows is a series of brief journalistic reports all strung on a chronological line. No attempt is made to be comprehensive or to analyze or to interpret. The purpose is merely to *show* what self-advocates have done in the past and how such rich nonconformist activities increase with each year.

An Unwitting Shutdown of the Human Spirit

This writer remembers working in institutions in the latter 1950s and the 1960s, long before self-advocacy became a fact. Large numbers of people with the same kinds of disabilities were housed together in these out-of-the-way places. The tasks of a good worker were clear and without equivocation:

- A good worker became the unquestioned mouthpiece for his or her "patients" ("We speak for those who cannot speak for themselves").
- A good worker made oft-repeated use of a single adjective, *appropriate* ("Joe, it's not appropriate for you to speak now," or "Sally, your behavior is inappropriate").
- A good worker hewed to the common denominator ("Bill, if I let you have this special privilege, then everyone on the ward will want it, too).
- A good worker utilized a herd mentality ("C'mon, gang. Let's head 'em up and move 'em out. We have five minutes to get to the dining hall").
- A good worker knew how to force the right choice ("James, if you straighten up you can stay in the day room. If you don't, we'll put you in the seclusion room. It's up to you").
- A good worker offered a badly paved, one-way street called *benevolence* ("We must always give to you, but we refuse to let you give to us").

Picture to yourself dorms for males and dorms for females — separated by expanses of grass. Picture a new innovation in the 1960s, the Saturday Night Dance, with visitors from surrounding towns coming to watch. Picture also a goodly number of institutional staff members being ordered to attend the dance as well. Specially trained staff members "worked" the dancing patients like cutting horses, employing the "one-two-three rule": A worker walked past a couple dancing too close. "Not so close," the smiling worker would say *sotto voce*, "This is warning number one." Any close dancers continuing until they got a smile and "number three" knew they would be restricted from dances for six months.

Don't picture it, but try to think about males who were castrated when they began to masturbate. Think about females being sterilized shortly after menstruation.

Think about people whose teeth were pulled for biting.

Think about "patients" lining up for medications prescribed not so much for their health, but to keep them docile and under control.

As painful and unbelievable as it may now seem, try to sense the clash between the formal inservice training of new workers and the everyday peer-group training on the wards. There was a day not too long ago when some veteran workers proudly called themselves *bughousers*. They expounded their own curriculum to young workers who took in their authoritative-sounding statements like baby birds in a nest.

("I remember the days when we only needed two drugs," one bughouser said. "If someone got too high, we knocked them out with chloral hydrate. If they got depressed, we cleaned them out with epsom salt." "It was those conscientious objectors during World War II who really messed things up," another said. "They were too soft. They never could control a ward like we could").

The Longing to Be Useful

On a Sunday evening in October 1963, Jimmy Briggs, a nine-year-old with severe disabilities, wandered away from an institution and became lost in the woods nearby. All off-duty personnel received calls to get to the institution as fast as they could. Everyone met in a large meeting room and received search assignments. As the staff members moved out, Ray King and Elmer Abernathy, two teenagers who lived at the institution, stopped this writer and asked if they could look for Jimmy, too. The superintendent was consulted. He pondered the situation for a moment, then said, "They can go if they stay close to you."

Ray and Elmer found Jimmy.

During the institution's Thanksgiving pageant, the superintendent called the boys to the stage. He presented them with certificates of appreciation for finding Jimmy.

Everyone cheered.

Much, however, remained unsaid: Ray and Elmer knew almost every hill, gully and tree in that wooded area. They moved out quickly that night. The real trick was to stay close to them! Better than 60 able-bodied teenagers like Ray and Elmer lived at the institution. They knew these woods, too. After all, the institution's recreation department used this area for hikes and campouts.

The Dignity of Risk

STOCKHOLM, SWEDEN, NOVEMBER 8, 1969. Ten persons with mental retardation and six university students — all good friends — came together for a special adventure. They met in a small room on the second story of a downtown building. They sat down and reviewed all of their plans for the day. Then down to the street they went. They moved through winding streets until they came to the Swedish Royal Theatre.

An employee greeted them. Together they moved to the dressing room of Anita Bjork, the star of the currently-running play *Karlson on the Roof.* They presented the actress a bouquet of flowers. She visited with them in a relaxed and gracious manner for at least 15 minutes. Then for the next two hours, with the employee leading, the group of friends moved frontstage and backstage, into every nook and cranny of the theatre.

They saw the set workshops. They looked at costumes. They examined the harness used by Karlson when he flew off the roof. One member was strapped into the rigging and the others pulled him along the cable. They even climbed up to the catwalks five stories above the stage and watched the workers below. It was a danger-ous perch, but everyone wanted to go up.

Leaving the theatre, the sixteen went to a coffee shop and discussed all that they had experienced. Everyone decided they wanted to see the play at a later date. So, right then and there, they began making a checklist of preparations. As they left, the group decided not to return to the club. They agreed to break up at this new and strange location and each find his or her own way home.

Later, Bengt Nirje, the director of the Swedish association for persons with retardation and the creator of the club system, explained what had just taken place. The system consists of 24 loosely organized clubs of 20 members each. Half the members of each club are persons with retardation; the other half are university students. Most of these small bands met at the same second-story room at different times.

The Nirje-designed guidelines for the clubs are interesting. There is no leader. Persons can only be members-in-full-standing after proving they can travel to and from the club on their own. For some this takes help and practice. Each excursion contains three separate movements: a meeting for talking and planning, going on the adventure, and a meeting for talking about what the members have experienced.

Nirje did admit to teaching a principle he called "hidden social training" to the university students before they became group members. This concept made a great difference. For example, one group went on a weekend outing, each with the equiva-lent of $15 in their possession. During the outing, the student-members were "called away," leaving those with retardation to spend the day alone. On the next day when the group was reunited, the members talked at length about what they experienced.

Nirje's program flew in the face of most professionals of that time. Most be-lieved persons with retardation must be protected at all costs. Nirje disagreed. "These people feel that human beings must never be protected from risk," he said. "To be allowed to be human means to be allowed to fail" (Perske, 1970, p. 17).

"We Are People First"

SALEM, OREGON, JANUARY 8, 1974. Eight residents or former residents of Fairview Hospital and Training Center met at Doris Brown's White House Home, a group home on Liberty Street. On that day, they officially initiated the first self-advocacy organization in the world. According to their historian, "It wasn't a very fashion-able birth for an organization that would in just five years grow up to become 1000 members strong in Oregon alone, and would have sister groups in three states, with 42 states requesting assistance for starting similar organizations" (Edwards, 1982, p. 13).

The seed for such an organization began to sprout after two workers and three residents of the Fairview institution attended a Canadian meeting on Victoria Is-land in 1973. The meeting had been billed as "The First Convention for the Men-tally Handicapped in North America." The Oregon contingent was touched by how the "conference participants spoke out firmly about their frustrations at being called retarded and being treated as though they were children their entire lives" (p. 10). The Oregonians began to build on this experience:

> The Canadian convention served as the stimulus. Those five partici-
> pants came home to Oregon anxious to explore the possibilities of
> Oregon's persons with retardation being able to speak out for them-
> selves. So, Dennis and Ann Heath, Nancy Hufford, and Patty Barney
> began telling people about their experience in Canada and their dream
> for Oregon. Unlike the Canadian meeting that was organized and di-
> rected by professionals, they dreamed of building a self-advocacy group
> that at long last would release them from the intentions of profession-
> als, organizations and agencies and allow them to advocate for them-
> selves. They, too, dreamed of a convention that would allow them to get
> together, but they wanted one that was organized and directed by them-
> selves, with helpers assisting only when they reached out and sought
> assistance (Edwards, 1982, p. 10).

By five months after the organization's first birthday, members were deeply involved in the rudiments of official meetings — the democracy, listening, speaking one at a time, making decisions, and voting. Much energy and arguing went into deciding the organization's name.

> All at once out of the back of the room someone suggested that the
> name ought to reflect what they were all about. Their name should say
> who they were and what they wanted. "We are people first," someone
> said in a loud voice. "PEOPLE FIRST!" As the vote was taken and the
> decision made, a real step was taken in giving a sense of identity to the
> group. From that day on people proudly identified themselves as PEOPLE
> FIRST (Edwards, 1982, p. 14).

Glorious Confusion

OTTER CREST, OREGON, 1974. The first self-advocacy convention took place on October 12-13, 1974, on the scenic Oregon Coast. It was the major flash of the year that was sparked by the organization's founding in January. Two hundred participants were expected, but 560 showed up!

> The registration area was jammed up with people, everyone was talking
> as old friends found each other and confusion reigned. There was a sea
> of bodies everywhere, but no one seemed to mind. There was too much
> to see and too many old friends to get together with for anyone to

mind. Everything was off schedule. Meals had to be double-shifted and rooms had to be shared, but no one got lost or forgotten; that in itself was a miracle (Edwards, 1982, p. 17).

Then came the opening session:

The earth moved just a bit when Valerie Schaaf, first president of People First, stepped onto the podium and spoke clearly into the microphone: **"This, The First People First Convention, is officially called to order!"** The room fell silent as all eyes turned their attention on Valerie.... Five hundred and sixty very special persons united and drew strength from one another during that first meeting. There was no doubt in anyone's mind that the beginning of a very wonderful revolutionary moment had begun! People First had carried off what had seemed impossible in many persons' minds just ten months earlier (Edwards, 1982, p. 18).

One Man's "Brainstorm"

OMAHA, NEBRASKA, 1985. Ray Loomis was a tall, rangy man with deep-set, piercing eyes and a brow he could furrow when struggling with a problem. Professionals tended to underestimate this man's power during his fifteen years at Beatrice State Home. When he was released in 1968, the superintendent predicted that he wouldn't succeed more than three days on the outside. He stayed out, but the going was rough (Shoultz, 1982, p. 19).

After seven years in the community, Loomis approached officials of the Greater Omaha Association for Retarded Citizens (GOARC) and the Eastern Nebraska Office of Retardation (ENCOR) with "a brainstorm."

He felt that people who were leaving the institution needed a group to belong to — a group whose focus was on helping its members to face problems. Although neither he nor any of the ENCOR or GOARC staff who helped him had ever heard of "self-advocacy," Ray knew instinctively that the group must be self-directing. He saw that the members of the group who were not mentally handicapped should be supporters and helpers but not leaders. He knew and acted on this even though it was two years before the group even defined itself as a group for mentally handicapped people (Shoultz, 1982, p. 19).

From that time on, natural leadership talents radiated from this man. Other former inmates from Beatrice State Home gathered around him and their leadership talents began to bloom as well. He even fell in love with a woman from the institution. He admitted to always liking Nancy Schwein, but the rules of the institution kept them apart. According to Loomis, the punishment for being with a woman was 12 hours of hard labor — waxing the same floor over and over.

He married Nancy. Later, a son, Billie Joe, was born.

Loomis proposed that the Omaha group be called "Project Two." His thinking: Community-based services served as the first project, and the self-advocacy movement was the second.

Loomis was a philosopher at heart. He led the group in thinking about basics: "What is Project Two? What is self-advocacy? What is the role of Shirley Dean, Tom Miller and Bonnie Shoultz [the group's helpers]?" He also saw that everyone needed to practice their leadership skills. So he worked on plans to rotate chairpersons (Shoultz, p. 23).

Interestingly, Project Two organized with the same fervor and reaped the same massive statewide results as their Oregon counterparts.

Then Ray Loomis died.

It was a time of heartbreak. On September 24, 1979, Loomis failed to recover from open-heart surgery. On September 24, Omaha's Holy Name Catholic Church was filled with over 250 persons from across the state who said goodbye to this well-loved self-advocate. Ten days after the funeral, Nebraska staged its second People First convention. Interestingly, Ray's wife, Nancy, and other members of Project Two, filled Loomis' leadership shoes. Over 220 attendees left the convention, vowing to keep his dream alive.

A Senator Gets His Mind Changed

OMAHA, NEBRASKA, 1979. It happened two months after Ray Loomis' death. Ten-year-old Jonathan Allen, a resident at Beatrice State Home, was visited by his mother. She found him badly bruised. She questioned the staff members. No one seemed to know what happened. She drove Jonathan to Omaha and placed him in the hospital.

As soon as the story came out in the media, some Project Two members visited the mother. Upset by the occurrence, Project Two went into session and struggled over what they might do. Then they moved.

They wrote a press statement, rehearsed for a press conference, and invited the media. With TV cameras running and reporters taking notes, the statement was read. It began:

> We believe people should be treated like human beings — with kindness, fairness and love. We are upset that a child may have been abused at Beatrice. Jonathan Allen could not defend himself. We believe that it is the responsibility of the State of Nebraska to provide more care and to watch over its residents more carefully.
>
> We also believe that all the people should be moved out of Beatrice into their own communities. We believe that all people, no matter how

handicapped they are, can live in their own communities. We think that
the money that is being spent right now to keep people in Beatrice should
be spent to bring them back here (Shoultz, 1982, p. 227).

Next, the members asked to meet with their state senator, Vard Johnson. Johnson
felt the institution should not be closed. To prove his point, he asked them to
accompany him on an unnanounced tour. They accepted.

The members who were chosen to tour took special training on how to conduct
themselves and what to look for. Of course, being former residents of Beatrice, they
already knew a lot about the place and the way it really worked.

Ten people — six Project Two members, two professional helpers, Senator Johnson
and an aide — headed for Beatrice. After a thorough tour, the self-advocates explained what they observed and what they heard from residents with whom they
once lived. Johnson was moved.

Things, however, did not stop there. After their discussion, the self-advocates
asked Senator Johnson to take one more tour with them — through the community-based services in the Omaha area. He accepted.

After the community tour, Johnson told the media that he had changed his
mind. The headline in the *Omaha World-Herald* proclaimed, "Visits to Retarded
Changed Senator's Attitude" (Shoultz, 1982, p. 17).

Kansas University Overpowers Self-Advocates
for Federal Grant

SALEM, OREGON, 1980. The accomplishments of Oregon self-advocates captured the
interest of many people across the world. They expanded their scope and became
known as People First International. The federal government was so moved by the
organization's success, its Developmental Disabilities Bureau sent out requests for
"technical assistance" grant proposals for starting People First organizations in other
parts of the country. The Oregon group applied for the grant. They never dreamed any
agency could be more in the running, considering their remarkable track record.

Nevertheless, Kansas University got the grant. Its University Affiliated Program received $75,000.

People First International reacted. They argued that after five years of experience in this "consumer movement" — inspiring and helping to start 270 self-advocacy groups in 41 states — they deserved the grant award.

The Bureau disagreed. It stoutly defended the selection of the University of
Kansas over People First International, saying the the Kansas application was "tech-
nically sounder" (Edwards, 1982).

Kansas University had used professional grant writers — even though their
experience in the movement amounted to one big zero. The grant request from
People First International was written largely by persons with disabilities.

Bernard Carabello Becomes Quick On the Uptake (1981)

NEW YORK, NEW YORK, 1981. Eleven years earlier, on January 11, 1972, Geraldo Rivera had met Bernard Carabello for the first time. Rivera, an ABC-TV reporter, was scheduled to interview the 21-year-old man with cerebral palsy and learn about his life in Willowbrook State School. The interview was held in the home of William Bronston, a medical doctor who worked at Willowbrook. "Because the palsy severely limited Bernard's control over his muscles," Rivera said, "he writhed in his chair and his arms were in constant involuntary motion. I was afraid he wouldn't be able to answer any questions, but he did." With struggling speech, Carabello talked about his 18 years as a resident of Willowbrook, about not being able to read, about being too old for the school program — and then he began to cry. That night, Rivera featured Carabello in his report on the evening news. He closed by saying, "My God. What a waste. Leaving a boy like that to vegetate on one of those stinking wards all day long. Just rotting away, when with more training he could become a productive member of society" (Rivera, pp. 63-66).

Later, Carabello moved into the community and Willowbrook was closed. Something else happened, too, that, to this writer, is just as touching: Rivera and Carabello developed a close, rich friendship that continues to this day.

The greatest happening, however, became apparent when Bonnie Shoultz interviewed veteran self-advocate Carabello in 1981:

> I'm much better at helping others. I talk to people. I got SSI for someone who really needed it. I got a home for someone else. That makes me feel really good.
>
> I try not to treat people "special." They don't need that. I have people come to me and talk down to me, as if I'm a child or hard-of-hearing: "How *are* you?" "You're a *good* boy!" I had a woman give me a dollar and tell me to go buy myself some ice cream. I said, "You need it more than I do." She said, "Thank you." Sometimes I'll jokingly say, "Hey, you've got to do this for me — I'm handicapped!" It makes a point. One time a salesman knocked on the door, and he saw me and said, "Is anybody home?" I said, "Who the hell do you think *I* am?"
>
> (Williams and Shoultz, 1982, p. 78)

Carabello still works hard at making his lips form the words he wants to say, but not quite as much as the day when Rivera first interviewed him. Also, one can't help but notice how Carabello's sentences are quick and effective, like a shortstop's throw to first base — like the sentences used by his friend, Geraldo. Copying the syntax of his friend and practicing in self-advocacy situations has paid off for Bernard Carabello.

Speaking For Ourselves

THE GREATER PHILADELPHIA AREA, JUNE 1982. A class-action lawsuit focused national media attention on the Pennhurst Developmental Center — for being utterly rotten about helping people develop. Consequently, the residents of this institution moved into community settings in the five counties nearby. Although these "brothers" and "sisters" were scattered, they came together as one of the most powerful self-advocacy groups in the nation. When the time came to give themselves a name, they decided to call themselves "Speaking for Ourselves." Later, member Roland Johnson was asked how they arrived at such a picturesque name. Mr. Johnson screwed his face up into dead seriousness. Then with the voice of a judge, he said, "Oh, can't you see it? What we call ourselves is what we do." Becoming even more somber, he said, "We simply refused to give ourselves one of those alphabetic names — like NARC or AAMD or TASH — and force people to sit on their hands for days trying to figure out what those letters meant."

Interestingly, most self-advocacy organizations chose descriptive names as well. People First continues to be preferred the most. Others, however, have come up with The Pioneer Club, Progress Ahead, Citizens United, The Trailblazers, and, of course, Project Two.

Investigative Reporters

SACRAMENTO, CALIFORNIA, 1983. When the state of California wanted inside information on its service system for persons with developmental disabilities, it chose six receivers of services to do the job. The investigators — Barbara Blease, James Drake, Tom Hopkins, Sandy Jensen, Connie Martinez, and John McMillan — were active members of People First of California.

Through oral training — not reading — the group gained a thorough understanding of the Lanterman Developmental Disabilities Service Act, California's own bill of rights and service delivery law. Each received training in the use of tape recorders. Then, with one advisor and a recorder/writer, they moved through the state. They traveled 1500 miles, talked to 150 people with disabilities and made 70 hours of recorded tapes.

They issued a scathing report of over 200 pages, showing how people were being *retarded* by the system and were struggling to *survive* it (People First of California, 1984).

Some interesting points were raised:

- "The Lanterman Act pushes for development, but the system pushes back" (p. 9).
- Some talked about being treated as commodities, not human beings — only things worth money to the agencies serving them (p. 8).

- Some described how case managers told them they weren't ready to leave a residence when they knew they were being held back because of the money they brought into the system (p. 56).
- Many voiced their hatred for going bowling and to movies in large groups (p. 14).
- Some felt successful services are rare because success is not rewarded (p. 58).
- The investigators felt that every service provider needed training in the Lanterman Act — like they received it (p. 33).
- Some talked about workshops that made them more retarded (p. 32).
- One workshop employee registered his utter disgust for making wind chimes (p. 66).
- Questions were raised about being a Boy Scout at age 35 (pp. 14-13).

Seizing the Moment and Grabbing the Power

PRINCETON, NEW JERSEY, MARCH 21, 1986. It was the first of a two-day "Interstate Seminar on Self-Advocacy for Persons with Disabilities." Agencies from Connecticut, New Jersey, New York and Pennsylvania funded a conference for 156 persons — professionals mingled with an equal number of persons having disabilities.

Professionals and persons with disabilities were paired together. Each pair shared a hotel room. They took their meals together and sat together during the sessions.

Even so, professionals felt some strange need to discriminate. They saw that all persons with disabilities received the title *self-advocates*. Everyone else became known as *advocates*.

Things went smoothly until after the first small-group sessions. In the general assembly that followed, small-group recorders on the front stage began giving their reports when Steve Dorsey of Pennsylvania stood up in the audience. **"I just wondered how come there aren't more self-advocates on the platform,"** he said.

Everyone became aware that all but one of the ten people in front were professionals.

Bernard Carabello of New York rose and voiced his disfavor with the way the term *self-advocate* was being used.

"Everybody should be self-advocates," T.J. Monroe of Connecticut said.

"If I'm a self-advocate, when do I become an advocate?" Linda LaCourse of New Jersey added.

These honest statements from persons with disabilities moved the professionals to slowly let go of the reins, and the so-called self-advocates — in their own ways — began to pick them up (InterServ, 1986).

Other moments at the Princeton conference:

- Warm and friendly joking went on between New York Commissioner Art Webb and his roommate, Bernard Carabello (**"I just got a call from Gover-**

nor Cuomo. He appointed me Commissioner of Mental Retardation and Developmental Disabilities. I'm sorry, Art Webb, your job is over") (p. 3).

- T.J. Monroe woke up his roommate, Connecticut Commissioner Brian Lensink, at 4 A.M. He wanted to know why professionals had been so lousy about teaching sex education (p. 3).

- In the general assembly room, every participant had a microphone and an on-off switch on a desk in front of them. At one point in the session, everyone wanted to respond to an issue at the same time. Too many pushed their mike buttons at the same time – knocking out the system (p. 5).

- Connecticut self-advocate Dick Nazzari, for the first time in his life, made a formal statement to a large assembly. He struggled painfully for each word. He paused. He spoke again. The audience quietly waited for him to get it all out. Then the whole assembly cheered and applauded him loudly (p. 5).

- New Jersey Commissioner Eddie Moore confessed that for the first time in his life, he not only heard how some self-advocates hated the word *retarded*. He also sensed how it could diminish them in the eyes of others (p.7).

- Polly Tulley, a parent, told the general assembly how much she had learned. She felt other parents should attend meetings like this. Someone in the audience disagreed. "All parents aren't like you," the person said. "We want our parents to come and observe — not participate" (p. 9).

- Karen Kreitler's father entered the back of the large assembly room unannounced to hear his daughter's keynote speech. Later, after being touched by what his daughter said, he asked a professional if anyone had taught her the meaning of the word *honorarium* yet (p. 10).

- Self-advocate Loretta Claiborne responded to another self-advocate in the assembly who had demanded a dishwasher in her new apartment. "I have two dishwashers — my hands!" Ms. Claiborne said (p. 15).

- Most memorable: Professionals – at break times – admitted to each other how much they used the word *mental retardation* in their everyday dealings, not really sensing how much that word could wound people. Some felt this single conciousness-raising issue made their attendance at the conference worthwhile (p. 17).

Well, It Seemed Right

SOMEWHERE IN CONNECTICUT, MARCH 28, 1986. Timothy Johnson (not his real name) left the Princeton conference and returned to his town and his job at a supermarket. He did it with new fire for taking risks.

On this day, while putting cereal boxes on shelves at the supermarket, a small child nearby began to cry loudly. The child's mother told the little one to shut up. The child kept crying. Finally, the mother reached down and slapped the child.

Mr. Johnson slapped the mother.

Mr. Johnson was fired.

Every Great Movement Has Its Songs

STAMFORD, CONNECTICUT, DECEMBER 4, 1987. The Communist Party has its *Internationale*. The U. S. Civil Rights Movement gained power and determination from *We Shall Overcome*. *Bread and Roses* raised the spirits of those in the Feminist Movement. Now the self-advocacy movement has its anthem as well.

Karl Williams, a songwriter who also works with persons with disabilities, came to the four-state (New York, New Jersey, Pennsylvania and Connecticut) self-advocate conference at Stamford, Connecticut. He brought his guitar and he asked to say a few words at the opening plenary session.

"I attended an earlier self-advocacy meeting," he said, "and I heard a leader say, 'You people are in a revolution, but revolutions have songs that keep them going. Where are your songs? Your revolution doesn't have any songs.'" (InterServ, 1987) Williams said he thought about that statement for a long time.

Then he wrote a song for self-advocates. It appears at the beginning of this section, opposite page 1 of this book.

He played the song for his audience. Everyone liked it. The melody was rich and the words were catchy. They liked it so much every plenary session opened with it for the next two days. By the end of the conference everyone sang the song along with him.

Today self-advocacy groups all over the world begin their meetings by singing this truly revolutionary song.

ADA: An Explosion of Fresh Directions

WASHINGTON, DC, JULY 26, 1990. Over 2000 persons — most of them with disabilities — traveled from all parts of the nation. They converged on the south lawn of The White House to witness President George Bush's signing of the landmark civil rights bill for persons with disabilities, the Americans with Disabilities Act.

"Let the shameful wall of exclusion finally come tumbling down," the president said as he signed the bill. Bush appealed to "my friends in the business community" to accept persons with disabilities. "You have in your hands, the key to the success of this act."

The act prohibits discrimination against persons with disabilities in employment or in limiting access to public accommodations, such as restaurants, stores, museums, and theaters. Employment provisions of the law will be phased in between 1992 and 1994, while the equal access measures take effect in 18 months.

While President Bush said the law would be implemented cautiously ("We have all been determined to ensure that it gives flexibility, particularly in terms of the timetable of implementation, and we've been committed to containing the costs that may be incurred"), many advocates and self-advocates expressed impatience with the slow pace of change.

Although the act has far-reaching implications, some basics are clear. It guarantees persons with disabilities access to:

- *Public Accommodations*: Must be accessible after 18 months. Businesses with 25 or fewer workers and gross annual receipts of $1 million or less have six additional months to comply; those with 10 or fewer workers and gross annual receipts of $500,000 have an additional year. New facilities must be accessible.
- *Transportation*: New buses, commuter-rail and Amtrak cars must be wheelchair accessible. One car per train must be made accessible within five years. Key stations and new stations must be made accessible within three years.
- *Employment*: After two years, businesses with 25 workers or more are required to disregard handicaps in hiring and make accommodations at their own expense for workers with disabilities, unless the cost is too great. After four years, the law applies to those with 15 workers or more.
- *Telephones*: Utilities are required to provide special services for customers with hearing and speech impairments within three years (Spears, 1990).

Most self-advocates see the act as a gateway to full citizenship in the United States. They intend to use the act in order to press for the same civil rights other citizens receive.

A Tribute to Today's Self-Advocates

Back in 1962, this writer conducted a group session with six teenage boys who lived in an institution for mental retardation. The session began with a film, "The Good Samaritan." When the film ended, the boys were encouraged to talk about the characters in the story.

Interestingly, all of them fixed on the man who was beaten up and left by the side of the road. Then they talked at length about all the mean and rotten things that had happened to each of them. No doubt about it, they had much to say.

Not one of them, however, talked about the magnanimous Samaritan!

They seemed unable to grasp and learn from such a lofty act of kindness — the binding of the man's wounds, getting him to an inn, telling the innkeeper to let him stay and rest until well — at the Samaritan's expense.

Why didn't they grasp the generally accepted focus of the story? Maybe they had received so little goodness from others that they had little to give. On the other hand, maybe staff members failed to grasp the high ideal that *these people could be helped to be givers in the world, too.*

When one watches a good self-advocacy organization in operation today, one gets a different picture. Of course, they work at fighting like tigers for their own dignity, respect and full citizenship! They, nevertheless, can also be seen working on the notion that it is more blessed to give than to receive!

This latter blessing showed itself vividly when some members of the new National Self-Advocacy Network read a report on Robert Wayne Sawyer. Sawyer was scheduled to be executed a few minutes after midnight on March 5, 1993 — even though recent evidence of mental retardation and brain damage had never been heard by a court. New evidence that might lead a jury to vote him innocent had not been heard as well (Perske, 1993).

Network members passed the word, and self-advocates from all over the U.S. *gave* of themselves quickly, writing letters asking for clemency from the governor of Louisiana.

Unfortunately, the cause was lost. Robert was executed.

Even so, my grateful response to this outpouring of sharing and concern went out to that national network. It was written in capitals because of a strong desire to get the message across. That letter appears on the next page.

Epilogue

Self-advocacy organizations are very much on the move.

Their beginnings were ragged.

They dared to make *their own* mistakes and they began to learn from them.

Now, however, they move forward with greater sophistication and confidence.

No one could have predicted this movement three decades ago.

No one can even predict where they will be in ten years.

They keep moving and nothing can stop them now.

They often amaze others in the field by what they are doing.

So how can we understand and help these people who call themselves self-advocates?

Only by watching them — simply *watching* them... and cheering them on.

MARCH 5, 1993

DEBBIE ROBINSON
THE NATIONAL SELF-ADVOCACY NETWORK
C/O SPEAKING FOR OURSELVES, ONE PLYMOUTH MEETING (#530)
PLYMOUTH MEETING, PA 19462

DEAR DEBBIE:

I AM WRITING THIS AFTER LEAVING THE LOUISIANA STATE PENITENTIARY
AT ANGOLA, LOUISIANA.

YOU AND YOUR NATIONAL SELF-ADVOCACY NETWORK DID A KIND THING.
YOU GOT THE WORD OUT FOR ROBERT WAYNE SAWYER.
GOVERNOR EDWARDS RECEIVED OVER 500 LETTERS FROM SELF-ADVOCATES.
THEY CAME FROM ALL PARTS OF THE UNITED STATES.
PLEASE THANK ALL THE PEOPLE YOU CONTACTED.
TELL THEM THEY DID THE RIGHT THING.

NOW IT RIPS ME UP TO GIVE YOU THE BAD NEWS:
ROBERT WAS EXECUTED AT NINE MINUTES AFTER MIDNIGHT THIS MORNING.
HE DIED EVEN THOUGH THE TRUTH WAS ON HIS SIDE.
IT WAS POLITICS THAT KILLED HIM.
POLITICIANS SAW HIM AS A SYMBOL.
THEY FAILED TO SEE HIM AS A HUMAN BEING.

LAST TUESDAY, WE BATTLED FOR HIM BEFORE THE BOARD OF PARDONS.
JIM BROLIN, EXECUTIVE DIRECTOR OF THE ARC OF LOUISIANA, SPOKE FOR
HIM. I TALKED ABOUT HOW EASY IT IS TO CONVICT PEOPLE LIKE ROBERT.
DR. RUTH LUCKASSON AND OTHER EXPERTS DESCRIBED HIS DISABILITIES.
IT WENT ON FOR SIX HOURS.
WE WERE CONVINCING. WE WERE SURE WE HAD WON.
THEN THE BOARD OF PARDONS VOTED, 3-TO-2, THAT ROBERT DIE.
THE GOVERNOR REFUSED TO OVERRULE THE BOARD OF PARDONS' VOTE.

DEBBIE, TELL ALL OF YOUR "BROTHERS AND SISTERS":
ALL ROBERT EVER WANTED WAS TO BE LIKED BY OTHERS.
HE WANTED TO HAVE GOOD FRIENDS.
HE WANTED TO BELONG TO GOOD PEOPLE--LIKE YOU.

IF LITTLE FIVE-FOOT-TWO-INCH ROBERT HAD BEEN IN A SELF-ADVOCACY
GROUP,
IF HE HAD BEEN SUPPORTED BY PEOPLE LIKE YOU,
HE WOULDN'T HAVE BEEN SO VULNERABLE.
SO MANY OTHERS WOULDN'T HAVE WOUNDED HIM THE WAY THEY DID.
HE WOULDN'T HAVE GOTTEN INTO THIS FIX, BEEN ARRESTED, CONVICTED,
AND KILLED.
I'M SURE OF IT.

WITH GRATEFULNESS FOR ALL OF YOU,

ROBERT PERSKE

References

Edwards, J. (1982). *We are People First*. Portland: EDNICK, Inc.

InterServ (1986). *Report of the first inter-state seminar on self-advocacy*. New York: InterServ, Suite 410, United Nations Plaza.

InterServ (1987). *Report of the second inter-state seminar on self-advocacy*. New York: InterServ, Suite 410, United Nations Plaza.

People First of California (1984). *Surviving in the system: Mental retardation and the retarding environment*. Sacramento, CA: State Council on Developmental Disabilities.

Perske, R. (1970). *Journal submitted to the Rosemary F. Dybwad International Awards Committee*. 18113 Town Center Drive, Olney, Maryland 20832.

Perske, R. (1972). The dignity of risk and persons with mental retardation. *Mental Retardation, 10*(1), February.

Perske, R. (1978). *The report to the president: Mental retardation — the leading edge — service programs that work*. Washington, DC: The President's Committee on Mental Retardation.

Perske, R. (1993). *Robert Sawyer scheduled for execution on March 5 — his mental retardation never considered by the courts*. Emergency newsletter to 400 selected colleagues who work with people having developmental disabilities. February 8.

Spears, G. (1990). Disabilities act signed by Bush. *The Philadelphia Inquirer*, July 27.

Rivera, G. (1972). *Willowbrook: A report on how it is and why it doesn't have to be that way*. New York: Random House.

Williams, K (1987). *Speaking for ourselves* (copyrighted song). Speaking for Ourselves, Suite 530, 1 Plymouth Meeting, Plymouth Meeting, Pennsylvania 19462.

Williams, P., & Shoultz, B. (1982). *We can speak for ourselves: Self-advocacy by mentally handicapped people*. Bloomington: Indiana University Press.

Section II

The Self-Advocate Experience

THE MARATHON MAN

Johnny ran.
that was his problem,
he was what the staff called a runner
logical since he ran whenever he could—

one minute
they thought they had him
three ways to Sunday
tied to the bedpost
    with someone else's soiled sheets;

then they'd no sooner turn around
and he'd be up to his harry houdini
routine all over again.

even the aides admitted he was pretty
smart for being a retard;
all the rest of them would sit and rock.

but not Johnny
he'd jump up
dart this way and that.

then the next thing you know
he'd find an open door
or leap through a window

and he'd be clocking the mile
on the institution's main drag
at three-point-ninety-two
like the long distance runner
    he longed to be.

they tried vinegar spray,
four-point restraints,
even leaden shoes.
nothing slowed his free stride
until they placed electrodes on his hide
and shocked him.

shocked him silly.

now he's on the back ward
rocking to and fro
to and fro
to and fro...

— *Bob Williams* (see p. xii)

3

"It's Been A Struggle"
Her Own Story

Barbara Goode
with an introduction by Bruce Kappel

In 1993, at the Third International People First conference, a new award was given for the first time. The Rosemary Dybwad Award is to be awarded to a female self-advocate who exemplifies the dedication and leadership that were exemplified by the life of Rosemary Dybwad. The first award was given to BARB GOODE by Gunnar Dybwad. We are pleased to have Barb share her personal perspective in this chapter.

Introduction

Barb Goode is my friend. Barb might never tell you all of the things she has done. She does not like people to think she is tooting her own horn. So I will.

Barb was the first president of one of the original People First groups in Canada. She was one of the people responsible for starting the National People First Project in Canada. She was the first self-advocate to be on the Board of the Canadian Association for Community Living (CACL). She was the first chairperson of the Consumer Advisory Committee to CACL. She was the leader of the first group of self-advocates to bring a case to the Supreme Court of Canada. She was the first self-advocate on the Board of the International League of Societies for Persons with Mental Handicap. She was the first chairperson of the League's Self Advocacy Committee. She was on the founding board of a service agency whose board members are mostly self-advocates. She was the first self-advocate to address the General Assembly of the United Nations.

Barb has a couple of part-time jobs and is on boards and committees locally, nationally and internationally. Barb Goode has been labelled M.R. She taught me that *M.R.* means "mighty remarkable." Barb is a remarkable person. And, like many other self-advocates, she has had her share of struggles. Barb has been one of the leaders responsible for many changes in Canada. We talk about those in the chapter on the history of People First in Canada. In this chapter, we talk about some of the struggles Barb has had in her personal life, particularly the difficulties she has had being listened to and taken seriously. For Barb Goode, the Goode life has been a struggle.

This chapter is by Barb Goode. I helped out by asking Barb some questions. Everything else is what Barb told me.

Getting Involved with People First

Barb, how did you get involved with People First?

In 1977, it could have been earlier, at a baseball game with some friends, we started People First as a social club. It started out being just a social club. Before I started, this group wasn't called anything. They had just started meeting socially. They were doing things like baseball and recreational things mostly. Then about a year went by and we started People First.

The social club was going already, so we just put People First with us. If people were interested in meetings, you went to meetings. And if you were interested in social, you went to social. If you were interested in both, you went to both. So you weren't forced to go to either one.

Were you involved in starting the social club?

No, it had been going before I started. I just went because I had nothing to do one day. Mom told me about this baseball group that someone told her about. So I went to just watch. Someone asked me if I wanted to get involved, so I just got involved.

Where did the idea to start People First come from?

The way I remember it was, there was going to be a big conference in the States. They asked me if I would be interested in going. I think I said "yes." So I went down and we got back.

We got a group of us together over dinner one night. A staff member cornered me with another staff. They cornered me near the kitchen, so I couldn't get out. They said, "You can't leave this kitchen unless you decide to be the next president." At the time, I remember I was going, "I don't think so," and they are going, "Yes, you are." So, we got a meeting going that way. Just getting people interested, and then we asked different people. Then we had an election and I was voted the president with some other people.

Living in a Group Home and Speaking Up

Were you living at home or in the group home at that point?

Half and half. I was just going to be moving into the group home after a few months.

How long were you in the group home?

A year and a half, one month, two weeks, three days.

Why do you know the precise time?

I just like remembering things like that.

How was it there in the group home?

It was OK. What really bothered me a lot was that when — I am a very clean person and always have been — and like when the staff put everybody at the house on a hygiene program. And what that meant was that you had to wash your hair, like you had to go from your hair downwards. When you had a bath, and they stood in the bathroom with you so you got it straight. And if you didn't get it straight, you would get told off.

And so with me, at the time, if you can believe it, I did not really speak out for myself. But anyway, so I ran away from home. I showed my disgust that way, because I could not tell the staff I couldn't cope with it, with them, having someone look after me in the bathtub. As I said, can't people wash their hair the way they want to, to have a bath the way they want to? I understand that there are safety factors, if someone is going to be unsafe in the bathroom. Like if you are going to have seizures. But if you aren't going to have seizures or if you don't need assistance to do things, why do you need someone to be in there?

When you ran away to home, did you ever go back to the group home?

Yeah, I went back. I mean I was just so mad at them for having someone invade my privacy. I also remember at the time, I was wearing my housecoat. It was a short one. It was not a long one, but I have never worn a short one since. And I can remember wearing the short housecoat. I was sitting in the living room with some other people. And the staff people told me I should go upstairs. And I went upstairs, and they followed me. They told me that there was one male staff, and I was embarrassing him by wearing this short housecoat. So they weren't going to let me downstairs any more with this housecoat on. So, if I wanted to wear my housecoat in the house, I couldn't do it when this man, this staff member, was around.

There were things like that I did not think were called for. I mean, can't a person in their own home wear a housecoat? I mean, it was not that short.

How did you come to leave the group home for good?

After being there for a year, I had said to the staff that I wanted to move. I felt that I had learnt all the skills that they could offer me. They said they did not feel that way. They said that I did not have any of the skills that you need to live on your own. So, for the next six months, they helped me do that.

But the other thing that kind of makes me angry, thinking back on it, I can remember them on a Sunday saying to me, saying to all of us, "Every Sunday is going to be chore day, and if you can't get your chores done by a certain time you can't go out for the afternoon or evening." But you had no other choice than doing them on a Sunday. In our family that is family day, and so I wanted to go home. And I couldn't go home unless I did my chores properly. That was frustrating.

You said you were ready, and they said you weren't ready, so what happened?

Well, we put this plan in action. A group of us, the staff and I and Mom and Dad, and we talked about what they would do to help me do that. What they did was, upstairs where I stayed there was this room off the live-in staff's room. It had a small kitchen, and I learned how to make my own meals, and how to look after the upstairs by myself.

It was frustrating for me at times, because it was like we had certain things we had to cook, like hamburgers, and if you didn't make them the right size that they liked, you had to do them over. And like we had to make pancakes, and if they were too doughy, you had to do them over again. And to this day, I do not like to make those two things. And the same with chicken. We had to cook chicken with "Shake and Bake." If you didn't shake them properly, they would get after you. Things like that.

So, the fact that you spoke up and said you wanted to leave really got a lot of stuff going?

I think it did. But in some ways I did not want to leave, but I did leave. I mean that because I did not know what it was going to be like. Why do people have to learn everything perfectly?

Did you move into your own place after that?

Uh-huh, after six months. I moved into an old house that had this bachelor suite. I lived there for a while.

Getting A Chance to Speak For Yourself

Why were you at the United Nations?

I was representing self-advocates from Canada, and it was because it was the end of the Decade of the Disabled. The Decade of the Disabled started in 1981 and it finished last year.

Were there other self-advocates, or were you speaking on behalf of self-advocates from around the world?

I was talking for everybody. That was a big role, to be able to talk for everyone. But it is really difficult for me, I have never figured it out, when I go to a conference, who am I representing — self-advocates, myself, the organization that paid for me to go? All of these things that I have to think about. And it is never really clear to me who I really represent but I think that I represented the parents, self-advocates, everybody involved with the committee.

What was that like, talking to leaders from all around the world?

In some ways it was scary, it was kinda scary. I think at the time I didn't realize who I was going to talk to. I hadn't really thought about it. I think the reasons being that when we got there, at the UN, it was in such a confusion that no one knew where anything was. No one knew where the name tags were. You had to be quiet. You had to wear these name tags. If you didn't wear these name tags, you couldn't go through point A and point B. It was a big hassle.

And finally when I got my name, I had someone else's, a completely different name on. So I felt like what happened was that they got my name tag, and I couldn't say anything. I had a man's name, but they thought it was a woman's name in someone else's country. It was really weird.

And then the night before, I was asked to look at the speech that Victor Wolstrom from the International League had written. He had written it, because he felt that I couldn't write a speech very well. So he took it on himself.

Jo Dickey and I had said to him that we wanted to change it, and he said he couldn't change it because of the translators. The translators needed to have it right away. Anyway, I changed the last paragraph. But a lot of people said to me "it doesn't matter about the words, it matters that you were there."

Is what was in the speech what you believe? When you got up to read it, did you feel uncomfortable?

Some of it was my ideas, but it was not my words. I wouldn't have put some things that way.

Like "We are people first and only secondly do we have a handicap." I wouldn't have put it that way. I would have said "We are people first, and handicapped second." That is the way I would have said it.

And then "We want to push our rights forward and we want to let other people know that we are here." I wouldn't have put it that way. I would have said "We want to learn our rights, and we want to let other people know that we are here."

Some people told you that it wasn't a big deal; what did you think? Does it bother you when someone writes a speech for you?

Yeah, if they had asked me before and said I am going to write your speech for you, that's fine. No — if they were going to write my speech, I would want to have input into it, and I would have wanted to go over it beforehand, instead of giving it to me at ten o'clock at night and at eight o'clock the next morning having to be ready to go over there. That is not my idea.

After about four years ago, we figured out the best way for me is for people to ask me questions, and like that we figure out a system of knowing the questions I want to be asked, instead of reading something when it sounds right, I am reading it, instead I want to be able to change it, if I need to. And if, like write down ideas I have. That is what I do sometimes. I write ideas down, and I look at them, and I know what I'm talking about. Instead of someone just writing down the whole thing. I think that's being fair to anybody, that you should be able to look at it beforehand, or help with it.

But I mean I understand why he [Victor at the United Nations] did it in some ways, but it still didn't make me feel any easier about it.

Does that happen to you a lot that people write speeches for you, or articles for you and you do not have a chance to have input?

With articles like, I write what I am feeling and I write it the way, like I jump around a lot, because I still think it is important that people be able to write their own way. That has been one of my pet peeves in the last few years, is to be able to write something without people judging me and saying "Oh, we can't put that, because it doesn't make sense." If it doesn't make sense, help me put it so it does make sense.

I do not write things in order. I might start with 1978 and jump to 1990. That's just my way of thinking. I think that I am not different from a lot of people. If I am thinking about something, I have to say it. Even if I write it down, I feel that I might lose it.

I don't really like people presuming that I don't know how to write. Because I think that I can write, but it may not be the way that they write, so they might not be used to it.

If they want Barb Goode to speak, let Barb Goode speak?

Yeah, yeah. And if they want me to write something, let me write it even if I fail and it doesn't make sense, I feel good that I did it. And the same with speaking. Like Peter and Pat are wonderful at speaking, *but I am not like that.* I have never thought that I am the best speaker in the whole world, but I think they're better because Pat has never used notes. Peter uses notes. But everybody has their own style.

And you know, to me, I guess it is OK that people want to help us, to go through it with someone who understands, but I don't want just anyone to go through it. It is like "The Voice," the newsletter that I help with. Many people don't understand that when I write articles, that's the way I want it, instead of their words and not my words. Even if it is in plain language, but not my words, I don't like it. Because they're doing it their own way.

There's another newsletter that I help with and the only thing they change is how you spell it. And if you don't spell it right and it doesn't look like what it is supposed to be, then they change it. Like if it is *know* instead of *no*, they don't change it, because that doesn't really matter. To me it doesn't. I mean, you're trying.

Who is "The Voice" for?

Self-advocates all over British Columbia. But we are trying to get other people to write it. But it seems only the same people write it. But we try and write it in a way that people understand. Like issues that concern people. Like the last issue, we talk about a radio show we're doing. A group of us have been doing this radio show. But I didn't get involved for the simple reason that I hate my voice on tape so I didn't want to do it. And the other reason that I didn't really want to do it, was that other people were involved and they don't all get along and so it would be a hassle to try and get along with everybody, because they want to be on at the same time.

And then we talked about the International Conference. We are trying to let people know about issues that concern them. Like co-op housing, I did one about my place one time.

That is the other thing, as a group, we stay with issues that we want to write about, but when it comes down to it we don't have the final say. It's the person at BCACL [the British Columbia Association for Community Living] because she said it's because they got the grant from the Law Foundation and they want issues that are about law. And so issues have to be about law, but the law gets very complicated, so if we changed it, it doesn't make sense.

It's a fighting battle.

Being Accused of Pretending to be Handicapped

Another battle you mentioned was people accusing you of pretending to be handicapped?

When you get, and I'm not bragging, when you get as well known as Peter and I and Pat, it is really hard, because people think that now you are pretending to be handicapped. That is a real big issue for me — to get people to understand that you are not over your label. Like you are always a man, and you do not stop being that. So, how can you not be a mentally handicapped person any more. To me it's an insult.

Why do you think people do that?

I think because we speak well, and we know all the issues, not all the issues, but we know the issues, and that people like yourself have helped us over the years...

Instead of disagreeing with what you say, they say you are pretending?

Uh-huh. It's because they cannot accept it. How can we come up with these big things that we are saying? Like it's hard for them to believe that any handicapped person can think that way.

So you are either pretending or some advisor is manipulating you?

Yeah, they're behind me talking for me. I've been accused of that before, you know that...

At a meeting I was at a few weeks ago, we talked about this, a friend of mine. It is hard to explain, but she thinks that people think that I'm pretending to be mentally handicapped because I come across so well and that they don't understand that it has been a struggle for the last ten or twelve years.

This one person said that they think, for a perfect example, is sometimes there are one-to-one workers that come to my apartment building. They come and see almost everybody in the building. This friend thinks that lately I have been trying to figure out a problem by myself and I've been asking them to assist me. And they have been saying they don't have time, and putting me off and all this.

So, this person says that all of a sudden come Christmas the problem will get worse and worse and all of a sudden I won't be able to cope and because they think that I am able to cope, that everything is hunky-dory. But someone told me a long time ago, that no one is a human if they don't have problems. Everyone has problems. And so, this friend was trying to point out to me that he thinks that it is his fault that people have put me up here [like on a pedestal] and they don't realize what damage it has done.

And I mean, sometimes it feels awful to me to be able to, I don't like that I can't do something, but I want to do something. That if I don't do something I'm letting people down. It's like I have no control over it. It's like I want to make people happy, but then when it comes to them making me happy, they don't worry about that. They think "Oh, everything's just fine." I don't know if that makes sense.

Not Being Listened To

Is being on the board at the International League different from being on the board at CACL [the Canadian Association for Community Living]?

I feel like I'm going back in time at the International League. I'm back in time, because I'm the only self-advocate. And it seems to me it's happening all over again. I'm the first self-advocate involved with the League. And I just think we're going backwards.

Like people aren't on committees. Like we have our special committee. And that was a big issues at the time at CACL, like that we [the Self-Advocacy Committee] were the only committee. We weren't on any other committees but this one. And that was one thing that we fought for.

So here's Barb Goode being the first again at the International League, and having to cut the road for everyone else?

And you know, in some ways I don't really like it. I mean in some ways it's OK, but in some ways I've been feeling like it's a lot of pressure, like to be the first at some thing. But then again it some times feels all right. Dulcie and I had a long talk about it. [Barb's friend Dulcie became the first woman to be the Ombudsman for a province.] When she got elected, it was like the first in Canada to have a woman, and so she says it's the same thing.

We're the first at some things, but we're not sure if that's how, if we like it that way. In some ways, that's a real hard question. It depends on the situation. If it's a good situation, like in a way, at the League. Like I'd been involved with them for 12 years or more before this happened. I can remember they asked if I could have my name go [for the Board]. And I said "I'm not sure, but anyway, go for it." So anyway, I remember some one else wanted the job. When it came to elections, it was really close.

I out won a non-handicapped person and I said to them at the time, I can remember after I won, I said to someone, "Let him have it." Because this person was totally upset with me for winning 'cause they wanted it. Because, like Canada has not been really involved with the League. And it's politics for me. And I never thought I was involved with politics before, I know I am, but I had never really seen it.

And it's really bugging me. That this person really wanted it. And I just said "Thank you." And this person was angry at me. And still is. And that kinda hurts, it really does. Like at the time I thought, "Go for it, let him take it," if he's so interested, let him have it. Let him struggle through. I mean, he wouldn't have to struggle. It would be easy. But I mean, I don't think he thinks I can do it. I really believe that, that he doesn't think I'll do a good job, that he'll do a better job because he's a non-handicapped person. And that's another thing, that people like himself, that have a high paying job, and that they can just go to conferences like that and they get paid. And how many self-advocates get paid being on a board? Like we don't have good jobs, so we can't just go away.

What other organizations are you active in?
A few years ago I was active with DAWN — Disabled Women's Network. I think the main reason that I dropped out was because, a lot of people don't agree with me, but this is the way I feel, a lot of other disabled groups don't want developmentally handicapped people involved. And they don't want us involved because they feel that we are not at the same level as them. Like their disability is more noticeable, and ours isn't noticeable, so to them — I think they feel they're more superior...

But I think all disabled groups should work together. I think we're all fighting for the same thing. Why should the wheelchair people ask for support when we are asking for the same thing from the government? No wonder the government gets confused about who the money goes to.

I was involved with CDRC, the Canadian Disabilities Rights Council, for a while. And that to me was the same kind of thing, they didn't really understand our kinds of issues. I can remember being at this session, and it was all on plain language. We made these placards, a few of us. We rated people, the speakers — like when they judge people for skating, like 9.1 or 9.2. And I can remember there was someone from Toronto there, David Baker I think, I gave him the worst marks possible. Because he really upset me. 'Cause he gave this presentation all in complicated language, so we scored him later and we said he was bad, like 1.1 or some thing. And he said, "How dare you!" He wouldn't talk to us. He told the person we were with he didn't like it. And then he came over and apologized later, after, because he knew he was in the wrong. But I'll never forget that. We had score cards, like "poor," "very good." And his was "very poor."

And that's another thing, people don't think we have a sense of humor, but I like saying I have one. It might be drier or wittier or whatever, but I have one.

Getting the Bills Paid

What keeps you going?

I just keep going because I just... but there've been days lately when I just shut down completely. I just get so frustrated I don't.... It's hard to talk about this. When I came back from Toronto last Wednesday, I just came back a nervous wreck. I didn't want to talk to anyone all that day. And I was glad no one was home where I live until 4 or 4:30 when most people get home. And it was just, to me, it seemed last the two times I've been away, I've come back and complained to my parents and I've just feel like a real crumb by the time I come home, because I don't feel like ... It's been nice to go away, but at the back of my mind it's been worrying me. Working and getting my bills paid.

And so people just think that I'm up, up, up all the time, but I have my low days. And it's just I try not to get people thinking that I have low days, but I do have them. And I carry on, because I know that I have to carry on.

You're worried because they cut your hours back at work? [Barb has a job as a visiting homemaker.]

Uh-huh. Yeah. In March I told them I was going to Toronto twice, and I'd work every other weekend, and I told them I could work every weekend that I was home. And they said "Forget it, just take all of the weekends off." So that's what is happening.

That is where I get my most money, because that 24 hours I get paid for. So that is a lot of money off.

So when you travel in your volunteer work you sometimes lose money because you can't work, and you lose even more money because they cut back on your hours. Do you think people who invite you to do things think about that?

I really don't know. I really don't know. But after talking to my parents about it on Wednesday, they thought that a lot of people, and I really hadn't thought of it, like CACL [the Canadian Association for Community Living] hadn't thought of it.

Because some people get a handicapped pension, and they're not working, and they don't have to worry about it, and that's how they go because they can go like just at the drop of a hat. But I have to be thinking about it all the time.

And even when I wasn't working, like when I was unemployed full time, that might not make sense but you know what I mean, I was asked to go to three or four different places. And the whole time, the whole time, I'm not kidding, I was away on these trips, like Paris and England, instead of going there and enjoying myself, I was scared silly that they were going, that UIC [Unemployment Insurance] would find out about me going on these trips, and they would discontinue it.

People kept telling me "Don't worry, don't worry, it won't happen." And when I got back there was a letter saying "We cut back your money, because we didn't get your report card." So they found out because I mailed them early and they didn't like that. And they figured out that I was away.

So I never got that money back, and that was for two weeks, and that's a lot of money. And people don't realize that. You know, to me, a lot of people don't understand. It's just a way I have. I can't really enjoy myself because I'm worried about the money — "Where's the next pay cheque coming from?"

I don't like to worry about money. I'd like to have just enough money to get by and pay all my bills, and then I wouldn't worry. But I'm constantly worrying about it. I know a lot of people who don't worry about it, but I do, I do. It's on my mind all the time. And a lot of people I know don't worry about it.

And that's another issue. A lot of people are in workshops, and people get a real job in the community, and then if they fail at their new job, they go back to the workshop. Because they get GAINS [the disability pension], they get their pension, they get dental-medical. But when you're out in the community, like right now I had medical-dental, but I couldn't stay on them because you have to work like forty hours a week. And I never got, like I was on medical-dental for two months, but now I'm not on it. I have to pay my own. And then when you're in a place like mine that's subsidized, like when you get handicapped pension, your pension gets lower. That doesn't make sense to me. That's never made sense to me. You get less money because you're in cheap housing.

When people are on handicapped pension, like you pay your bills, like next Wednesday people get paid, at the end of the month, and they get their bills all paid up. Then it comes to the middle of the month, people have to eat macaroni and cheese or things like that. Because they can't afford things. I mean, that's what happened to me. I can't afford it. Like lately, I've not been doing very well in that department because I can't afford the rent. You know, you get two steps ahead, two back.

People Think It's All Glory and Good Times — It's Not

It's hard work, and people think going into hotel rooms, and having free meals, and travelling all over the world, is like easy as pie. It's not.

It really bugs me. I like doing things. I like talking now. But sometimes I just feel like a welcome door mat. That people are walking all over me.... And how do you get people to understand that it is a lot of hard work. And that it's not easy. It has not been easy. And how do you get people to understand that I'm not doing it just because, I'm doing it because I want to help other people. But it's getting to the point where that there's other self-advocates I know who won't have anything to do with me, because they know that I'm involved with all of this, and I'm getting all the glory and they wonder why they're not.

... I can remember going to a hotel in Toronto, and they wanted my credit card. And I said to them "I don't have one," and they said "You can't have a room unless." But CACL and the Institute have this agreement, that all self-advocates get a room. I mean you don't have to pay for it. So we get this room, but they don't like it.

So they said "Well, we need a credit card." And I said "I don't have one," and they got me really upset. So they said, "It's $75 dollars and tax." I had $75 so I gave it to them. And I phoned the office [CACL] right away, and I said "They're charging me $75 or more," and they said, "We'll be right down."

They took two hours to come down. I sat in the lobby for two hours, steaming mad at the hotel. I told them when they got there that I was leaving, that I wasn't going. And so, they finally got the money back. The staff were accusing me of all these things, that I didn't have a credit card. And no apology ever. They apologized to them, CACL, but not to me. So I said I wasn't going there any more.

And after a long time I finally got this credit card, but they all said I didn't make enough money. Like you need to make a certain amount, but they never told me how much you needed to make. So anyway, a friend and these other people wrote this letter. And the bank wrote one too. And they said I deserved one and that's how I got one. But I use it for I.D. only, when they ask for it.

Getting A Pizza

And then there was another time, a few years ago I was at this meeting, and I was volunteered to phone for pizza. So I phoned for this pizza and the lady at the other end said "You can't order," and I said "Pardon me?", and she said "You can't order, you're a teenager." And I'm going, "Oh." But I got really angry.

Then I got off the phone and wouldn't talk to anyone, I was just walking around. And so I told this friend finally. And she said "Let me phone." So she phoned and got through, and told them what had happened to me. And they said they couldn't do anything. So we got this pizza finally and it was cold.

So I thought, with this friend's help, we wrote this letter. We wrote this letter saying. We got around ten or twelve people to sign it. I took it around to different people, and they all signed it. But it took a long time to get the address. The pizza company, they wouldn't give you the head office address, because they didn't know what we were doing, or they wouldn't give us the manager's name. So we just tried to do undercover work.

So we finally got this letter back saying something about, no "sorry" or anything, other than "If your friends and you are unhappy, and you are, it sounds like, we will put a special gadget on my phone, the management's, so I'll know it is you." And we all said that is not what we want. If anything, we want pizza and an apology. And we all said they were the worst pizza I've ever had, it tasted like cardboard. And we told them that, and he didn't believe us.

So I mean, I don't go there. So as a result I tell people "don't go somewhere" and we all ban them. Like we don't go there.

Something to Be Proud Of

What are some of the things that you are proud of being involved with?

OK, I think the name change, the Eve case, and then advising and assisting National People First. And then there is LMCBSS [Lower Mainland Community Based Services Society]. That is a group that I helped start five years ago. It is basically self-advocates. I was the president, the first president. As you know, it is unheard of for self-advocates to be running associations. So I started it with some other people.

We are unique in that we have five self-advocates on the board. We sign the papers, do the contracts that most normates do. I'm just very proud of it, because we've done so many things. I like to be able to do things a lot of people say I can't do, and this is one of them. The executive director and other people have got flack in the past. Other people say how can we as self-advocates sign papers when we don't really know what they mean. You know, the same old thing.

Where did the idea to start LMCBSS come?

The way that I remember it, there is two things. One being, there was a conference with BCACL [British Columbia Association for Community Living] that they had called for different associations to start talking, and to start new groups. And so Cam Dori, he's the executive director for the Burnaby Association, got this brain wave about what he wanted to do. He got himself and his wife and three or four other couples together, I was not one of them at the time, I was just as a consultant.

And so they got these three or four couples together and just talked about it... They talked about that for six or seven months. And they thought they should get some self-advocates together. So we started talking about getting incorporated and signing papers, but we didn't start having meetings. We just started talking. So we started having meetings amongst ourselves, and we got incorporated.

So, we got together, got incorporated, and then I got to be president and some other people got to be different things. From there we got eight houses. We helped hire the staff, some of them, the first supervisors in some of the homes. We went to visit people in Woodlands and Glendale [two institutions], to meet the people.

We met with the Ministry [the government department], met with different people that we needed to talk to.

Up to a year ago, we never had an executive director. And so almost six months ago now, we hired our own executive director.

So how many people do you support?

Around 24. And we are getting a new home. We're looking into ideas for homes, other than just group homes. I like to say that we are unique because we have one group home that has two people in it. And when we opened that house it was unique because the Ministry doesn't usually fund for two people. And it is unique in that it was funded through both Ministries. One person was funded by one Ministry, and the other person was funded by the other. We did it that way.

We share a office space with two other associations. We all support each other...

We have a lot of different ranges of people. Like I don't like giving people labels, but like some people are semi-independent, some might want to move into a group home in the next year. They are getting help to look for a new place, if that is what they want. Or there could be two people that could live at home all their lives, if that's what they want.

And then we have another home that is quite different also. The Ministry is helping fund it. It is for one person with 24-hour care who lived a long time in an institution. And that is different.

So LMCBSS is one of the things you are proud to be involved with?

Very proud. I mean I am proud to be involved in all that I've got going, thinking back on it. You know, the other day I was asked about all my accomplishments, and I'm not bragging, but when I looked at it, I couldn't believe how much I've done over the years. It's kind of amazing. It's mighty remarkable.

4

Handicap Consciousness

translated from the Swedish

ÅKE JOHANSSON, then-President of RFUB Grunden (a national organization of persons with intellectual disability under the auspices of the Swedish ARC) and the first person with intellectual disability to sit on the national board of the full parents' association, gave this opening speech at the international conference of the Nordiska Forbundet Psykisk Utvecklingshämning (Nordic Association on Intellectual Disability), August 4-8 1987, at the University of Uppsala, Sweden.

I think it is important to go back a little before speaking about what it means to be handicap conscious.

In my case, I have lived in institutions for 32 years of my life. First I went to a school home, Hallagården. I was sent to school there because I was weak, so I was told. But this was not the whole truth.... Hallagården was a home for mentally handicapped children. When I went there we were divided into two groups. There were the mentally handicapped who could be educated and the mentally handicapped who were not capable of being educated. It's frightening, thinking back to those times, that not everybody was allowed to go to school. For my part I had the honor of going to school, if it can be considered an honor to go to school in Hallagården.

When I was 18 I was sent to a work home, Rönneholm Castle, which is in Skåne. Now Rönneholm was an open institution. Hallagården on the other hand was a closed institution. But living in institutions for so many years makes it very easy for a person to become passive. It is something you become without noticing it yourself. In the long run, a person can be very hurt by living in institutions. It can be very difficult to break away from the passive life one leads. You have to work very hard with yourself to make a recovery. Which brings me to the question of handicap consciousness.

I've thought a great deal about why nobody told us who were living in the institutions, why we were there and why we should be there. Little by little I came to the
conclusion that they didn't believe we could understand what it was all about. In the
first place, nobody said the words *mentally handicapped* or told us why we should go
to the place we were going to.

As a mentally handicapped person, as I see things today, when I was at the
institution there were very bad attitudes towards us who were mentally handicapped.
I feel today that there was a wall between the staff and us who were living there.
Then I ask myself why it was so difficult to talk about the words *mentally handicapped*.
Now I want to say how important it is that one talks about the words *mentally
handicapped* and what sort of handicap it is. To be able to get a handicap consciousness it is important that one finds out about it, as early as it is possible to speak
about mental handicap.

If I think back to the time when I was at the institution, I would have liked to find
out that I was mentally handicapped. But this is what we did not find out, and that is
the big mistake that was made, that nobody told us what was wrong. This played a
large part in making our situation so difficult.

Should I have been able to become aware of my handicap much earlier than I did?
It is not right that one should have to go and wonder why one is in an institution, why
one is there.

It's the same for those living at home with their parents. They too go around
wondering why they are as they are. And if one doesn't get an explanation at an early
age, well, one goes around imagining what can be wrong, and then one gets a totally
wrong picture of what the matter is. It also makes it difficult to respect oneself as a
mentally handicapped person in the future.

I can understand it in one way. It is so that there is a fear in everybody which
stops us speaking with the handicapped person. But it must not be like that. The
important thing is that we try, all together, to speak about the words *mentally
handicapped*.

Now, I am aware that this is difficult. But we must do it to get a handicap
consciousness — everybody in society. To get a handicap consciousness, that means
that one goes through a series of crises with oneself. It may be a very difficult time
which one has to go through because there are many crises and it is the same for a
person who is not mentally handicapped. The first step one tales is that one talks
about the sort of person one is and the situation one is in. After a very long time one
comes to the point when one learns to say "I am mentally handicapped."

But it is very difficult to say that I am mentally handicapped. In the first place,
there is so much feeling in these words. In the second place, I cannot do it until I
have respect for myself, that I am a mentally handicapped person.

Now, one cannot talk about oneself all at once. I know from my own experience that it takes a very long time. And today, I usually say that it is good if it takes
time, talking about oneself, I mean. Because there is so much one must learn about

oneself, because being handicap conscious means knowing that it is a question of myself.

Now this cannot be done all at once. It is something that one must work on for a long time. It is a crisis which one must struggle with. Because it must come from inside, and by that I mean that one has to search for the handicap one has. This is the crisis which can be very difficult for some people. Because it is now one asks oneself, "Am I mentally handicapped?"

What one needs now is the help of somebody who is not mentally handicapped. I said a moment ago that one must struggle oneself. Well, this is true to a certain degree. It is so that one cannot become handicap conscious all by oneself.

When I had come to this point in tackling my situation, it was very easy for me to overemphasize my handicap. Now, you shouldn't think that you who are not mentally handicapped do not overemphasize our handicap, because you do. You can overemphasize it in such a way that you find it difficult to accept a mentally handicapped person.

When we have come this far in working with our situation, then it may be difficult to accept that one is mentally handicapped. It is then very easy for us to do things which are too difficult for us. We do this only to prove that we are not mentally handicapped. One undertakes things which one knows "I can't do this really, but I will do it anyway.

This has a lot to do with the difficulty I have in seeing my limitations. I want to be as good as possible, and then I think it will be easier for me to get understanding, It is now that I need help. Now it is not possible to struggle alone with myself any longer. For me to get a handicap consciousness, there must be two of us.

What makes it so difficult to get a handicap consciousness? Well, I suppose it has a lot to do with the fact that we still have many prejudices and also we don't have the right attitudes towards the handicap. Then there are some walls which prevent us from speaking about the words *mentally handicapped*. It is the wall of disrespect which must be pulled down. I know that is the wall which is most difficult to pull down. One wall which we must break through is the wall which prevents us from getting understanding

Now I come to the difficult part. That is, to get a positive handicap consciousness. This is when the big crises hit us. Because the handicap itself is a part of my own picture. It can be both painful and difficult to accept help if one doesn't know what one is capable of. Then being helped can feel insulting for a person. I must be able to feel secure, be able to take an initiative, be independent and have a sexual identity. But the difficult part of being able to get a positive handicap consciousness comes when I have to learn that my picture of myself is a part of it.

If I have come through these crises, I can discover other mentally handicapped people and feel solidarity with them. One gets strength to deal with the sorrow caused by the handicap. Knowledge of my handicap makes it possible for me to accept responsibility for myself. This is when I can say that I have a Positive Handicap

Consciousness.

But then we have something called Negative Handicap Consciousness.... I know that there are many more people who are negative than there are positive people.

When a mentally handicapped person comes and asks "Am I mentally handicapped?" — the fact that a person asks a question like that is because he has been going around thinking "What am I and what am I not?" Now it is very important that one doesn't just answer "Yes, you are mentally handicapped," but one must try to get to the bottom of his question. It is now that the best time has come to speak about the words *mental handicap*.

I will go so far as to say that a person cannot answer this question if he or she does not have a positive handicap consciousness. If a person is negative, they will do anything not to be mentally handicapped, One cannot feel any solidarity with others who are mentally handicapped either, because one wants to be better than one is all the time.

Moving away from a negative handicap consciousness towards a positive consciousness is very difficult. One needs a lot of help because it is very difficult.

5

Thoughts in Me

Elisabeth Broberg
translated from the Swedish

The speech by ELISABETH BROBERG *excerpted below was a keynote address at the Nordic Association on Intellectual Disability Conference in August 1987. Elisabeth Broberg was the first person with intellectual disability to be proposed for Woman of the Year, in recognition of her self-advocacy efforts as an employee of her church, as a volunteer with the Swedish ARC, and through her numerous interviews in newspapers and on national television.*

I shall present myself through describing my life, how I have had it. Next I shall speak of human dignity. That is what is most important in my life.

When I was born I was very sick. My doctor said:

- I would never talk.
- I would never be able to walk.
- I would never be able to take care of myself in the community.
- I should live in a home for children. I should not live at home.

So I lived in a home for children. From that time, I don't remember so much. There are few people now who have stories for me from my infancy....

When I was 17 years old, I joined a church. There I felt valuable and important.

During this period, a number of things happened in my life. I put forth questions and demanded to have answers. I went to FUB's [the Swedish ARC] partnership training, that gave me a great deal of power....

But today I live in a group residence. I have my own apartment; there I am doing well. I don't know what the future holds for me; that has to be seen. So it is for persons of all ages. It shall be enough to not be unemployed.

Why am I here today? What is human dignity? What does it mean for us who have an intellectual handicap?

Human dignity is my greatest question. Human dignity is needed by a person who has it hard. All people like to be valued very much. All must, at some time, have the same thoughts as everyone else. Human dignity means that one shall be able to live with others. Human dignity is to be able to move about freely in the community. Human dignity can also be to take time for other people who are severely handicapped, to talk with them the same as one would talk with others.

For development, it means to have the power to do things. To develop is important for all people. We need everyone's development. But how does one develop? Does one develop by living in an institution? Does one develop through just being intellectually handicapped? Or only write a paper with a new law? [a reference to the 1986 Act of Parliament which mandates the closing down of all institutions, hopefully by the year 2000] No, it does not mean that.

I think that one's best development has to be in the community; I have to learn to be myself, Elisabeth Broberg, or to be who I am.

I have gained experience being Elisabeth Broberg. I have met others to whom I have mentioned human dignity. I have said, *Don't judge others by appearance only*. If only you could combine this with human dignity. That is so important for us intellectually handicapped; that we get to feel that we have value like others.

There was a debate in Borås [Elisabeth's home town] a few years ago, that dealt with whether or not intellectually handicapped should have to live in a regional villa. One feels inside oneself a common disappointment with these persons. One could feel oneself to be not worth anything since that day, so I said to myself: "Now I will go out! I will go out and inform about my life, about FUB, about human dignity."

To be taken seriously is very important. I, Elisabeth Broberg, have not always been taken so seriously. It has felt bad to be judged by appearances only, but it doesn't mean anything.

We must be taken seriously.

We are every bit as valuable as any of you.

We will live and we will reside in the community where everyone has to get along together and all are very valuable.

Take just one example: a girl in a wheelchair. When she goes into a grocery store, she doesn't feel valued that day. When one comes into a grocery store, so many commonplace objects are so high, she must have help, she can't take care of herself. One doesn't feel very valuable when one constantly is anchored in situations where one can't do for oneself and always needs to ask for help. That's it. You must learn that first....

Don't you and I have the same color of hair?
But we are precisely the same in value.

Aren't you and I the same in height?
But we are precisely the same in value.

You can learn things much faster than I.
But we are precisely the same in value.

So. I could continue here as long as you would like. I could put forth many questions in me. Here I will give you a greeting. I have been a Christian for six years. I have carried inside of me a feeling of my full value.

THOUGHTS IN ME

Thoughts go up and down in me!
The future!

Yes, what will happen with me and
my friends next?

Do we need a law
which is just for us?

Or can we be in the community
on our own terms?

Can we live and work on our own terms?

We are people who will live,
Live together with you.

Will we have that?

Address to the National Conference Of and For People with Intellectual Disability

Gothenberg, Sweden, 1987

Thomas Holmqvist
translated from the Swedish

THOMAS HOLMQVIST is a person with intellectual disability who has been a leader of FUB Grunden *in Gothenberg, Sweden. FUB is the national organization originally developed by and for parents; Grunden is the newer section of FUB, comprised of people with intellectual disability. FUB exists solely for education, advocacy, supports to families, and research. In this speech, Mr. Holmqvist reported his impressions of the last full national FUB meeting, and explained the purpose of the FUB Grunden conference.*

We in FUB are happy to welcome you warmly to this conference which we organized solely for us intellectually handicapped in FUB.... It was hard [at the last full national parent FUB meeting] to understand from their [self-advocates'] point of view, and it went too fast. They didn't understand everything that was said. That made it hard to understand their recommendations. It became hard for the intellectually handicapped representatives to support each other.

We come here out of this need for our own major meeting solely for those with intellectual handicap. At this meeting we can discuss common problems which we find in our everyday lives. We can make recommendations which can be motions to be considered at the national meeting. Thus it can be seen that we can make recommendations for change in our own lives.

We show also that we can understand those who have severe and profound intellectual handicap. They are the ones who need the most support and help from the community. But it is important that it becomes their wishes coming out of their needs (not just what the community thinks)....

We can talk about how it feels when others decide for us. And how it feels when people talk over our heads and make decisions about us. It feels dumb and sad and one feels violated. That is how it has been for us every time. That feeling is common for us who have intellectual handicap. That we understand only too well....

Ten years ago it was demonstrated that intellectually handicapped people in institutions should have their own room. Still, many of them are together. [Seventy percent of people living in institutions had rooms of their own in 1987.]

It was long ago that we recommended that they create more jobs in the open market. But the majority are still in day centers and sheltered workshops.

I hope that folks will soon take our recommendations seriously....

Again, a warm welcome!

Parents' Expectations and Demands

Åke Johansson
translated from the Swedish

ÅKE JOHANSSON lived in Swedish institutions for people with intellectual disability for 32 years. He was chairman of the 1987 National Conference Of and For People with Intellectual Disability, held in Gothenberg, Sweden. In the speech below, he requested compassion for the parents in FUB — the national parent association — and proposed recommendations for consideration by the conference committees.

The changing and, at times, very negative and unsympathetic, attitudes toward intellectually handicapped also had negative consequences for their parents. They often felt neglected by others. Combined with the lack of support and care from society this was a heavy burden to many families. Feelings of guilt and shame made practical and economical difficulties even harder to bear.

Some of the parents followed the advice of the experts and abandoned and tried to forget their intellectually handicapped child. Those who stayed in contact with their child got an insight into institutional care which they had to accept even though they saw the disadvantages. Some parents, however, decided to manage on their own without intervention from others. They didn't want to be a "burden to society." Maybe they also understood that, after all, the intellectually handicapped child could benefit from belonging to a family.

These experiences don't only apply to the situation for intellectually handicapped persons and their relatives in the past. Many parents of adult intellectually handicapped persons in day activity centers today have similar experiences. It can be difficult for these parents to accept and believe in information about new ambitions within the services for intellectually handicapped persons. This might be one of the reasons why it takes time to develop cooperation between relatives and personnel. If parents experience that society earlier treated them and their child poorly, that will influence the attitudes toward the persons who are today caring for their adult child.

The respect for parents' demand for and need of psychological and practical support when their children have grown up has developed not least through the National Parents' Association for Intellectually Handicapped Children, Youth and Adults [RFUB], which started in 1956 and has more than 135 local branches with more than 30,000 members. Within RFUB it was early realized that parents of intellectually handicapped children need someone to contact for support and help to express their needs. [They conduct no residential nor work programs.] Thus the consultative activity started, which today is complementary to the support given by the personnel within the [state-administered] services for intellectually handicapped persons (social workers and psychologists).

Today, the importance of parents' emotional experiences when having an intellectually handicapped child is recognized. There is a growing understanding that flexible, practical help, also has a psychological value. But we must remember that the parents, whose children now are 35–40 years old, have received very little support from society. This goes for all kinds of help: economical, pedagogical, psychological, and social. Many times this has led to a situation where the family takes total care of the intellectually handicapped child and doesn't live a normal life. This pattern has developed over many years and has become a way to live. Sudden changes in such a situation can arouse very strong feelings. It is therefore especially important for professionals to cooperate and consider the needs of parents as well as those of the intellectually handicapped child.

A decision has been made that every institution shall be closed, and I think that is a good decision. When I say every institution, I mean every one, including the Annedal Institution in Gothenberg. Doctors say that these children have to live in a hospital. It concerns 21 severely intellectually handicapped children. What shall I think of doctors when they talk like that? I would go so far as to say that I don't believe they know as much as I am *supposed* to believe they know! I thought I could expect more from doctors. But I obviously can't. Hearing these words from doctors makes me doubt their understanding of what it is like to be intellectually handicapped.

RESIDENCES

Every residence should have a bathroom and a small kitchen, so you can make your own coffee.

The law says that you are entitled to choose who to live with. But this is not so

---

* At this time, when a child with disability is born, the family learns they will receive from the government such entitlements as: an income supplement of more than $8,000.00 yearly; free loan and repair of state-of-the-art equipment (prostheses, wheelchairs, communication boards, etc.) and toys from Lekotek libraries; home health aides (in-home child care) on a sliding fee scale; respite care; and subsidized taxi service, where the person with disability pays the equivalent of a bus fare and an escort rides free.

in reality. I think those who move from an institution to a group home should have a say and not be persuaded, as happens today.

It is a citizen's right to have access to a residence, and this goes also for handicapped persons. But the individual needs must be adhered to. The residence must have a design which corresponds to the demands of each handicapped person.

The intellectually handicapped person needs extra resources because of his disability. This means more concretely that we, the intellectually handicapped — regardless of degree of handicap — are in need of residences that are adjusted to each individual.

What I have said is very important. We must face the fact that a person might live in his residence for the rest of his life. Those 7,000 intellectually handicapped persons living in institutions today have been denied their social right to adequate residence. They need a place of their own and they have a right to get it.

THE RIGHT TO DAILY ACTIVITY

In the rural community, the mildly and moderately intellectually handicapped had a task and were able to contribute to the maintenance of the family. At the so-called "working homes," the intellectually handicapped had the same kind of tasks. They worked with farming and gardening; the women were cooking, weaving and knitting.

At that time, many intellectually handicapped adults also were placed in "family homes," which meant that they helped farmers at the lowest possible payment. Many had to work very hard — and some even had to live with the animals. Even though we don't have these horrible family-home conditions today, there still remains a lot to be done concerning work for intellectually handicapped people.

Our first wish is that our work at our day activity centers throughout the country is regarded as important…. it makes it possible for the intellectually handicapped person to participate in the community….

Many intellectually handicapped persons today want a salary instead of a pension. I agree, because I think these people are aware of the fact that they are worthy workers. All these people should not stay at day activity centers. They should have a job, at first in a small group of intellectually handicapped persons within a company, with a prospect of being individually employed. Then it is time to demand a salary. In my opinion this is the right way to go.

With these words I now declare the work of the national meeting opened. If we work together I know that we will succeed in the hard work we have in front of us.

3

Self-Advocacy and the International League

Robert Martin
with Desmond Corrigan

ROBERT MARTIN and DESMOND CORRIGAN live in New Zealand. This paper was presented to the eleventh World Congress of the International League of Societies for Persons with Mental Handicap (ILSMH) in New Delhi, India, in November 1994, and to the Inclusion Internationale Conference on Human Rights for Persons with Mental Handicaps in Central and Eastern Europe, October 1995.

Self-advocacy is an empowerment issue which affects the lives of every person who has an intellectual disability or handicap. In the past, most professional people and many of the groups who provided services for people labelled disabled, believed that we, the disabled community, had little to offer and should not participate in the making of decisions which affect our lives.

How wrong they were.

I have been involved in self-advocacy for the past 20 years. I did not know what it was called at first, but I knew I was tired of being told what I could and could not do. I had feelings, I had a belief in myself — although others often did not see it.

During the last few years we had seen a growing self-advocacy movement through-out the world for people labeled intellectually disabled or handicapped.

The People First movement has been started in many countries and is growing in strength. More and more self-advocates are wanting to have control of their lives and to make the decisions that affect them. This led to the International League setting up a Committee on Self-Advocacy. This committee of self-advocates has met twice. The first meeting was held in the Netherlands and the second meeting was held in London.

At these two meetings, we as self-advocates wrote down what we believed are the important beliefs, values, and principles for self-advocacy throughout the world. With the help of the League, a booklet on our Beliefs, Values and Principles has been written. I hope you will all not only read it but think about what it means to us. We have spoken out about why our friends must not be left in institutions, why we must be seen as **People First**, and why it is wrong to be labelled disabled.

I, along with many of my friends, grew up in an institution — in fact most of the first 15 years of my life was spent in institutions. I know the damage this has done to my life. Institutions must close, but when people come from institutions to live in their community they must receive support or they will fail. They do not deserve to fail.

We are people first. We deserve to have the same rights and protection of the law as our fellow countrymen. I am a New Zealander and very proud to be one. I am the same as every other New Zealander. I am not someone less than others or someone to be ignored or treated badly because I have an intellectual disability.

Being labelled disabled often makes you feel bad inside or not worth much as a person. Others often look down on you or call you names such as *dummy, stupid, moron,* to name just a few. I have been called those names and when I lashed out I was then seen as a challenging behavior. A challenge to whom?

As a child, I sat with my head in my hands for weeks at a time. I did not want to live in a world where I was teased and ill-treated. Then I discovered sports — something I was very good at — and my world started to change.

Everyone in this room today has abilities. I want you to remember that is true as well for us who are self-advocates. We have a lot to offer. Let's get rid of the labels. Our disabilities are only a small part of our lives. We are people too and we want to join you and not watch the world pass us by.

Self-advocacy or the ability to make your own decisions is the one thing that most people take for granted — until this right or ability is taken away from them. Everyone at this Congress is a self-advocate.

Self-advocacy starts with the small decisions — what clothes will I wear today? what radio station or television program will I watch? will I go and see a friend today? Yes — we all take this for granted until it is denied to us. Many people labelled disabled lose all their rights to make these decisions. Others — be they family, staff or professionals — make the decisions for them. They become powerless and feel useless as people. Self-advocacy is about supporting people so they can make their own decisions and have control over their own lives.

People with greater levels of disability also have the ability to make their own decisions. The key is communication. Many of us at this Congress do not speak the same language, but we can communicate with each other by simple signs and body language. It is no different for those self-advocates who cannot speak. We must learn to watch their body language and understand what they are telling us. Self-advocacy is for everyone, including those with greater disability.

As we look forward to the year 2000 we want to see some changes. Negative labelling and the stigma that it gives must go. We want to be seen as *people with abilities*; while we accept our disabilities, they are just a small part of our lives.

We want to see the institutions closed forever. All people need support to live in their community. Some of us need more support than others. With a supportive community, institutions will close and all people will live a valued life.

We want organizations and service providers to support us, to recognize our worth as people, and to involve us in their decision making as of right now. Without us, they would not exist. We have a lot to offer, and given the chance, we can make good decisions.

We want to see people who have been labelled disabled being supported to live a full and meaningful life in their own community, within their own family and with their own friends.

We want self-advocates to be empowered to make their own decisions, to have control over their lives, and to have a real say in their everyday lives.

We want the *chance* to live alongside each and every one of you, to share the joys and hardships of life, and to be responsible citizens.

Much has changed — most of it for the good. More of us are living in the community, many of us now work at real jobs, and as young people many of us are able to attend regular school.

I ask each one of you to make a personal commitment to help us to open the doors into our own community for each one of us who has been labelled disabled. To keep those locked doors open. To never allow them to close again. We are all people together, and together we can achieve anything.

Section III

Self-Advocacy Around The World

"Le National"

(Refrain)
Le national il a grandi
dans le coeur des gens aussi
dans notre pays.

De Vancouver à Sydney
des personnes ce sont regroupées
pour défendre leurs propres droits.
C'est ainsi que le mouvement est né.

(Refrain)

On a lutté pour notre liberté
en tant que personnes handicappés
bien trop souvent laissées de côté
par des blessures tant affligées.

(Refrain)

On a été étiquetés
des personnes handicapées
Mais aujourd'hui, tout a changé
Nous sommes capable de nous affirmer.

(Refrain)

Au fil des années
le mouvement y'a poussé
On a réalisé
nos rêves de liberté.

(Refrain)
People First of Canada has grown
in the hearts of the people
and in our country.

From Vancouver to Sydney
people formed groups
to advocate for themselves.
That is how the movement started.

(Refrain)

Once trapped by a label,
too often abandoned,
and so often hurt,
we fought for our freedom.

(Refrain)

There was a time
when we were labeled handicapped,
but today, everything has changed
and we can assert ourselves.

(Refrain)

Over the years
the movement has grown.
We've fulfilled
our dreams of freedom.

— Denis Laroche
President, People First of Canada
(see p. 128)

"In Their Best Interest"

How Self-Advocacy Came About in the ILSMH

Helmut Spudich

HELMUT SPUDICH is an Editorial Writer for the Salzburger Nachrichten, *Austria's leading newspaper. Earlier, he served as Executive Director of* Lebenshilfe, *the Austrian association of families of persons with mental handicaps. In this chapter, he shares his experiences with self-advocates' participation at several meetings of the International League of Societies for People with Mental Handicaps.*

In the beginning there was a simple telegram. The time was early summer 1978, when preparations for the seventh World Congress of the International League of Societies for Persons with Mental Handicap (ILSMH*), to be held that fall in Vienna, were fully underway. It was Rosemary Dybwad who put this question to the organizers: Can you accommodate a "group of young people" from the Bancroft School at the Congress?

Of course we could. We were putting up 1500 people from around the globe, offering day care to parents, so what could possibly be the problem with 10 or so "young people" traveling with some of their teachers and counsellors?

But at the time, we did not really grasp the essence of the question. It was not just accommodation that the Congress organizers were asked for. It really was a quest for participation: being empowered to take part in a Congress that discussed questions of everyday life affecting the students of Bancroft School as well as thousands of other people around the world — who were the objects of the discussions, though themselves neither invited nor present. All that was provided for at this

---

* Formerly the International League of Societies for the Mentally Handicapped (ILSMH), "The League" continues to use the old acronym even after reformulating their name to incorporate "people first" language.

international gathering was good, old-fashioned "day care" — in other words, the hidden message was *Keep Out* of our expert meetings."

So when the group from Bancroft, accompanied by friends, helpers, and Bancroft's director Clarence York, finally arrived in Vienna in October 1978, they were well received as special guests, but not as regular participants. To be sure, these young people were visiting sessions, meeting people and making friends, dancing Viennese waltzes at the Mayor's reception. Undoubtedly they enjoyed an eventful and enjoyable week.

But although their presence was well noted in the halls of the fancy imperial palace during coffee breaks and the social events of a splendid week of thoughtful deliberations, even slipping in and out of sessions to listen in, they were not there as equals. Rarely did anybody bother to stop the flow of talk to ask or explain.

Still, these early self-advocates at the 7th World Congress of the ILSMH drove home a strong message. Gunnar Dybwad, who was elected president of the League after having served so well as program chairman of the Congress, in early 1979 founded a standing committee of the ILSMH on "Participation," under the skilled chairmanship of Eleanor Elkin and Clarence York. Its goal was to ensure the inclusion of persons with mental handicap in the work of the League — as well as to serve as an example for national associations on how to pursue participation of self-advocates, in questions of everyday life just as much as in policy forming. So Vienna, with its semi-open doors, after all had an impact on the kick-off of the international self-advocacy movement.

Slowly but steadily, the participation committee covered ground. In itself it was an exercise in full participation, consisting of self-advocates as well as advocates. One of its prime objectives was to accomplish the participation of persons with mental handicap at the next Congress of the League, to be held 1982 in Nairobi, Kenya. Through correspondence (at the time much slower before the advent of fax and electronic mail), occasional meetings, and enduring discussion, Eleanor Elkin and Clarence York prepared an organizational scheme that turned out to be very successful.

Before this international debut of participation went onstage, the International Year of Disabled Persons (1981) provided another milestone of self-advocacy. At the United Nations Center in Vienna, a preparatory committee of the UN in 1980 agreed to hear a statement from a self-advocate from Austria. For the opening session of the final meeting of this international planning group, one self-advocate from Vienna was able to deliver a message of participation on behalf of persons with mental handicap. The statement, prepared with the help of the Viennese Parents' Association, was received well by the official UN delegates as well as by a national TV audience in Austria. Most important, it did away with the notion of many that people with a disability could not speak for themselves, and certainly broadened the meaning of the UN year: "Full Participation."

Personal Stories Made Their Point

Very elegantly, this first internationally heard strong claim for self-advocacy served as a prelude to the successful participation of self-advocates in the League's participation in Nairobi. It was an exciting moment when finally, after several years of arduous participation, a group of 30 persons from nine countries, accompanied by friends, helpers and relatives, crowded into the meeting room on the fourth floor of the Kenyatta Conference Center. The air was busy with whispered translations to cope with the Babylonian language problem, ranging from Arabic and Kiswahili to German, Swedish, English, and French. Where the "regular" Congress participants required a team of 18 translators to handle just three languages, this group attacked the cross-cultural barriers with volunteers, humor, patience, and resourcefulness. Communication throughout this week of intense discussions never seemed to be a problem.

Indeed, communication was what this whole week was about — talking with someone who has shared the same experiences of being set back, of being secluded in an institution for years, of not being listened to, of not being understood. On four days of the week, the talk and discussion centered around the basic facts of life: about the workplace, about friendship, about being listened to and heard, about making your own decisions, about going on vacations and leisure opportunities, about marriage and children.

There was the young woman who flushed when she talked about her wish to marry her boyfriend and demanded the right to share her life with him, a life not decided upon by others who pretend to speak "in her best interest." Looking around the room, you could see nods and understanding on the faces. Much of the discussion, of the frustration of past experience, of hope for the future, focused on the most central aspect of human life: the need to belong and to relate to others.

Others, like Åke Johansson from Sweden, had experienced the total control exercised by institutions over their lives. Between the ages of 10 and 46 Åke lived in an institution before he was able to attend school and move on to a life on his own. At the meeting he was able to relay his work experience to others — like explaining to Mark about labor unions. It took three different takes and the support of other conference participants for Mark to catch on — but catch on he did.

A set of questions that the participation committee had prepared for this international meeting helped steer discussions throughout the week. Samples: "Can you choose the person or persons with whom you live?" "Can people with mental handicap get married in your country?" "Do you want to have children?" "Are you represented on your society's board or committees?" "Do you have a choice of where to work?" "How does it feel to be out of work?"

People quickly learned the rules of the conference game, and worked out some rules of their own. The plenary group learned how to tackle discussions in smaller working groups and report back to the whole. After the first day, impatience with the many observers grew and a new rule was established: "No more than two outsiders allowed for each meeting." Some self-advocates had traveled to Nairobi with their parents, who even accompanied them to the meeting. It took some doing to slip out of their shadow. But throughout the week, one could see the growth in self-esteem as other self-advocates lent support to their colleagues.

Hard Work Yields Progress

After three long days filled with discovery, hard work and excitement over a newly formed bond of international solidarity, the "parallel" program finally became one with the Congress at large. Self-advocates presented their opinions and conclusions to the Thursday morning plenary session and to the hundreds of participants from around the world, mostly parents and professionals of various disciplines. The group had chosen a panel of speakers to represent what came out of three days of separate meetings of self-advocates. And although many of the general Congress participants showed their support for the representation of persons with mental handicap, there was also a sense of the old benevolent mistrust. To those, Åke Johansson from Sweden had this to say about self-advocacy:

> There must be information about how it is to be mentally handicapped.... We must dare to talk about ourselves and our situation. We can do that by showing we can do a lot despite that we are mentally handicapped: by putting our foot down, when being treated unfairly; by letting us participate in difficult matters.... We must participate in boards and committees in our organization. But is it possible to participate in a meaningful way in boards and committees? We think it is, because one meaningful way is to work in smaller groups and smaller committees. But the members of the board must not go through the questions too quickly, because then it is difficult to understand, especially when it comes to economic questions.

One is tempted to add that this is a meaningful proposal for almost *anyone* on the governing boards of organizations — not just for those who have to cope with a disability.

Åke Johansson also countered the skepticism sometimes expressed that it was only those with a slight impairment who were able to be self-advocates.

> Who should speak for the mentally handicapped? The mentally handicapped shall speak for themselves. We know what is best for ourselves. When it comes to the severely and profoundly handicapped, we think a person who is very close to her or him should do the talking.

It was impressive how this panel of self-advocates handled the many questions that the plenary session put forward. Samples:

- "How do you feel when you are included in the services for severely handicapped persons?"

  Michael Ahlbin from Sweden had this to say in response: "I think it's
  good we can help them. We can understand them — when they are worried,
  when they are sad, and then we might be able to help them."

- "How do you decide whether or not to get married?"

  David Mogamba from Kenya: "When I decide to marry I will choose my
  partner according to the character she has."

- "Do you think you should have children?"

  Barbara Goode from Canada: "There are a lot of so-called normal people
  that have kids and they can't look after them, I've been told. But no one
  makes up their minds for them, so no one should make up our minds."

After hours of presentation and discussion, one Congress participant summed up
the feeling of the audience by saying, "I would very much like to express my sincere
congratulations to all the participants, not because they are mentally handicapped
but because they have answered so very well on these very difficult questions, both
mentally and intellectually."

More Progress In Nairobi

Nairobi was the birth of the international acceptance of the right and need for self-
advocacy, for "full participation," as called for by the International Year of Disabled Persons. By organizing such an impressive meeting of self-advocates and
overcoming the barriers of international travel, different languages, and the benevolent prejudice of "speaking for those who cannot speak for themselves," the
ILSMH effectively challenged itself and its national members to do likewise. No
more conferences and meetings could be called without this nagging question to
organizing committees: What about "participation"?

From the conference of self-advocates came a set of recommendations that were
presented to the ILSMH. Some of the proposals were practical, to overcome the
handicap of "normal" persons when it comes to dealing with "the handicapped":
"We wish we could have translation with the earphones. We would like everyone to
speak slowly so that we can understand. Sometimes the speeches are too long and
too technical." (Who would not agree on that?) "We will need money if we are to be
effective. Our national parent associations should sponsor people with mental handicaps to come to the Congress." Other recommendations challenged the basic way
persons with mental handicap have been dealt with so far. "We see ourselves as

equal partners. It is important that we be called adults and that we be treated like everybody else." And finally, the demand for full participation on all levels: "Each national and local association should have persons with mental handicap on their board."

In the years to follow Nairobi, it was the self-advocates who emerged as the best watchdogs of their "best interest." One event describes how this shift in representation, from protected to protectors, took place — not without (unintended) hurt to the caretakers. In Hamburg in the fall of 1983, the first European Congress of the ILSMH was to take place. The German parents' association *Lebenshilfe* had learned their lesson from Nairobi, or so they thought. With great perfection, a parallel program was set up in which several hundred persons participated.

But the parallel program turned out to be a separate program. The meeting places were remote from the conference site in the downtown area. "Technical reasons" were quoted for having the sessions of self-advocates take place in workshops on the outskirts of the city. Communication with the "regular" conference participants was limited to a large social event. But the self-advocates knew how to gather attention: at the closing session of the Congress, they marched into the hall in protest, carrying banners and angrily demanding the stage to express their outrage over being shut out from the regular Congress proceedings. They certainly caught the attention of the participants, as well as of the media. The protests were heard not only in the conference hall, but nationwide through newspaper headlines and TV reports.

Participation Today

Participation has become a natural feature of ILSMH events since Nairobi. Still, progress can be a slow-moving snail. It took another ten years before the League effectively dealt with one of the central recommendations made at Nairobi: that self-advocates be represented on the board. It was only at the League's general assembly in April 1992 that Barbara Goode, founder of People First of Canada and one of the panelists at the Nairobi conference, was elected a regular board member of the ILSMH. In ten years' time, full participation within the League has finally become a reality.

What's next? Will it take another ten years for the League to elect a self-advocate president of the organization?

10

The Right to Self-Determination in Sweden

Patricia McKenna, M.S.

PATRICIA SHEA MCKENNA, speech-language pathologist, was awarded a scholarship by the Rotary Foundation to study the evolution of the Normalization Principle with Bengt Nirje, its author, and Lars Kebon, chair of the Psychiatric/Psychological Research Team at the University of Uppsala, Sweden, in 1987–1988.* Stipendium guidelines required basic mastery of the Swedish language. Because she has cerebral palsy, Ms. McKenna feels people with intellectual and physical disability greeted her in a spirit of genuine solidarity. They were generous in sharing their personal and political struggles and patient with her attempts at their language.

While preparing for my year in Sweden, I wondered how many new ideas would really be encountered. After all, we have an abundance of creative people and programs working in state and charitable associations at home and around the world.

In the first four sections of this chapter, I will share with you examples of the startling discovery that many people with intellectual disability — that is, mental retardation — have developed their capacity for deep self-knowledge, critically analyzing quality of life issues, engaging in thoughtful deliberations with service providers and politicians, and initiating informed (even bilingual) cross-cultural discourse.

The rest of the chapter explores three aspects of Scandinavian culture, increasingly systematized over the years, which encourage such personal and collective strengths. In essence, they acknowledge that *all people have the right to food, clothing,*

* The author would like to thank Bengt Nirje and Lars Kebon for their assistance in the preparation of this chapter.

shelter, health services, education, training, and employment. People with disability participate in all this; when environmental upports and technical aids are needed, they
are provided from tax monies. They discourage charity drives, which become exercises
in privilege and teach generations of people to pity the recipients. The Scandinavian
environment, then, liberates everyone to strive for personal and cultural achievements over and above basic human needs in a climate of egalitarianism.

So it was a year of learning and experiencing ideas very new to me. I welcome
this opportunity to bring them to you, with warmest thanks to all my Swedish
teachers.

I. International Conference of the Nordic Association on Intellectual Disability, Uppsala, August 1987

My study year began with attendance at this conference. For the first time in over
100 years of quadrennial meetings, *people with intellectual disability were among the
keynote speakers!* (Two of their speeches have been included as Chapters 4 and 5 of
this volume.) They, who understand best of all the disabilities and circumstances of
their lives, stood shoulder to shoulder with parents, professionals and politicians
in the great hall of the University of Uppsala, a 500-year center of scholarship, to
share their insights and wisdom. From their own manuscripts, they asked the 100
listeners to learn from history in order to create a better future.

The energy generated from these messages rippled throughout the audience
and brought us to our feet with ovations surpassing the magnitude I observed four
months later at the Nobel award ceremony in Stockholm. Like witnessing an Olympic
victory, we thrill, we know when we are present at a breakthrough moment in hard-
earned human excellence.

I resolved then to meet these speakers and their colleagues, to learn from them.
I wanted them to teach me how they came to such deep self-knowledge and how
they put it to community education and political use.

My research team advisors introduced me to leaders in this movement for self-
determination. They, in turn, invited me to additional national and regional conferences: one in Gothenberg (October 1987), and one in Tranås (December 1987).

II. National Conference Of and For People with Intellectual Disability, Gothenberg, October 1987

The three-day convention was held in Dalheimers House, a fully accessible hotel,
and was attended by about 100 people with intellectual disability plus about 20
advisors. They had traveled from all parts of Sweden to study issues together and to
prepare recommendations for the entire FUB national parents' meeting (to be held
the following year in Luleo, Sweden) to promote regional initiatives with service
providers, politicians, and the whole community. It was called to order with a

welcome from Thomas Holmqvist, whose speech is excerpted in Chapter 6 of this volume. He was followed by Åke Johansson, who presented a rationale for empathy with the parents' views and for the committee work to come, excerpted in Chapter 7.

These speeches and this conference must be considered against the backdrop of their parents' organization functioning as an umbrella to the group comprised of people with intellectual disability. Thus, these sons and daughters are struggling (with support from FUB staff) to establish their adult identity on personal and organizational levels simultaneously.

Conference leaders invited participants wo select a committee and work on it for the entire weekend. They could choose to work on one of several topics: residence, work, education, or free-time issues. They were charges with the responsibility of reporting recommendations at the final conference meeting. I joined one of the free-time groups for the weekend. It was composed of about 12–15 persons, including 3–5 *handledere* (advisors) who offered occasional assistance. The chair, Mikael Ahlbin, and the secretary both have an intellectual disability. Using parliamentary procedure, they led a discussion and wrote the minutes, focusing on that which is good and that which is needed for quality free-time opportunities.

The committees met about three times. People were well practiced in processing content and form.

During the closing sessions, everyone reassembled to report on committee recommendations. Only the delegates with intellectual disability were allowed to have the floor. One *handledere* persisted in raising her hand, rising to her feet and trying to speak. Åke Johansson used the power of his person and position to call her out of order, brought down the gavel, and she was ruled to sit down without being allowed to say a word! This conference was solid upon its foundations, or *grunden*. Recommendations included:

RESIDENCES
- Staff should help out and be supportive, but not make the decisions.
- Home health aides should be available for each and every need.
- It is important when moving to a residence that a person is well prepared. One must be mature to move.
- We should decide ourselves where to live and who should share the group homes.
- Persons with intellectual handicap should decide who will be employed as staff.
- *All* people should have a room of one's own (98% of persons living in community residences reportedly had a room of their own in 1987).

WORK
- All workplaces should be adapted for multi-handicapped persons.
- One should prepare well, beginning with the specialist training before taking

the specialist job.
- Many jobs must be created for the intellectually handicapped in the public sector.
- There should be more worker union education for intellectually handicapped persons.

EDUCATION [The following references are unique to Scandinavia and will be discussed in detail later.]
- More places in Folk High Schools. They are important and good for confidence.
- Study circle time is too short. It should be lengthened.

FREE TIME
- It is important that hotels, restaurants, public places and transportation are handicapped-accessible.
- Free-of-charge companions should be easily available — for example, for vacations.
- Intellectually handicapped people should have self-management education to participate in public leisure-time projects.
- Work schedules of personnel shouldn't hinder free-time plans of people with intellectual handicap.

In his closing address, Lars-Åke Martinsson said [translated]:

We in FUB Grunden here in Gothenberg will thank all of you for a really fine conference. It has been wonderful to have you here.

Work in the committee groups has been very good and we think that all have gotten to say what they think. *Handledere* were careful about not talking too much themselves, weren't just pushy and were helpful. Discussions have been interesting and worthwhile, exactly as we had hoped it would be. We have come together and made recommendations, proposals and motions, and said how we intellectually handicapped persons will live our lives. A life which we ourselves will and should decide about, to have it as we want it.

All who spoke here at this regional conference, shall in *Grunden* continue further to our local groups and to the national group. We think and hope that they shall listen more to us in the future and our ideas and recommendations will be taken seriously.

To accept one's own handicap is important; then it is easier to live as one is. It is sufficiently important to change attitudes and prejudices among people in our own neighborhoods and among people in the community. We must get to be heard and accepted. Intellectually handicapped persons shall not be satisfied with being the worst-off in the future.

Finally, *Grunden* will thank all personnel at Dalheimers Hotel for a really fine job and service. We will even thank the governing board of FUB and Barbro [past president of the FUB parent association] for backing us and giving us a jump forward into an enlightened future.

Friends and acquaintances! Thanks again for a fun and successful weekend, and we hope that our work gets results and that we intellectually handicapped persons continue to meet at such conferences in the future!"

III. A Regional Conference Of and For People with Intellectual Disability, Tranås, December 1987

At a hotel on Lake Vatten, a group of 50–60 persons with intellectual disability and 10–15 *handledere* (many of whom had attended the FUB-Grunden National Conference one month earlier in Gothenberg) gathered together for a weekend retreat of study, discussions, reflection, expressions of art, dance, drama, socialization. Such weekend retreats are popular throughout Sweden. One study circle coordinator alone has formed 35 weekend and week-long retreats in one year to bring together various groupings of persons with disability, parents, and personnel from services, social clubs, educational circles, etc. The primary focus is on improving communication, understanding, and attitudes.

This group of people had been meeting like this twice a year for 8 years. The year before, a few had asked if it should end, but the question was answered with a resounding *no*; so it continued with renewed energy.

One afternoon was filled with a visit from a service provider and a legislator. They had been invited by the participants to hear and discuss many of the same issues which were raised at the Gothenberg conference. Only the persons with intellectual disability addressed them. The officials listened attentively, asked questions, and debated. They sometimes tended to respond with general statements, saying they would take some of the ideas into consideration but others would be too expensive to be implemented just yet. Overall, the people with disability were taken seriously.

Inviting otherwise powerful personages to this neutral place was an equalizer. The tone of the retreat itself had been one of encompassing purposefulness and congeniality. In that environment, then, the initiation of discussions — preceded by hours/years of preparation in hometown weekly study circles — suffused the participants with a kind of confidence which comes from a substantive information base of democratic, participatory, continuing education and a sense of solidarity with one's peers.

IV. Informal Conversations

This depth of thinking and clarity of expression which you have just read about was paralleled by numerous informal conversations. Many people with intellectual disability approached me to commence conversations filled with well-informed statements and questions, sometimes using English as a second language. Typical examples:

- "Do people with intellectual handicaps in the United States live in institutions or in the community?"

- "Is it true you have homeless in the United States?... But you have so much money there! What kind of people are you?"

They were interesting, interested, knowledgeable — and this visiting student was incredulous! (As I was struggling to learn the basics of *their* language and culture.)

Halfway through my study year, I purchased a video camera and now have hours of tapes, wherein people with intellectual disability — mostly using the English language — present their homes, marriages, children, workplaces, social clubs and adult education dynamics, and thoughts about self-determination and solidarity with others.

V. Analysis

My whole study year then became a continual search to try and answer these questions:

- How is it that there are so many who continue to mature with quiet confidence, deepening self-actualization, expanding knowledge, and a sense of society as a family of humankind on a fragile planet?
- How is it that from a large and diverse group there emerges some who grow into leadership and political activism, working for progressive changes in their own organization, in the counties, in the country, and internationally?

The clues, even answers, that gradually emerged seem to be directly related to the sturdiness of three foundational cornerstones of Scandinavian culture:

1. Trust in their system of governing.
2. A history of envisioning and acting upon the "Principle of Normalization" and the "Right to Self-Determination."
3. Participatory, democratic, continuing education outside (and sometimes within) Systems and Provisions.

TRUST IN THEIR SYSTEM OF GOVERNING

Everyone has the right to housing, transportation, education, employment, vacations, 18 months maternity/paternity leave and 60 days annually for child/family illness at 90% of salary, tutorials in native language/culture for immigrant children, universal health care, etc.

Quality of life for everyone. Sweden is a democracy with a capitalist economy which emphasizes people's *inter*dependence. For example, they have spoken of their whole nation as *Folkhemmet*: "The People's Home" (Åberg, 1987), where everyone is valued because s/he exists — and they govern themselves accordingly. Thus, during the income-producing years of 21-65, they pay progressive taxes at an average of 50% of their wages (Fact Sheet on Sweden, 1986: Taxes in Sweden). This is viewed as a lifetime insurance wherein they take care of one another during the non-income years of childhood and old age — and sometimes in between: accidents, illness, disability, etc. (Fors, 1969; Morris, 1988; The Swedish Immigration Board Information Division, 1987). They appear to have eliminated observable poverty, in that one finds no class of homeless people, no slums. Lifestyle seems to be guided by their slogan *Lagom ar bäst:* "Everything in moderation." People own or rent comfortable attractive homes or apartments enriched with original art works, and often an additional (inherited) little cottage in the country. Families own just one car and depend otherwise on the well-developed mass transit system. They have the right to take 5 weeks paid vacation; those who can afford it travel to the warmer climes of southern Europe.

Quality of life for people with disability. "The Swedish view is that everyone has the *right* to help from the community when they need it. Voluntary efforts can only supplement those of the community, and their value lies precisely in offering something beyond the routine. But charities must never be an excuse for public neglect, or delay efforts financed by taxation. Only public services based on taxation can be the legislated right of all citizens" (Fors, 1969). Charity drives, in fact, are exercises in privilege for givers and receivers; they teach society, generation after generation, to pity people with disability and systematically *prevent respect.*

The Swedish disability movement consists of 26 organizations *of* and *for* people with disability (with the single exception of persons with intellectual disability who remain with in the patronage of the parent association). They receive financial support from the state, counties and municipalities (The National Council for the Disabled [HCK], 1987).

Furthermore, "A handicap in Sweden and the World Health Organization is not looked upon as a characteristic of a person with a disability caused by injury or illness, but a relationship between the person and the environment. *It shifts the handicap from the person to the environment.* This is important, because it places a responsibility on all organizers, both public and private, to see that activities are accessible to all, *thus preventing a disability from becoming a handicap*" (Fact Sheets on Sweden, 1986: Support for the Disabled in Sweden). People with and without disability, therefore, see each other enjoy a comfortable standard of living and do not need to advocate for basic survival (housing, health care, etc.)!

People are relatively safe from crime on the streets of Sweden (especially during the dark hours, which can be lengthy during winter months). In the absence of poverty, the crime rate is low and the vulnerable are less likely to be victimized. People who have a disability, the elderly, and others can lead busy lives after work hours because they have access to affordable transportation; walking, riding (curb-climbing) electric wheelchairs, bikes, buses, subsidized taxis, and cars. They can also come together in social and sports clubs, adult education centers, for shopping, etc.

The cornerstone of trust in their system of governing themselves is based on a value system which believes in assuring the collective well being.

A History of Envisioning and Acting Upon "The Principle of Normalization" and "The Right to Self-Determination"

I suggest you treat yourselves to a rereading of Bengt Nirje's "The Normalization Principle" and "The Right to Self-Determination."

"The Normalization Principle." From his Scandinavian roots, Nirje developed and articulated an ideology for persons with intellectual disability which has revolutionized our thinking, frames of reference and actions forever. Although some facets of "The Normalization Principle" have been achieved by people in many cultures, much has yet to be realized. Nirje's works are more than famous documents to be honored; for many people with disability around the world, they are blueprints for action.

"The Right to Self-Determination." People who are working on acceptance of their disability, who are struggling "to be one's self among all others," who aspire to work as advocates, who demand that democracy include informed participation by all citizens — we all embrace Nirje's "Right to Self-Determination" as a classic source of information and inspiration.

Nirje included in this essay a brief report of what is thought to be the very first national conference of persons with intellectual disability. It was held in Sweden in 1968. The second conference, in 1970, was a full-scale 3-day conference attended by 2 elected representatives from 24 of 25 counties and 2 Danish guests. Nirje described the process and content of the conference. Although the process was nearly identical to that of the 1987 Gothenberg conference, it is noteworthy that the content differed in that many of the 1970 recommendations have meanwhile been implemented. Examples of success:

1970 "Travel should be prepared, with courses in the language, manners, and habits of countries we visit."

1988 People are introduced to English language beginning at 9–10 years of age in elementary school. Those with interest can continue, even in adult years within adult education study circles. Such adult courses can be taken to study any language/culture.

1970 "We want to have apartments of our own and not be coddled by personnel; therefore we want courses in cooking and budgeting."

1988 Many now have apartments of their own. Courses are offered in adult education study circles, at day occupational centres, as well as naturally, in one's own or nearby supervised apartment.

A *gode man* can be hired by a person who lives independently and needs to learn budgeting. The *gode man* may at first have full responsibility for paying the rent, banking, etc. He or she gradually helps the person to learn to handle money with knowledge and increasing independence.

1970 "We want the right to move together with a member of the opposite sex when we feel ready for it, and we do want the right to marry when we ourselves find the time is right."

1988 It is common in Sweden for people to live together as husband and wife, whether married or not (*Sammanboende*). So, too, can people with intellectual and physical disability, living within or outside of the supervised residences; they can marry if they wish.

1970 "The home shall be small."

1988 Parliament passed an act in 1986 stating that all institutions will close (hopefully by the year 2000). All options for residence, education, work, and free time will be in the community.

One to 8 persons live in each residence (the future calls for no more than 4). Ninety-eight percent of people living in the community and 70% of those living in institutions have rooms of their own. To assure privacy, people are taught to lock their bedroom doors.

1970 "We ask for adult education in the daytime, either in study circles a few days a week or during a longer continuous period."

1988 People with intellectual and physical disability now have a wide range of adult education choices, with study circles days and evenings in municipal (integrated) centers, sometimes in day occupational centers, plus weekend or year-long (integrated) residential education at Folk High Schools.

1970 "We want employee councils at our sheltered workshops."

1988 Union-type work groups exist in many sheltered workshops. Leadership
and participation is within the power and the privacy of the workers, with
assistance from an advisor (usually from the adult education center) until
the group functions independently.

The cornerstone of belief in Sweden is that people with intellectual disability
have a right to a "normal rhythm of the day, the week, the year, the life cycle;
normal interactions in a heterosexual world; normal economy and environment;
normal respect, and the right to self-determination" (Nirje, 1969, 1972). This belief
has been firmly embedded in Scandinavian history for more than a quarter century
(Bank-Mikkelsen, 1959).

PARTICIPATORY, DEMOCRATIC, CONTINUING EDUCATION

Outside the System

The Adult Education Association (*Vuxenskolan*) and FUB have paid and volunteer personnel who lead study circles in integrated and segregated centers. They
recruit for leaders those who are open, who value people for themselves, and who
believe in the potential for all persons to learn and to grow in self-confidence.
Within conferences and retreats, social clubs, municipal study circles, and Folk
High Schools, these personnel serve as combined leaders and advisors, according to
circumstances. Several groups in Borås and Gothenberg impressed me with their
creative vitality: acknowledging the need and possibility for improved communica-
tions, understanding, and attitudes inside all of us, they seemed to be continually
planning new learning opportunities for each other, various groupings of persons
with and without disabilities, parents, service personnel, etc.

Social Clubs. Social clubs exist throughout the country. The one I attended in
Uppsala met weekly in a church-owned building shared by various groups. It included 20–30 members, most of whom had intellectual disability and others who
volunteered from FUB and church groups.

Early in the evening, people mingled, chatted, played games or musical instru-
ments, read poetry, and purchased snacks or a light supper. The gathering was
unstructured, and everyone was free to be self-directed: a person could be alone and
quiet. A volunteer might invite people to join in somehow; if they did not wish to,
that was OK too.

After a while, people gathered for a business meeting to plan social events.
Following parliamentary procedure, the officers with disability led the meeting,
with coaching provided as needed by a volunteer. The mood was friendly and
relaxed.

The group might decide to study social issues, or to invite speakers versed in
certain topics; some speakers might address political activism. This, in fact, was the

path followed by Connie Berqvist and some of his friends in Borås, in the south of Sweden. During the late 1970s, they became active members in their local FUB club. After a while, they began to say among themselves that it isn't easy to be in society when people don't know how to participate effectively in groups. About 5 persons from the club began a study circle with a leader from the *Vuxenskolan* Adult Education Center. They wanted to become more clear about: "What is FUB? Why am I a member, and why is FUB important to me as a person with intellectual disability?" Connie says:

> It is very important first to learn what one's handicap is and to be able to accept it. Next, it is very, very important for others to know about my handicap, because I don't want to be alone with it. If I need help from others and they accept me and my handicap, I can ask for help and get it in the right way.

After several years of weekly study circles and weekend courses, Connie's group said, "Now we want to meet the politicians and tell them what we think is good for us." With knowledge of issues, self-confidence, and solidarity, they grew into political activism.

Examples of successful dialogue with the politicians:

1. The county and *Vuxenskolan* pay all expenses for attendance at weekend study retreats (including this guest student).
2. People now use money instead of vouchers to make purchases.

Examples of continuing dialogue with the politicians who say, "We are working on it":

1. People with disabilities should have ordinary jobs with salaries.
2. When staff are recruited, people living in community residences want to be part of the hiring process.
3. Money to pay personal assistants to accompany us on vacations should be available.
4. If a group home will be built, don't inform the neighbors first! No one else does that! We can live anywhere in society! After we move in, we can invite the neighbors when we wish. (McKenna video, 1988)

I visited a newly rented space in Gothenberg where the people with disability and a few FUB personnel were deciding how to decorate their own club house. As in Uppsala, several large rooms with wide doorways flowed into one another. People could use it creatively for simultaneous small-group meetings or a large one. Here, too, the tone was quietly relaxed and totally inclusive.

Over the years, these clubs have provided at least weekly opportunities for:

- taking charge of one's own leisure time, in the company of others;
- practicing organizational/leadership skills;
- acquiring information to form opinions;
- growing in the confidence that one can find meaningful socialization in widening circles of community groups;
- having fun!

Folk High Schools. One uniquely Scandinavian form of adult education is the Folk High School. They were founded in the mid-19th century as an alternative to traditional higher education. The purpose was to give better opportunities to young rural adults. Today, students come from all ages and locales to learn, reside, participate in self-government and immerse themselves in personal and communal growth — for just one weekend, or for as long as 3 years (*The Swedish Folk High School*, 1986).

Vigorous outreach to people with physical and intellectual disability, to immigrants, and to housewives was initiated in the mid-1960s. In Sweden today, there are some 125 Folk High Schools which enroll about 250,000 students annually. No tuition fees are charged; financing comes mainly from tax-based public funds, with lesser contributions from nonprofit organizations, trade unions, and private companies. There is no official compulsory syllabus; the teachers of each school, in cooperation with students, determine the curriculum within the guidelines of the Folk High School Code ("Adult Education in Sweden," 1986). State supervision consists of the National Board of Education providing counseling and support rather than control (*The Swedish Folk High School*, 1986).

Bengt Nirje and I visited Kjesäter Folk High School together. Pupils included people with moderate to severe intellectual disability. The school was integrated during meals and free time. Classes were offered in Swedish, Math, Current Events and Social Studies, Botany, Psychology, Arts and Crafts, Physical Education, Music and Dance, Social Living Skills, English, and Typing. Studies are individualized (within the classes) as much as possible by the special education and Folk High School teachers. Free-time activities are planned by committees of people with intellectual disability, and facilitated by recreation leaders ("Courses for Mentally Retarded at a Swedish Folk High School," 1988; McKenna video, 1988).

On a feeling level, one senses tranquility in the buildings of this manor, which was once owned by nobility and is settled snugly with in a patch of Swedish forest. The spirit can expand to overflow from itself and soar with the birds — whose song was all that we heard beyond our own voices (McKenna video, 1988).

Envision, then within this milieu, opportunity for fulfillment of the form and content of Folk High School activities as stated in the statutory confirmation by the Swedish Parliament in 1977:

- Increase the student's awareness of his or her own circumstances and those

of the world at large.
- Deepen and enlarge the student's sensitivity and experiential capacity.
- Develop critical sense, independence, and capacity for cooperation.
- Develop the student's creative potential.
- Strengthen the will and ability of the student, in solidarity with others, to play an active part in working life and the life of the community.

(The Swedish Folk High School, 1986)

One Folk High School teacher has said that the difference between these schools and traditional education is that in the former, one can think for oneself as compared with the rote learning expectations in the latter. Folk High School, she stated, can be:

> an opportunity for people with different backgrounds to meet and listen to one another.... an opportunity to spend a relatively long period trying another way of living, so as to show oneself and the rest of society that it can be done (The Swedish Folk High School, 1986).

Adult Study Circles. Like the Folk High Schools, Adult Study Circles started as a popular alternative to traditional higher education, over 100 years ago. These circles have participated in outreach to persons with disability for nearly 25 years, but are not residential. Organized by the local branches of Sweden's educational associations, they are centrally located in most communities, and by far the largest number of today's adult learners attend them ("Adult Education in Sweden," 1986).

Although Adult Study Circles receive financial subsidies from tax-based funds, nonprofit organizations, trade unions and private companies, the participants must also pay a small tuition ("Adult Education in Sweden," 1986). People receiving disability or retirement pension paid 225 SKR ($37.50) for one course each term during the 1987 school year (Dubiel interview, 1987). Study Circles are supervised by the National Board of Education, which ensures that the courses comply with the general guidelines of the government and Parliament ("Adult Education in Sweden," 1986).

Study leaders at all levels of responsibility stress that each circle consists of "participants" and "leaders," not "teachers" and "students." Those who recruit circle leaders require no formal educational credentials of the applicants. They must demonstrate knowledge of their subject and of study circles, and "be open." In fact, there is preference for non-educators with practical experience who work days and want to lead studies during evening hours. This is thought to contribute to the spirit of equality among circle members. Once hired, regular in-service training is provided. Leaders are salaried and unionized (Author interviews with Study Circle administrators, leaders, and participants in Borås, Gothenberg, Stockholm, Södertalje, and Uppsala, Sweden, 1987/88).

The focus and methods of studies are democratically decided by participants themselves. To be eligible for a subsidy, a study circle must have between 5 and 20 members ("Adult Education in Sweden," 1986). Ideal group size when members have intellectual disability is 4–5 plus the leader. More importance is placed on development of self-confidence, attitudes toward humankind, disability studies, and feelings than on academic achievements. There are no degrees awarded; they might decide upon certificates of attendance (Author interviews, 1987–88).

Courses which have been requested and taken by people with intellectual disability include: Literature, Swedish and foreign languages, Civics/Voting, Math, Music and Dance, Drama, Art, Botany, Reading, Writing, Community Orientation/Transportation, Leisure Choices, the Psychological Study of One's Own and Others' Disabilities, Disability Attitudes and Issues, Peace, and the Environment (Author interviews, 1987/88).

Music circles are favorites with people who have severe to profound intellectual disability The focus is on receptive and expressive language within salutations, names, body parts, etc. (Author study visits, 1987/88).

A class studying the Swedish language utilized textbooks and workbooks which we summer session foreign students had used during our orientation program. The subject matter was interesting and appealing to adults (Author study visits).

Easy Reader books and newspapers. Easy Reader books and newspapers are easier to read than books and papers in general. They combine literary and easily-read qualities. They are written for all people who are at a very basic reading level (immigrants, foreign students, people with dyslexia or intellectual disability, etc.). Easy Readers include textbooks to accompany some adult education courses, newspapers, fiction, poetry, documentaries, and biographies. They are available in schools, bookshops, and public libraries ("Easy to Read: A News Service for the Mentally Handicapped," 1985).

Developing an Easy Reader book is a long and experimental process. Between 1971 and 1986, 184 such materials were published in Sweden. They are written by a variety of authors, illustrated by many artists, and published by different publishing houses, all in close cooperation with a foundation funded by the National Swedish Board of Education. High artistic quality is essential because of the belief that complicated messages can reach even poor readers when accompanied by pictures with artistic authenticity ("How to Publish Easy Reader Books: A Model," 1986).

The Swedish Parliament has established that "Cultural policy shall help to protect freedom of speech and to create such conditions that this freedom shall be enjoyed in reality." It is well known that many people suffer from such severe impediments to reading and communication that it is necessary, somehow, to make literature available to them. This need has led to the publication of Easy Reader materials, books on tape, in Braille, in manual sign and in Blissymbolics ("Easy to

Read Books on the Readers' Own Terms," 1982).

Although quality production is a long and detailed process, Sweden is an example of one country which has undertaken such a project. It has been projected that the number of English-speaking readers, worldwide, would be vast enough to support such a major industry internationally. The author refers readers to the National Swedish Board of Education as a helpful resource which provides detailed information, on request, in English.

The right to such educational opportunities is a foundational cornerstone precious to Scandinavians. For the last quarter century, they have opened their halls of higher learning with creative adaptations to extend this valuable right to all members of their society. And now they can count increasing numbers of people with intellectual disability among their scholars: those who love learning for its own sake and go forth to stimulate thinking with their original contributions.

Within the System

During his tenure as Head of the Division for Handicapped People in the National Swedish Board of Health and Welfare (1961–1987), Earl Grunewald, M.D., promoted the practical application of "The Normalization Principle" throughout the land. An overriding theme was that a person's ability to shape his or her day-to-day existence must be fostered and developed (Grunewald, 1987).

Thus, for example, Swedish psychologists have been actively opposed to the use of behavior modification; they see it as a shallow 'Band-Aid' approach which acts upon or against one's personhood, thereby preventing internalized maturation and not getting to the root of problems. Instead, they, too, have promoted all facets of "The Normalization Principle" with emphasis on building meaningful relationships, individually and in small groups.

Individually: The environment will be adapted. This includes the hiring of a personal assistant who will help a person one-to-one, daily, trustingly learn to adapt to changes which are difficult for psychological or physical reasons.

Small group: The SIVUS group dynamic method has been growing in use within worksite, residential and leisure time decision-making in Sweden since 1974. SIVUS is the acronym for *Social Individ Via Utveckling i Samverkan,* which translates as "Socio-Individual Development through Cooperation." Some of the basic principles of the SIVUS method are based on the results of a 3-year experiment (1962–65) in Indonesia, led by psychologist Sophian Walujo, Ph.D., in order to work up and test an appropriate education method for extension university students, so that they could cope with both their work in the mornings and their studies in the evenings.

In 1974 the SIVUS project started at ALA, a research group associated with FUB. Since 1970, the project has been administered by the National Swedish Board of Health and Welfare and led by Dr. Walujo. By 1987, the method was being used in about 250 Swedish settings, plus many more in at least 30 other countries, with children and adults across the range of cognitive abilities.

SIVUS is based on the knowledge of how all human beings develop, both as individual and social beings: *from* our own needs, experiences, and interests, *through* our own efforts, *to* our own experiences, results, and development. Thus, where SIVUS is practiced, a heterogenous group of people with intellectual disability congregate in the educational/work/residential setting, with the personnel whose attitude must be that of leading/guiding rather than authoritative.

Daily, before activities begin, everyone meets to make a plan. Each person says what he or she will do, and that is written on a chalkboard or in a log book by one of the persons with disability. Next, everyone leaves the meeting to work on the plan. The supervisors should continue as gentle teachers.

Finally, at the end of that activity or day's work, a final meeting is held where everyone self-evaluates, reading first what he or she had originally planned. If the job/activity was done well, one can say so and feel good inside. If not, the members encourage the person to take it as a learning experience and try it in a different way next time (McKenna video, 1988). "Emphasis is on each person's existing abilities and possibilities as positive aspects to be developed further, rather than on his deficiencies..." (Walujo & Grunewald, 1984).

Thus, individually and in small-group settings, people have the daily opportunity at work, at home, in leisure and educational planning to democratically participate in deciding what will be done, do it, and pace their growth through self-evaluation.

Summary

Clearly, Swedish society has developed enriched resources to draw upon: the natural capacities inside people, generous and compassionate governing, meaningful evolution of "The Normalization Principle" and "The Right to Self-Determination," love of continuing education, respect for the common good. One wonders how soon people with intellectual disability in Sweden will establish their own organization independent of their parents. When will they apply for government grants, join the National Council for the Disabled (HCK), hire advisors of their own choosing, welcome friends from FUB to join them as equal partners, and — as Elisabeth Broberg said in Chapter 5 of this volume — really "be in the community on our own terms"?

References

The Swedish Institute (1986). *Adult Education in Sweden.* Stockholm, Sweden: Author.

Aberg, Å. (1987). *A Concise History of Sweden* (pp. 92-94).

Bank-Mikkelsen, N.E. (1969). A metropolitan area in Denmark: Copenagen. In R. Kugel & W. Wolfensberger (eds.), *Changing Patterns in Residential Services for the Mentally Retarded* (pp. 227-254). Washington, DC: President's Committee on Mental Retardation.

Broberg, E. (1987).. Keynote speech presented at Nordiska Forbundet Psykisk Utvecklingstorda Conference, Uppsala, Sweden. August 1987.

"Courses for Mentally Retarded at a Swedish Folk High School" Kjesäter Folk High School, Vingaker, Sweden.

"Easy to Read Books (ER Books) on the Reader's Own Terms." 1982. national Swedish Board of Education. Bureau 6. "The Working Groups for ER Books" S106 42 Stockholm, Sweden.

Fact Sheets on Sweden. 1986. "General Facts on Sweden." The Swedish Institute Box 7434 S103-91 Stockholm, Sweden.

Fact Sheets on Sweden. 1986. "Support for the Disabled in Sweden." The Swedish Institute Box 7434 S103-91 Stockholm, Sweden.

Fact Sheets on Sweden. 1986. "Taxes in Sweden." The Swedish Institute Box 7434 S103-91 Stockholm, Sweden.

Fors, Å. (1969). *Social policy and how it works.* K. Bradfield, Translator. Kugelsbergs Botryckeri. Stockholm, Sweden.

FUB (1987, September). *Bidrag and formaner* (Allowance and benefits). FUB KONTAKT, nr. 4 (pp. 13-18). Riksforbundet FUB, Box 5410, S114 84 Stockholm, Sweden.

Grunewald, K. (1987). Human dignity: Respect and consideration for mentally disabled adults. The National Swedish Board of Health and Welfare. Spangsbergs Tryckerier A.B. Stockholm, Sweden.

Holmqvist, T. (1987). Keynote speech presented at RFUB-Grunden conference, October 1987, Gothenberg, Sweden.

"How to Publish Easy Reader Books: A Model." (1986). Beata Lundstrom and Elsie Bellander

TFLA Conference Paper: Tokyo General Conference. Swedish Board of Education. S 106 42 Stockholm, Sweden.

Johansson, Å. (1986). Keynote speech presented at the ILSMH World Congress in Rio de Janeiro, 1986, and at the Nordiska Forbundet Psykisk Utvecklingstorda Conference, Uppsala, Sweden, 1987.

Johansson, Å. (1987). Keynote speech presented at RFUB-Grunden conference, October 1987, Gothenberg, Sweden.

Levander, K. (Ed.) (1986). *Sweden: A general introduction for immigrants* (p. 79). The Swedish Immigration Board, Information Division. AB Faiths Tryckeri. Varnamo, Sweden.

Martinsson, L.Å. (1987). Keynote presentation at RFUB-Grunden Conference, Gothenberg, Sweden.

McKenna, P.S. (1987-88). Rotary Foundation Scholar. Research Project: Directed study of "The Normalization Principle" and "The Right to Self-Determination" with the author Bengt Nirje and Lars Kebbon, Ph.D., Associate Director of Psychological Unit, University of Uppsala, Sweden. Unpublished raw data: course notes, personal observations and experiences, photographs, videotapes.

Morris, D. (1988, Fall). Local self-reliance: A Swedish lesson for America. *Building Economic Alternatives* (pp. 3-4).

The National Council for the Disabled (1987). Disability Politics in Sweden. Box 7779 S 103 96 Stockholm, Swden. Norstedts Tryckeri, Stockholm, Sweden.

The National Swedish Board of Education. Bureau 6. S 106 42 Stockholm, Sweden.

"A News Service for the Mentally Handicapped" Reports DsU 1985:6 and DsU 1985:7. The Committee on Spoken Newspapers. Ministry of Education and Cultural Affairs. Tallidningskommitten. Stora Nygatan 2A. S 111 27 Stockholm, Sweden.

Nirje, B. (1969). The normalization principle and its human management implications. In R.B. Kugel & W. Wolfensberger (Eds.), *Changing patterns in residential services for the mentally retarded,*

Chapter 7 (p. 179). Washington, DC: President's Committee on Mental Retardation.

Nirje, B. (1972). The right to self-determination. In W. Wolfensberger (Ed.), *Normalization*, Chapter 13 (pp. 176-193). Toronto: National Institute on Mental Retardation.

Nirje, B. (1980). The normalization principle. In R. Flynn & K. Nitsch (Eds.), *Normalization, integration, and community services*, Chapter 2 (pp. 39-42). Baltimore, MD: University Park Press.

RFUB-Grunden Conference: Final Reports. (1987) Gothenberg, Sweden.

National Board of Education (1986). The Swedish folk high school. Bureau 6. S 106 42 Stockholm, Sweden.

Walujo, S (1984). *Group dynamic method for the mentally retarded (SIVUS)*. The Swedish National Board of Health and Welfare. Division of Services for the Handicapped. S 106 30 Stockholm, Sweden.

11

A History of People First in Canada

Bruce Kappel

Bruce Kappel is a longtime friend of the self-advocacy movement in Canada. His work on this chapter, and his assistance in the chapter by Barb Goode, stem from his work on a project to develop an oral history of self-advocacy in Canada. Bruce acknowledges the advice and expertise contributed by Peter Park and Pat Worth, two self-advocate leaders, and Beth French, self-advocacy advisor, whose contributions to the oral history are excerpted in this chapter.

Summary

This chapter gives some of the history of People First in Canada up to the early 1990s. First, we tell you some things about Canada. If you are from another country, this will help you find out where we are, how many people live here, and some thing about our country. Then, we answer four questions about the history of People First in Canada:

- How did People First get started in Canada?
- What are the National People First Project & People First of Canada?
- What are some of the issues that People First groups have taken on in Canada?
- What works? What doesn't?

An Introduction to Canada

Canada is a very big country. It is also a very small country. It is the biggest country in the world now that the Soviet Union became smaller countries. It takes more than seven hours to fly from one end of Canada to the other end. Three oceans surround us. The Atlantic is to the East. The Pacific is to the West. The Arctic

Ocean is to the North. The United States is to the South.

Canada is a small country because there are only twenty million people living here. Most of them live in cities along beside the Great Lakes and the St. Lawrence River. Toronto and Montreal are our biggest cities. But people live all across the country.

Because there are not many people here, there are fewer people to keep in touch with. Because our country is so big, it is hard to have meetings that include people from across Canada. People have to travel very far for a meeting.

Our country is divided into ten provinces and two territories. These are like the states in the United States. Ontario and Quebec are our biggest provinces. There are People First groups in all the provinces and territories. There are provincial or territorial groups in Ontario, Quebec, Manitoba, Nova Scotia, Saskatchewan, and British Columbia. There is People First of Canada for the whole country.

People speak many different languages in Canada. English and French are the two official languages. So, we have to make sure there are translators at meetings. We translate many books, newsletters, minutes of meetings into both French and English. In the parts of Canada where people speak English, our groups are called People First. Sometimes, however, people use the term *People's First*. The French name for People First is *Personnes d'abord*.

The Association in Canada is now called the Association for Community Living. It used to be called the Association for the Mentally Retarded. People First members worked long and hard to get the name changed. When we mention the Association in this history of People First in Canada, we will use the current name. That way, the old and offending name will not be used.

People with disabilities have been fighting long and hard for their rights in Canada. There have been major victories. In at least two provinces, there are no children labelled mentally handicapped living in institutions any more. Many provinces have said they want to close all of their institutions. In some provinces, there are no more segregated schools. In some communities, students with disabilities go to the same classes as other students. The law of Canada says that all Canadians have the right to equal protection and benefit of the law. This includes people with disabilities.

There have been victories, and there is a lot to do.

How Did People First Get Started in Canada?

People First got started in several ways in Canada. In one way, People First started in Canada in 1973. The British Columbia Association organized a conference for people who had lived in an institution. This was the first time that people labelled as mentally handicapped had come together in a conference in North America. According to Peter Park of People First of Canada, "It was just a self-advocacy session in that conference. The Association organized it. As a result, it fell apart. It was not supported." (Park, 1992)

Some people from Oregon attended the 1973 conference in British Columbia. After that they wanted their own conference "that was planned by and for people with disabilities, with assistance from advisors only when needed" (Park, 1992).

> In the course of planning the convention, the small group of planners decided they needed a name for themselves. A number of suggestions had been made when someone said, "I'm tired of being called retarded — we are people first." The name *People First* was chosen, and the People First self-advocacy movement began (Heath, 1985, pp. 6-7).

Because the name *People First* started in the States, some people say the People First movement started in the United States. According to Peter Park, "If a person says to you People First started in the States, it actually started in Canada. The first time self-advocates were involved in a conference was in British Columbia, one of the western provinces of this great country of ours."

People First also started in Canada each time self-advocates got the idea to start a People First group. People got involved in many different ways.

In 1974, the first People First group in Canada began in British Columbia. It was started by some women and men who had been living in institutions. They wanted to live in the community. They needed help because life in an institution is very different from life in the real world. They had not been taught what they needed to know to live and work on their own. They needed to make their own decisions and speak for themselves.

Peter Park describes how he got involved in Ontario.

> I read about People First when I was in the institution. I said to myself, "This sounds like a good thing." It was called People First. I decided I wanted to do it, and that was that. I decided to read what there was. There wasn't much, but I read everything I could. (Park, 1992)

Peter does not remember exactly what he first read about People First. It may have been an article called "People First: Evolution Toward Self Advocacy" in the *Canadian Journal on Mental Retardation* (Heath, Schaaf, & Talkington, 1978.) The article described the history of People First in Oregon.

Peter got out of the institution in February 1978. He moved to a group home in one town, then he moved to a group home in another town. By August, he had a People First group going. Peter decided to call a meeting. He put notices up in the group home and the sheltered workshop. Somebody helped him get a meeting room at the local YMCA. I asked Peter what he did at that first meeting.

> At that meeting it was decided that people wanted an organization sepa-
> rate from the local Association [called the "Association for the Mentally

Retarded" then], to do something for themselves. To do something period, and to learn about their rights as individuals.

That first meeting was more — where do we go from here, who do we invite, do we have a next meeting, who knows about rights? We decided to meet again in two weeks time... And, we would ask David Baker [a lawyer active in fighting for the rights of people with disabilities] to come in and tell us about our rights. (Park, 1992)

Pat Worth got started in a different way.

I could not find anyway to talk to the people in the workshop or the group home about my frustrations. Except, we started talking to each other at lunch time and at break time. There was a few of us, three or four, who were talking about the same issues at the same time — real pay, being labelled "retarded," about what was wrong with the group home. But we could not find time to talk privately. We were always worrying about the staff overhearing. Sometimes they did, and we got a lot of shit.

Sara Cravitz [a local Adult Protective Services Worker] convinced Sheridan College to give us free office space on Monday nights so we could get together and do some planning. We said we wanted to. She helped us with the workshop and the group home. They stayed off our back for a while.

What started as a group of four people became a large group because it caught on. (Worth, 1992)

Pat's group was not called People First in the beginning. It was just a group of people who got together to talk about issues. Peter Park came to their second meeting. He talked about People First.

So, people like Peter Park and Pat Worth deciding to start People First is one way People First got started. Some groups got going because people wanted to deal with an issue. Often the issue would be about the group home, the workshop, pay, or the name of the Association. Some groups started, especially in the early days of People First, so people could organize recreation. They wanted to go bowling, have dances, have coffee together, or go on trips.

PEOPLE FIRST AND THE 1973 CACL CONFERENCE

People First also got started when some people from across Canada met for the first time in 1979. The Canadian Association for Community Living was having its national conference and annual general meeting in Vancouver, British Columbia, that year. There was a self-advocacy session at the conference.

The people who became some of the leaders of People First across Canada met for the first time at that conference. Peter Park and Pat Worth already knew one another. At the conference, they met Barb Goode from British Columbia. Peter Park remembers that first meeting:

> I had heard of Barb Goode before, but never met her. There was this person in B.C. [British Columbia], Barb Goode. She was a self-advocate, spokesperson, and she started a group in Vancouver, or somewhere in that area. (Park, 1992)

For Pat Worth, "that was my first initial start with politics in associations." There were a lot of things wrong with the conference. In the first place, self-advocates were supposed to stay in a group home. Pat Worth remembers some things about that.

> CAMR [the national association for community living] was trying to get some of us to go to a group home to save costs. Some of us revolted. Some of the members were put in group homes while the conference was going on, but it did not work out. They were not willing to obey all the restrictions. They had to be home by curfew hours....
>
> We thought it was unfair since CAMR was footing the bill for a lot of other people at the hotel. (Worth, 1992)

Peter Park remembers it slightly differently:

> We were supposed to be billeted at a group home, but we were not as there was something contagious at the group home. We lived in a very ritzy hotel called the Bayshore Inn in Vancouver for about 6 days. (Park, undated)

At first, Pat felt out of place at the conference.

> It was like nothing I had every seen. It was my first time at a rich fancy hotel, the Bayshore Inn. I did not know what to wear. I was travelling in boots at this classy hotel. I was wearing nothing but jeans and a plain shirt. When I got to the hotel and saw all these people in suits, I thought I should be back on the plane. I remember Peter telling me it did not matter at all. (Worth, 1992)

Peter Park got into trouble because of some literature he brought.

> We all took some literature. I remember because it got me into trouble. The Executive Director of the Ontario Association [for Community Living] said I could not have written it. He told the Executive Director in Brantford that I could not have written it.... It was my life history. And I thought, "I know it. I was the one who lived it." (Park, 1992)

... the Executive Director of the Brantford Association said that I couldn't possibly have written the leaflets that I passed out. According to him the advisor (Jane Anderson) must have manipulated my thinking. Have I got news for that old fuddy duddy. The thing that hurt the most was that I had to be told second hand about this. I was told afterward by the Executive Director of OAMR that Jane Anderson had put her job on the line when telling this nobody that I did it. She only got me photocopies.

The Adult Protective Service Worker had it typed in Brantford. How in the devil is someone in Toronto going to see it or have any idea of what I might say. Needless to say I wouldn't say I hadn't written such and such even though he threatened to have me moved out of the Brantford residential setting. I remember saying "let him try and see what I do."

(Park, undated)

The advocacy session at the conference gave self-advocates a chance to speak up. But they could only talk to each other. Pat Worth remembers:

That was the very first session where I saw things actually being talked about in a large audience. People were talking about what that name had done to them, about institutions, about long-term workshops, about service providers always telling them what to do.

We talked a lot about money, because a lot of other people had control over our finances. They talked a lot about FBA [the disability allowance in Ontario] and what they had to do to get it, signing up to be permanently unemployable. Most of us never even saw the cheque. It went to the institution or the group home...

The self-advocacy session was organized all wrong. It was a good beginning for us, but the only people who came to that session were the self-advocates. Nobody else was interested in going. So, all we were doing was talking amongst each other. We were all very pissed off that nobody from the association or service providing agencies came to our session....

We got a good feeling, and that led to making decisions about the name changes, and sterilization, and workshop wages. (Worth, 1992)

A number of things came out of that conference. It was the first self-advocacy meeting at the national level. It brought together Barb Goode, Peter Park, Pat Worth, David Lincoln, and others. Together, these self-advocates formed an alliance that has lasted for years.

It also marked the beginnings of the Consumer Advisory Committee for the Canadian Association for Community Living. At that time, the Association used the word "consumer" to describe self-advocates. The importance of the Consumer

Advisory Committee, in the early days, was that it provided a way for People First leaders from across Canada to meet on a regular basis.

Some of the things that happened, at that time and afterward are:

1974   The first People First group in Canada begins in British Columbia.

1978   Local People First groups form in Prince Albert, Saskatchewan, and in Edmonton, Alberta. Groups are active in British Columbia.

1979   People First groups form in Brantford and Oakville, Ontario.

1980   Self advocates in Ontario hold a conference at Mohawk College in Hamilton, Ontario and decide to form a provincial People First organization.
        People First groups began to form in Manitoba and Saskatchewan.

1981   Provincial conference of People First in Ontario held in Toronto, Ontario. About 650 people attend.
        International People First Conference in Oregon.

1982   Meeting of self-advocates organized at the 1982 World Congress of the International League of Societies for Persons with Mental Handicap in Nairobi, Kenya. Barb Goode represents Canada.

1983   People First of Ontario formed.
        People First groups have formed in New Brunswick, Nova Scotia, Quebec, Prince Edward Island, and Alberta.

1984   National Self Advocacy Development Project begins. Project soon becomes known as the National People First Project. First issue of the newsletter of the project ("The National Organizer") comes out in July.
        International Self Advocacy Leadership Conference in Tacoma, Washington. People First leaders from British Columbia, Quebec, Manitoba, and the National People First Project attend.

1985   British Columbia forms provincial People First organization.
        In Ontario, there are 34 known groups.
        First meeting of the Halifax/Dartmouth, Nova Scotia People First group.

1986   Conference of People First leaders from Canada and the United States held in Bolton, Ontario.
        Self Advocates organize a "Workers Council" in a sheltered workshop in Nova Scotia.

1989   There are 19 People First chapters in British Columbia.
        Nova Scotia provincial People First group begins.
        Saskatchewan and Manitoba also have provincial organizations by this time.

1991   Founding Convention of People First of Canada.
        Provincial organizations alive and well in British Columbia, Alberta, Saskatchewan, Manitoba, Ontario, Quebec, New Brunswick, and Nova Scotia.

The National People First Project and People First of Canada have had a lot to do with the growth of People First in Canada. We talk about them next.

What Are the National People First Project
& People First of Canada?

The history of People First of Canada goes back about ten years. David Lincoln was President of People First of Ontario. He had a dream of starting People First of Canada. He worked with Jacques Pelletier of the Canadian Association to get funding to start the organization. They were having good luck in their talks with Health and Welfare Canada, the government department that funds that sort of thing.

The problem was that David Lincoln had not talked to other People First leaders about his idea. He was getting funding to start an organization that nobody had heard about. They were not sure they wanted it. People First leaders from across Canada got together to talk over the idea.

That was in 1983. At the time, there was People First of Ontario. In every other province, there were only local groups. People First leaders were worried about two things. First, they did not like it that David Lincoln had gone ahead with this idea without talking to anybody. They thought this was against what People First stands for. Second, they thought we needed help in developing People First in each of the provinces. If People First of Canada started too early, it would take attention away from helping people at the local and provincial level. Mainly, they wanted time to think and talk about it. They wanted to see what other people thought about a national People First group.

The Consumer Advisory Committee (CAC) of the Canadian Association was where most of this talking was going on. The CAC asked the Canadian Association to help it put its ideas together. The CAC wanted to talk with Health and Welfare about a plan that everybody liked. The Canadian Association asked a Board member and a staff member to help. Marjorie McPherson was on the Board then, and Bruce Kappel was on the staff. They helped the CAC develop a proposal.

They came up with the "Self-Advocacy Development Project." The idea was to get money for some staff. One would be an advisor, and one would be a self-advocate. There was an advisory committee made up of People First leaders and supporters from across Canada. The job of the project was to help organize self-advocacy groups across Canada. They got the money from the government to run the project. The project was called "The National People First Project." In the end, the project lasted six years. When it ended, People First of Canada was born.

The Project staff started on March 5, 1984. The first staff were Bill Worrell and Bob Berthelot. Bob had to leave the project shortly after he started, and was replaced by Peter Park. Bill Worrell was the Project Coordinator, Peter Park was the Self-Advocacy Specialist, and Maha Toubassy was the Assistant and Secretary.

Everything the project did was approved by the People First Advisory Committee. The people who were involved from the beginning of the Advisory Committee were:

- Gordon Fletcher (British Columbia)
- Harold Barnes (Alberta)
- Neil Mercer (Saskatchewan)
- Pat Worth (Ontario)
- Denis Laroche (Quebec)
- Barb Goode (British Columbia)
- Marie Gallagher (Alberta)
- Judith Snow (Ontario), and
- David Reid (New Brunswick).

Later, they were joined by Beth French (Ontario) and Andrea Feunekes (New Brunswick). Beth, Andrea, Judith, and Marie were advisors and supporters on the Advisory Committee.

In 1989, Bill Worrell left the Project. The staff who saw the Project through to the end, and the beginning of People First of Canada, were Peter Park, Pat Worth, Beth French, and Verlyn Rowett.

The purpose of the project was to help organize self-advocacy groups across Canada. The Project did a lot to do that. They

- wrote books – *Advice for Advisors* and *Leadership Training Manual* (both available in English and French)
- made videos about People First (*We Can Do It*) and jobs (*Speaking for Ourselves*)
- organized conferences at the local, provincial, national, and international level
- did training all over the country
- published a newsletter: *National Organizer*
- organized People First of Canada
- kept People First groups in touch with one another and the movement
- did all kinds of advocacy work

In 1987, People First members wrote some letters about what the National People First Project did. Gordon Fletcher (1987) from People First in British Columbia wrote:

> This project has enabled consumers to organize a provincial body in two years where it would have taken longer. The National People First Project has shown us how to get things together... You two [Bill and Peter] have given us advice on how to organize conferences... People First in Ontario held some conferences and then we learned from them... B.C. People First really got started back in September 1984 in Vancouver, B.C. That meeting would never have happened without the help and support of Bill

and Peter. It was that small group that was the beginning of something that is getting bigger and stronger every day...

Denis Laroche (1987), from Chicoutimi, Quebec, wrote:

The National People First project has worked hard to support us, to build groups everywhere. It hasn't always been easy especially in the past year, when the money has been tight. It's hard to make plans when you're never sure if you have enough finances to continue.

We have greatly appreciated the effort you have put into producing everything in French and English.... We know that when you travel somewhere to work with People First in another province that you will bring back important ideas for all of us to learn from. You have build bridges between groups across Canada. Your direct support to our work in Quebec has been very helpful — ideas on how to tackle issues and get results, how to prepare meetings and conferences and technical support...

Harold Barnes (1987), from Red Deer, Alberta, wrote:

Through newsletters such as the *National Organizer* and newspaper articles by People First members we have made the general public more aware of our wants and needs. People First is working now on issues like work, real jobs and the name change just to mention a few. The project has made the people in the community aware that these are *real* issues.

The project has information it passes on to the people it effects — us folks at the grassroots. In each province there are key leaders who share ideas with other provinces. We can keep in touch with each other through telephone calls and the exchange of addresses.

A valuable thing that they have shown and told us is that you start small then you grow to become large, strong and powerful...

David Reid (1987) from New Brunswick People First wrote:

The project has helped me and Andrea a lot, getting People First organized in our province. It taught us some valuable things such as where we might go for more information on People First, how we might start to network... and so on. The project taught us that there is more to People First than just a name. There is work as well. We aren't just a social club.... We learned that people want to deal with day-to-day concerns, usually something that affects them.

In February, 1990, Patrick Worth was the President of the National People First

Advisory Committee. He wrote an article for the *National Organizer* that talked about starting People First of Canada.

> The National People First Project has been in existence for five years. The main priority of the project was to support the People First movement in Canada by developing leadership in order for People First members to take control of their own movement. Now we need a movement not a project. Our project was temporary and does not have a Board, where members can have their say. In a People First movement, members from across the country will be connected through a board that we elect. We will make decisions together and fight for our rights. *That is what People First is all about.*
>
> The National People First Advisory Committee... now feels that the project has completed its task and the People First members of Canada must work together to support the creation of PEOPLE FIRST OF CANADA. (Worth, 1990)

The founding convention of People First of Canada was held on April 6-7, 1991, in Saint John, New Brunswick. Thirty-two delegates who were People First members were present. They had a vote to represent each province and territory. They approved a constitution and voted on a number of resolutions. The resolutions tell us what People First of Canada (1991) thinks is important. These resolutions were passed:

1. Because guardianship and orders of supervision take away the rights of individuals:Therefore be it resolved that People First of Canada oppose all legislation putting people under these acts.
2. Be it resolved that People First of Canada lobby the province of British Columbia to increase the number of low-income housing units. Be it further resolved that People First of Canada urge that the maximum shelter costs be adjusted to reflect the income levels of each area in the country.
3. Be it resolved that People First of Canada launch a public awareness campaign about the need for institutions to close now. People First of Canada should consult with the provincial and territorial People First groups about the role they will play in the campaign. National and provincial Associations for Community Living should be asked to support this campaign.
4. Be it resolved that People First of Canada along with their provincial organizations strongly lobby the federal and provincial governments to close all institutions and ensure that all services and resources are available for all individuals.
5. Whereas people described as having a mental handicap are typically given very limited employment opportunities in jobs that pay very little, require few skills, are boring, and provide little security and chance for advance-

ment: and whereas many people still have no real job opportunities:

Therefore be it resolved that People First of Canada, in cooperation with Canada's business and labour community, work to develop meaningful and valued career opportunities.

6. Be it resolved that People First of Canada help Quebec with the employment problem by pressuring the government and the employers.

7. Whereas many people who are labelled mentally handicapped are living in boarding homes and being treated poorly and the owners of these places make a profit from the people living there:

Therefore be it resolved that People First of Canada should make a public statement that no one should be allowed to make a profit from people who are described as having a mental handicap. And it be further resolved that People First of Canada call for the closure of all for-profit boarding homes.

Founders Awards were presented to Patrick Worth, Barb Goode, Peter Park, Harold Barnes, and Denis Laroche. People First of Canada is incorporated as a non-profit organization. It is still seeking charitable status.

The Board of People First of Canada is made up of Denis Laroche (Quebec), Paul Young (Nova Scotia), David Reid (New Brunswick), Arnold Bennington (British Columbia), Harold Barnes (Alberta), Norval Sears (Ontario), Shane Haddad (Saskatchewan), and Catherine Fortier (Quebec). The Executive Committee is Denis (President), Paul, David, and Harold. All but one of the Board members is also a President of a provincial People First group. Quebec gets two seats on the Board, so one of the members is not the President of the Provincial group. Andre Blanchet (British Columbia), Beth French (Ontario), Bruce Kappel (Ontario), and Jim Oulton (Nova Scotia) are regular volunteer advisors to the Board and Executive Committee. George Bartoszewicz is the translator.

What Are Some of the Issues People First Groups Have?

People First groups are known across Canada as people who take action. People First groups have taken their issues to the Supreme Court of Canada, the highest court in Canada. They have held demonstrations at provincial government buildings and had a sit-in at a minister's office. (A "minister" in Canada is an elected leader who heads up a department of government such as social services.) People First groups have had letter-writing campaigns to the newspapers, governments, and Associations for Community Living.

People First groups have taken on a lot of issues. Some of the ones that stick out for everybody include:

- The "Eve" Case (1981 to 1986)
- The Name Change (1979–1985 and beyond)

- The Poster Controversy (1988)
- Discrimination at the Burnaby Inn (1984)
- Human Rights in Saskatchewan and Alberta
- Fighting Institutions in Quebec, Ontario, and Nova Scotia
- Group Homes, Workshops, and Pay (Everywhere, All the Time)
- Autonomy from the Association.

1) THE "EVE" CASE (1981 TO 1986)

In Canada, men and women who have been labelled mentally handicapped were often sterilized without their permission. Harold Barnes (1987a) described what sterilization is.

> [Sterilization] is an operation performed on mentally handicapped and mentally retarded people so that they cannot give birth. This operation is performed on people in institutions and group homes. It is never explained to them so that it can be understood. Nobody ever says how it might affect them in years to come. It was done to stop people from having babies that could be born with mental retardation. It was done largely for staff convenience (they wouldn't have to clear up messes) in institutions and group homes. I think it is wrong.

Thanks to People First leaders, the Supreme Court of Canada decided that "*no one* will be sterilized without their permission. People should be protected from being sterilized against their will. No one should be denied the right to give birth for non-medical reasons" (Park, 1987).

That victory happened on October 23, 1986. The fight began in 1981 when a woman called "Eve" (not her real name) came to the attention of People First leaders.

When Eve was 21, she was going to a segregated school. She made friends with a guy at the school. They liked each other. Barb Goode (1991) describes what happened next.

> When Eve's mother saw Eve holding hands with the young man, she became worried about the risk of her daughter becoming pregnant. Mrs. "E" felt Eve could not cope with being a mother, and decided that her daughter should be sterilized. She went to the Supreme Court of Prince Edward Island to see if she could get the court to agree with her. The court said no. Eve's mother took her case to the Appeal Court of PEI. The Appeal Court agreed with her and decided that Eve should be sterilized. After the Appeal Court ruling, an Official Trustee of PEI took the case to the Supreme Court of Canada in Ottawa on behalf of Eve.

The Consumer Advisory Committee, made up of People First leaders from across Canada, thought that the Canadian Association for Community Living should fight for Eve's right to not be sterilized without her permission. The Advocacy Committee of the Canadian Association for Community Living thought so too. When the Board of Directors of the Canadian Association talked about Eve's situation, they could not make a decision. **"The Board was undecided because some of its members were parents, professionals, doctors, etc. It is a very touchy issue or you could say a hot potato, because a lot of parents supported Eve's mother, not Eve"** (Park, 1987)

Barb Goode was chairperson of the Consumer Advisory Committee, and a CACL Board member. She spoke up at the board meeting. She said that since the Canadian Association could not make up its mind, it should help the Consumer Advisory Committee fight for Eve. Barb asked the board to **"approve funds required to present the views of the handicapped people we represent to the Supreme Court as intervenors in the case of 'Eve'."** The Board of the Canadian Association approved $5,000. One member of the board was a lawyer named David Vickers. He agreed to help the self-advocates fight their case.

Today, a lot of people think it was the Canadian Association that took on the Eve case. In fact, the Canadian Association could not decide what it thought was important. The Consumer Advisory Committee did not have any trouble. It stuck up for what it believed. It convinced the Canadian Association to support self-advocates' fight for what they believed in.

This is what the Consumer Advisory Committee (1981) decided the Eve Committee should fight for:

- Eve is a human being and should not have something done to her that she hasn't asked for.
- We believe that except in emergency cases people should not be sterilized without their consent. It might take us longer to understand, but one day we will and then we can make a decision for ourselves.
- Sterilization doesn't stop sexual needs or prevent a person from being raped or harassed.
- With help and support, handicapped people can bring up children. For example, a former member of our committee who had frequent seizures now has a healthy baby and is taking good care of her with proper help and guidance.
- As human beings in this great country, we all should have the same rights as we all have the same needs.

That is how the "Eve Committee" got started. The Eve Committee was made up of Barb Goode, Peter Park, Harold Barnes, and David Lincoln. Each of them was a People First leader. Barb, Peter and Harold stuck with the Eve case for five years! They started work in June, 1981. With the help of their lawyers, they got permission from the Supreme Court to get involved in the Eve case when it came to court. They worked with their lawyers to prepare their case.

> Barb was extremely good as a chairperson — she shared what she had learnt with other members. She phones our [CAC's] lawyer at least once a week. Barb was asking of him where we were so far, what we can do now, etc. She phoned the lawyer in PEI that Eve's mom had and told him to get his act together and get his factum into the Supreme Court and our lawyer.
>
> We were told we ought to have a backup plan or secondary stand on the issue by our lawyers. We took one stand even though it was contro-versial and stuck by our guns. One of the biggest victories was the day the decision was handed down. Handicapped people had won a great thing. This was tremendous. (Park, 1992)

In 1985, the case finally went to court. It took more than one year for the judges to make up their minds. Barb Goode described the victory:

> It was the first time ever that people [labelled] with mental handicaps have taken a case to the highest court in Canada. It took a long time to get there — seven years we were waiting. I am very glad we had a long time to understand the case really well.
>
> Before, people were just given the operation. We were not always given the choice. It is now against the law to be sterilized without you saying whether you want it or not. But some parents want to have control over their son's or daughter's lives. Some of these parents and doctors still want us to have operations we don't need. They won't believe that we understand the effect of the operation on our bodies. We should be able to get information on the operation. The nine judges agreed with us that Eve should not be sterilized without her saying her own decision or choice.
>
> Peter Park and I were very involved in the case with other people [labelled] with a mental handicap. It was a great day for all of us. It tells everyone that people with a mental handicap can make up their minds given the proper information, and the information is explained to them. (Goode, 1987)

The "Eve" Case was important to the People First movement in Canada. It proved People First leaders could stand up to the Canadian Association, and win. It proved that self-advocates could take their issues to the highest court in the land, and win. People First leaders learned how to use the courts and work with lawyers to fight for their rights.

2) THE NAME CHANGE (1979–1985 AND BEYOND)

The Eve Case was easy compared to the fight that People First members had with Associations all across Canada about the name of the Association. The fight to change the name was a priority for People First groups across the country. It was important to them. The name change was an issue that brought self-advocates together to fight for something that was important to them.

The issue was very clear. Right across Canada, most Associations called themselves Associations for the Mentally Retarded. That name hurt people who had been labelled. The name of the Association was exactly the opposite of the phrase *people first*. It put the label right up front. It was the opposite of the rallying cry for People First members — **LABEL JARS, NOT PEOPLE.** Ann West (1985) from People First in Mississauga put it this way in a letter to the Board of Directors of CAMR:

> We don't want the name "Mentally Retarded". We get called "Mentally Retarded", "Retarded", "Lame Brain", and we don't think it is fair.
>
> We want to be treated like adults. We want to have equal rights like anyone else. We want to work and enjoy ourselves just as anybody else does.
>
> We would like C.A.M.R. to change their name to something that explains what the Association is doing, and what we want.

It is hard to find out exactly when the fight to change the name started. Pat Worth remembers the first conference of People First of Ontario in 1981. The organizers were expected about 250 people to show up. They were wrong. About 650 people came!

> We talked a lot about the name change. At that time OAMR [the Ontario Association] committed itself to aid us, if we came up with a particular name they would agree to.
>
> We sent around a petition at the sessions and the banquet about what name OAMR should change its name to. *Community Living* was voted unanimously. Not just some, but all, every self-advocate at the hotel. That started a feud between People First and OAMR.
>
> A year later, at the Association annual general meeting, where the name change was voted, People First was in favour of *Community Living* and the association turned us down. (Worth, 1992)

Peter Park remembers that some things started when he, Pat Worth, Barb Goode, and Harold Barnes first met each other at the same time in 1979. They were on a boat ride around the harbor in Vancouver. They talked about the idea of having a self-advocacy committee at the Canadian Association. "We shared the idea of the name needing to change. We did not know how to go about it or anything like that."

By 1980, they knew. The People First leaders who were part of the Consumer Advisory Committee of the Canadian Association decided they should try to get the national association to change its name. If national changed, then others would too. In 1980, the Consumer Advisory Committee suggested three names to CAMR. Peter Park (1985) describes what happened then.

> They were *Integration Canada, Community Living,* & *Choice.* In 1981, CAMR confused things by putting forth another name. It was *Options.* This made it so confusing that CAMR didn't change the name.
>
> In 1982 the CAC proposed the name *Community Living,* but CAMR voted it down.
>
> In 1983, we thought we, the CAC, were going to win on the name change — needless to say we did not.
>
> In October of 1984 consumers and interested people spoke for the name change, which was voted down again. They got up and left the meeting room as emotions ran high. [This was an organized walkout by self-advocates and supporters. When the name change was voted down, they stood up and walked out of the room single file. It got everyone's attention.]
>
> Since the vote was so near and yet so far, a Special General Meeting was called not later than June of 1985 to deal with the name change only.
>
> At the June 1985 meeting the name *Community Living* was voted down on the first ballot. This brought such a silence you could have heard a pin drop, and you didn't known whether to cry or what. Luckily someone wisely asked for a break at this time. Believe you me it was a very long coffee break.
>
> Back everyone came for the next vote — here it was passed and then some extra.
>
> It was about time that the Association realized that consumers do not ask for much with the exception of the name change, which most consumers wanted, and some service providers didn't. We had to overcome obstacles in our fight to the finish —*WE WON.*

The struggle to change the name was a hard one. Many parents and professionals in the Association argued that no one would know how to find the Association if the name changed. It would cost too much money to change the letterhead and signs. Some troublemakers in the Association argued that People First members were being manipulated by staff and People First leaders. They tried to undermine People First. They said most people who had been labelled did not care. They ignored the fact that everyone, all 650 people, at the People First of Ontario conference voted to change the name.

During the name change fight, many People First members learned to stand up to professionals and parent leaders. When People First members came up with an idea on how to change the name, and it did not work, they came up with new ideas. Just like with the Eve Case, people did not give up.

For many People First members, the whole fight around the name change was hurtful. The Association just would not hear what people were saying —"The name hurts us." All the excuses for not changing the name hurt people.

The vast majority of Associations in Canada today are called Associations for Community Living or something like that. Some people still complain about the name change. They do not understand what the big deal was. They do not understand how the label and the name hurt. This became very clear in October of 1988, when there was the Poster Controversy.

3) The Poster Controversy (1988)

After the name change, some people at the Canadian Association decided they needed to promote *Community Living*, and let people know the name of the Association had changed. The Canadian Association developed a public education campaign complete with posters and television spots. Pat Worth (1992) describes what happened.

> There were supposed to be a whole series of cartoon campaigns. One of them was supposed to be a 30-second cartoon on CBC [a national television network] which People First had several concerns about.
>
> One, it identified us as children. Two, it was a cartoon using a story that was not true. It had advertised this poster that was part of the campaign. It looked like a child reaching through a wall taking another child out, taking a child out of an institution all of a sudden. On top of the poster was a sign that said "the mentally retarded". In the cartoon, the wall falls down, the name *mentally retarded* blows up and *community living* comes out.
>
> We were very concerned about CACL using that old name again after we fought a long hard victory to get the name changed. They were going back to using the labels again.
>
> Anyways, at the CACL Annual Conference and General Meeting, we realised we had to organize fast. We had a meeting with People First members from all across Canada. We organized to stop this. I was also invited to be a speaker at that conference in a session with Michael Kendrick. I forget the topic, but I pulled the rug out from under CACL. I talked about something else, I talked about the whole public education campaign. It felt good.
>
> At the A.G.M. [Annual General Meeting] we went to the microphones

and told them why they should kill the campaign. It was like the name change all over again. In the end, the campaign was voted down. It did not go through. I will always remember that moment. CACL had established itself as a big giant in public education. At that conference we showed them who the giants were. It was sneaky business that backfired.

But the sneaky business continued.

Because of that experience, CACL did make a commitment to communicate with us for future campaigns. They developed a public education campaign that was much better. But, we were still not satisfied because they used the name "mentally retarded". We did not, and never will, go along with that. They went ahead anyway. (Worth, 1992)

4) Discrimination at the Burnaby Inn (1984)

It may seem that People First only does battle with the Association, but it also fights for rights in many other areas. One example of other kinds of struggles is what happened in Burnaby, British Columbia. Gerry Juzenas (1989), of B.C. People First, described the events.

On May 8, 1984, two advisors and some members of the Burnaby People First went to a restaurant to order a meal. The proprietor refused to serve us because he said we had upset the waitress and some of the customers by causing a loud disturbance. He also said that we had made a mess on the floor. We decided to write to the Human Rights Branch in British Columbia to see if legal action could be taken. They assigned us a lawyer since we couldn't afford one on our own.... We won the case! We were the first People First group to win a discrimination case like this. We received a $500.00 cash settlement. Two hundred dollars went to the Burnaby Sports Club and the remaining three hundred dollars was put in our bank account.

5) Human Rights in Saskatchewan and Alberta

In many provinces in Canada, there are laws called Human Rights Codes. Most provinces said that it is against the law for people to discriminate against other people because they have a physical or mental disability. People First members and other advocates were active in getting these laws passed. When Canada was developing its constitution, People First was active in getting the Charter of Rights and Freedoms to guarantee that people with disabilities have the right to equal protection and benefit of the law.

This kind of protection in the law is what made it possible for the People First group in Burnaby to take action against the restaurant that kicked them out.

Two provinces, Saskatchewan and Alberta, took a long time to change their Human Rights laws to protect people with disabilities. According to Pat Worth (1992), "People First in Alberta and Saskatchewan had a long fight with both of their governments... That seemed like a fight that would go on forever. They kept at it until it got done."

One of the ways that People First got the job done was by writing letters to the government. The Saskatchewan People First Council and local People First groups in the province wrote letters similar to this one from Ron Carpentier (1989) from Moose Jaw, Saskatchewan, People First. The letter is to the Attorney General of the Province of Saskatchewan.

> Dear Mr. Andrew:
> The members of the Moose Jaw chapter of People First urges you to amend the Saskatchewan Human Rights Code to include [people who are] mentally disabled. Given a chance we are productive and responsible citizens as well as anyone else. It isn't encouraging to know that if we go out to apply for a job, rent an apartment, etc. to know that people can discriminate against us on the grounds of our mental disability. A few of us who are fortunate to hold real jobs and pay taxes find it very upsetting that as taxpayers our rights aren't guaranteed the same way our fellow workers rights are....
> The Moose Jaw chapter of People First wishes to see that all people whatever disabling factor be included into the Saskatchewan Human Rights Code, and that we are individuals protected from discrimination the same as our fellow citizens. After all we are People First, and should be considered in that light with our disability as a secondary issue.

Today, the Saskatchewan and Alberta Human Rights Codes protect people with disabilities. This kind of law helped People First in Quebec fight for people in an institution there.

6) FIGHTING INSTITUTIONS IN QUEBEC, ONTARIO, AND NOVA SCOTIA

People First groups in many provinces are involved in fighting institutions. People First has used the law, the media, meetings with government, and public demonstrations to make its case.

Denis Laroche is very active on the board of People First of Canada and a leader of the Quebec People First Committee. In 1991, People First won a big victory for freedom. Denis (1991) described that victory:

We as handicapped people fought for a cause that we believed in. Now looking at this victory, we see a beginning for people fighting for their freedom.... and this is only a beginning.

Saint Theophile was an institution in the Province of Quebec near Montreal. The people who lived there were forced to do the work around the institution for nothing. They were treated very badly.

Parents and advocates saw how terrible things were and obtained the services of a lawyer to help them to get the people out. They had public demonstrations, they involved the media and they launched a human rights complaint. Last year the institution was closed and the people moved into group homes in the community.

Near the end of January 1991, the human rights complaint was won... The Human Rights Commission decided that people who lived in Saint Theophile were exploited and treated badly. They were awarded one million dollars ($1,000,000). For the first time in Canada, this money goes directly to the people who had to suffer through life in an institution.

People First of Ontario has been very active in fighting institutions. The struggle has been about two issues. The first is the Ontario government's policy on institutions. The government decided to make some institutions smaller, and close other ones. Recently, it slowed down the progress it was making. There were also problems with the way that people were being moved to the community. The second thing was that in two institutions a lot of people died.

Norval Sears (1991), President of People First of Ontario, described the struggle.

In November [1990], we heard about the deaths of 17 people who had lived in an institution named Brantwood in Brantford, and 16 people who died in an institution named Christopher Robin in Oshawa.

The Executive Committee of People First of Ontario heard about these deaths after many other people already knew. We felt that People First should have been told first before anyone else because these are our people and we should know what is happening to them.

Many of the people who died were children who will never grow up to see what the world is really like. They died in these institutions and no one really knows what happened to them there. They no longer have a voice to speak out about the way the staff was treating them in the institution....

We believe that these people died because they were being neglected, we know that they were not given enough food and drink to eat and many died of choking. These people were labelled "medically fragile" — this means that they were treated with kid gloves and expected to die early in their lives.

The Board [of People First of Ontario] felt very angry that the government was not going to hold an inquest and look into all of the deaths. The government said that they felt the staff had been doing a good job and that they didn't suspect any problems.

The Board was also very upset that the Minister of Community and Social Services had put a freeze or stop on all people coming out of institutions. She said she was going to look into conditions in institutions. We felt she was listening to the staff and the unions more than us.

...[W]e decided to take action and force the minister, Ms. Akande, to meet with us and hear our side of the story. We thought she should know what it is really like in an institution and that people are not getting treated fairly. We postponed the board meeting and took the entire board to her office at Queen's Park. When we got there we marched up to her office and requested to see her. They gave us all kinds of excuses why she couldn't meet with us. We said we wanted to meet with her if it took all night. They tried to get us to meet with her assistants and we said no, we wanted to talk to her in person. We waited and waited. We had a sit-in in her boardroom. We waited and waited...

When the minister met with us we gave her our demands. We told her we wanted full inquests into the deaths. We told her we want these institutions closed. There are too many deaths occurring.

The only thing she agreed with was to have an advocacy commission set up so that we could put in complaints of abuse.

After the meeting we met with reporters and told them that she didn't give us a good enough answer. We said that she hadn't listened to us.

Since then, we have met with Ms. Akande and other committees and told them that we feel strongly that the inquests into these deaths be carried out by people in the community, by advocates and not by nurses. We told her as well that institutions must be closed.

We have a lawyer from [the Advocacy Resource Centre for the Handicapped] to represent us at the inquest. People First want to be at this inquest so that we can be heard. We are advocates. We advocate on behalf of other people who cannot talk for themselves...

In Nova Scotia, Paul Young (1991), President of Nova Scotia People First, described what People First did in response to the death of a man named Harold in an institution.

His death came about when he was strangled to death by the straitjacket he was forced to wear. This aversive [punishment] technique was inhumane and a destruction of the human spirit.

The group [Nova Scotia People First] wrote an article and mailed it to all local papers so our position would be publicly known. We requested an immediate inquiry into his death and demanded the Nova Scotia government to accept responsibility for this tragic event. The opposition parties were also contacted with our concern and requested to help press the Government for immediate change.

Once the government informed us that the R.C.M.P. [the police] was satisfied with the investigation and concluded the institution was not negligent, we immediately demanded a copy of the report. We were denied. We feel that through all of this we stood our ground. The Halifax Rehabilitation Centre, where all of this occurred, voluntarily banned the use of all restraining devices, such as straight jackets, within the institution. We feel this was a result of the public pressure from groups and the general public who felt this death was not necessary and could have been prevented.

The group feels that we could have applied more pressure but the event was being shoved in the closet so it would be forgotten. This made it difficult to address the Government further. We feel, however, we did enough to prove that these techniques are not justified and change must occur. Hopefully in the near future these changes will take place....

7) GROUP HOMES, WORKSHOPS, AND PAY (EVERYWHERE, ALL THE TIME)

Wherever there are People First groups in Canada, there are issues about group homes and sheltered workshops. Many People First groups got going because of issues around these services.

When Peter Park and Pat Worth first got involved, their issues were about where they lived, the work they did, and getting paid for that work. Peter remembers those early days.

In 1978, I moved to a Group Home in a local city called Brantford. When I moved from my previous place I told the Association in no uncertain terms that I wanted an apartment of my own.

After People First got started in Brantford, we invited the President of the Board of the AMR, the Executive Director of the AMR and the coordinators of the workshop to a People First meeting. We did this as we wanted to know why the association had an apartment program for girls and not guys.

The association as a result invited People First members to a meeting and heard their side of the story. Soon there were apartments for guys as well as girls. After about 2 or 3 months, I moved out of the Group Home to an apartment I shared with 2 other guys...

In the workshop, wages were low and we (People First members) talked about this at our meetings and in the shop... People First members told the Board [of the Association] how they felt and were pleading with the association to let them make at least money that they could live on.

We did not get all we wanted but there were some improvements. 1) The Association started to ask us for some input. 2) A new wage policy was drawn up and posted in the shops where we could see it. Even if some couldn't read these who could would read it to them. This was something new. It was new for the Association. Wages for a two-week period became as high as $20 or as low as $5.50 in 1979. (Park, undated)

In Nova Scotia, a People First organization was started by Helen Cronin in Wolfville. The group calls itself a Worker's Council. The group started because Helen was upset at the workshop. Jim Oulton was the group's advisor. He wrote a paper about it.

Helen brought her frustration and anger to me. She felt tired of coping and acting like everything was O.K. when it really wasn't. She thought that no one understood her problems and that the workshop staff were purposefully ignoring her concerns. Helen said she found no support; only closed doors. She hated the stigma of mental retardation; she felt powerless and alone with her troubles. (Oulton, 1990-91, p. 2)

Helen and Jim found out about People First and started a group they called the Worker's Council. Eventually, the Council had an Executive Committee that met with Jim every week.

We would analyze the information from the minutes of the meeting, as well as the methods of interaction within the group structure. We looked at alternative ways to achieve effective communication within the larger organization of staff, management and Board of Directors [of the workshop]. Together, we prioritized the Council's business, not only as it related to the present, but also as it contributed to the fundamental principles of the "People's First Movement" which held a vision of not only self-advocacy but of developing a group advocacy movement. (Oulton, 1990-91, p. 9.)

At first, the Worker's Council spent a lot of time on social activities. They formed a dance committee, a bowling and movies committee, and so on. These committees gave people experience in getting organized and working together for things that were important to them. Then things began to change.

As the work of the Worker's Council grew, there was a necessity for increased support. Other staff at the agency had been watching the ups and downs of the group, and at the request of the Worker's Council, many were willing to get involved. Committees were formed to decide everything: from what colour to paint the bathroom walls, to establishing of canteen services, to Ethiopia Relief fund raising.

(Oulton, 1990-91, p. 12)

The Worker's Council has tried to get higher pay at the workshop. Helen has joined a local anti-poverty committee to work with others on the issue of poverty.

People First of Ontario and People First of Canada have also gotten involved with other groups to fight for their rights. People First is part of a coalition for employment equity. Pat Worth talked about what that has meant.

> We learned about our rights by being involved with the Employment Equity Coalition. As a rule, we were able to teach our members across Canada what minimum wage is all about. The Employment Equity Act says all employers must pay people minimum wage.
>
> We helped our local groups develop regional meetings for the purpose of having one-day workshops on real jobs. That took a whole lot of education because a lot of our members are people that did not understand that workshops were not real jobs. They did not understand the idea of minimum wage and how they were deprived of earning a salary like anyone else. A lot of us were conned into believing that a disability pension was actually a salary.
>
> It took a whole lot of education to teach our members that they could earn more money by working for an employer in the community. Most of them were earning 50 cents or 10 cents an hour. What they did not understand was that they could be earning four or five dollars an hour in the community. They were also worried about losing their benefits, and having to pay for their own medical and dental plans. That is still a fear today.
>
> They were so convinced by people, we were all convinced, especially by service providers that we could not do anything, because we were so disabled that we could not develop our own dreams. Most of us were put into workshops doing the same thing every day for 20 years, for very little money, for nothing, because people thought we were too disabled.
>
> When some of our members actually left the workshop and started to get jobs, it started to change the way people think. When we started to show up at Association conferences and described how we got jobs and the kinds of jobs, it was a real eye-opener for people... (Worth, 1992)

People First of Ontario started an Employment Equity project. They established an employment action plan.

The Board voted in favour of a couple of People First members to travel across the province of Ontario to visit local groups and to attend conferences and explain what employment equity means to People First. That was very helpful because an awful lot of people did not understand the meaning of employment equity. (Worth, 1992)

People First of Ontario was able to stop the government from passing a law about pay that People First did not agree with.

When Social Services in Ontario decided to develop a proposed policy to allow employers in communities to pay us less than minimum wage, we decided to have a march and demonstration around Social Services, outside of their office.

The wage policy was part of a plan to close down workshops, but it was done in such a way that was still discriminatory to our members. It got started as two pilot projects in London and Thunder Bay. Our members in London and Thunder Bay were told that they were going to get paid a minimum wage by their employers. That did not turn out to be so. What actually happened was that they got an equivalent, which allows the employer to pay them a dollar an hour, or more or less. So it was up to the employer to decide whether they got minimum wage or not. The rest of the money came from FBA [the disability allowance] which meant that they still had to stay on Family Benefits, and get a dollar or two or three dollars from their employer. It went against the Employment Standards Act which said all employers must pay people at least a minimum wage.

[To protest this policy,] the demonstration was held during our Conference and Annual General Meeting. And there was also a press conference. It was extremely successful. It led to People First of Ontario being invited to many conferences to talk about the wage policy. Nobody was listening to us before that. After the conference and demonstration, Social Services started inviting us to the table.

Anyways, the wage policy never got to legislation. We stopped the policy... We stopped it from being a law. (Worth, 1992)

8) AUTONOMY FROM THE ASSOCIATION

The history of People First in Canada is filled with confrontations with Associations for Community Living. The Eve Case, the Name Change and Poster Controversy, and issues about services are just some of the examples.

It is also true that Associations have helped People First. Staff of local, provincial and national association have been friends and advisors to People First. Some have been instrumental in helping to start People First groups.

The relationship between People First and Associations has had its ups and downs. In many cases, People First groups are fighting with the Association. At the same time, groups think they need the support of the Association.

People First of Canada decided to come to grips with this problem. The first thing it did was to write a short paper called "What Autonomy Means to People First." This is a short introduction to the importance of autonomy and principles of autonomy. The Executive Committee also wrote a longer discussion paper so that People First groups could talk about the problems.

This is what the paper said about what autonomy means to People First:

> It is very important for People First members to be able to speak for themselves.
>
> People First members must be able to tell their own stories about their lives. We must be able to tell our stories our way with our own words. That is one of the reasons we have People First. The movement belongs to us. It shows we are capable and responsible.
>
> Being able to speak for ourselves is called *autonomy*. Autonomy means we have OUR OWN VOICE. It means we have OUR OWN IDEAS.
>
> Autonomy means that we know what we want to say. It means that we have our own way of saying what is important to us. It means People First members are the people who talk about what People First is all about.
>
> Speaking for ourselves does not mean that we need to do everything by ourselves. We need to change things for people who have been labelled. To do that, we need friends or allies.
>
> When we work with other groups who support what we believe in, that is called an alliance. We need to make alliances with other groups. But, we do not need those other groups to tell us what to say or what we should think. (People First of Canada, 1992, p. 1)

People First of Canada has identified many things and people that threaten the autonomy of People First. Three of the things that really threaten People First are:

- groups that ignore us and use us
- the ways we get pulled away from People First
- sometimes, the way People First members act

There are many examples of how other people and groups ignore People First. There are many examples of how other groups use People First. One example involved the Canadian Association for Community Living.

> Something that happened recently is an example of this. In October, 1991, People First of Canada had a meeting with leaders of the Govern-

ment of Canada. We went with leaders from the Canadian Association for Community Living. The CACL people made the government think that the People First members were from CACL. CACL wanted the government to see how powerful CACL is, so CACL used us to look more powerful.

When the Canadian Association told its members about this meeting they did not even mention People First! In the Winter 1992 issue of *Newsbreak*, the newsletter of CACL, CACL mentions that Patrick Worth and Denis Laroche were at the meeting. But they do not even say that Pat and Denis were there representing People First. This is an example of how other groups use us. (People First of Canada, 1992, pp. 3-4)

Another example is about people trying to get People First members to think their way, rather than listening to what People First members think.

One example of this is when People First advisers start talking about issues between themselves and ignore what People First members have to say. Or, advisers put things on the agenda of a People First meeting, and those things are only important to the adviser, not People First.

We get a lot of this when we talk to Associations about the name change. Board members keep telling us that it is not practical to change the name. It would mean having to print a lot of new letterhead. They tell us the public will be confused. They are so busy thinking about their own ideas, they do not listen to People First members who say they are hurt by a name that labels people. (People First of Canada, 1992, p. 4)

Another way that the ability of People First to speak up is hurt is when other people and groups pull members away from People First business.

It is very important that People First members know what they think and have a chance to speak up. This is hard work. It takes time. If we are to have our autonomy, we have to do the work we have to do, and take the time to do the work.

One of the ways that other people threaten our autonomy is when they make it very easy for us to do things that are not People First work.

One way this happens is when Associations have dances and segregated bowling nights when there are People First meetings. This makes it easy for People First members not to go to People First meetings.

This also happens when agencies and Associations set up consumer advisory committees, or invite self-advocates to join their Board of Directors. When self-advocates join consumer advisory committees or a Board of Directors of an Association, they have less time to spend on People First business. This weakens People First. Self-advocates feel im-

portant when they sit on committees and Boards. But People First often
becomes less important to them. (People First of Canada, 1992, pp. 5-6)

People First of Canada also thinks that the way that People First leaders act
sometimes can take away autonomy.

> The ability of People First to have its own voice depends a lot on leader-
> ship.
> One of the worst things leaders can do is get power hungry. It is
> important for People First members to share power. We get into trouble
> when one person becomes the only person that speaks for People First.
> We know we are in trouble when leaders start saying "me" instead of
> "we". We know we are in trouble when People First members start
> talking about self-advocates as "they" instead of "we."
>   (People First of Canada, 1992, p. 6)

It is always a big problem when People First members and advisors fight the Association.

> An example of this happened at the 1991 Annual General Meeting of the
> Canadian Association. People First wanted to get a friend of People First
> elected as President of CACL. Many of the members of the Association
> were opposed to this. Some People First members were threatened by
> Association members. They were told they would lose their privileges,
> such as being on Committees, if they voted the wrong way.
> People First advisors may have the same kind of problem when they
> work for the Association. It means they may have to say tough things to
> their boss. People First members have the same kind of problem when
> they work in the workshop. Some times they have to speak up and take
> on the staff member who is their boss at the workshop.
>   (People First of Canada, 1992, p. 15)

People First of Canada has done a number of things to protect its autonomy.
One thing is to move its office out of the Canadian Association building. Another
thing is to make sure that when People First of Canada and the Canadian Association do things together, everybody makes it very clear that People First is a separate
organization. People First of Canada has also asked that, from now on, the Executive Committee of the Association meet with the Executive Committee of People
First. This means that the leaders of both groups meet with each other. Before, it
was the staff of the Association who would meet with People First. Or, a member of
the Association Board would meet with People First. Now, things will be equal.
A few years ago, People First was fighting to be heard by the Canadian Associa-

tion. It won votes for People First from each province at the Canadian Association's Annual General Meeting. This meant that People First could vote for Board members and resolutions about what the Association believes in and does.

People First of Canada thought about autonomy and the Canadian Association. People First decided that if it was going to have a partnership with the Association, it would be an equal partnership. This meant that if People First had votes at the Association's annual meeting, then the Association should have votes at People First. People First decided it did not want this to happen. So, it has asked the Association to change the rules so that People First no longer has votes in the Association. That was hard to do.

What Works? What Doesn't?

Over the last ten years, People First has learned a lot about what works and what does not work. In 1987, there was an article in the *National Organizer* that described some of the problems that People First groups have. The problems were ones that People First groups had talked about with the National People First Project.

1. *Groups fall apart.* Some of the reasons we heard for this problem:
   * the members weren't interested anymore;
   * nobody wants to do the work;
   * the President and other leaders weren't doing anything;
   * our advisor left and we can't find a new one;
   * we were fighting each other too much; we couldn't agree on anything;
   * we don't have a reason to meet anymore.
2. *Groups that meet but have nothing to talk about.*
3. *Losing members*
   * Getting members involved — how do we get more members to come to meetings and get involved?
   * Sometimes parents or staff keep members from attending meetings.
4. *The advisor runs the group and doesn't let the members make their own decisions.*
5. *Money.* Several groups have told us that they would like to try some new projects but they didn't have enough money. Others complained that they spend so much time fundraising they never had time to do anything else. Another problem is that money has been lost or stolen.
6. *The association runs the group.* When People First is a part of the association, the members are afraid to speak up about problems they have in the workshop or in the group home.
7. *Swelled heads.* Sometimes a member gets elected president or onto a board. All of a sudden the person thinks they can boss everyone around or not do any of the work.
8. *The public doesn't listen to us.* We aren't taken seriously, and it is hard to

change attitudes in the community. (*National Organizer*, 1987, pp. 6-7)

Some of the same issues and some different ones were identified in Ontario. In 1991, John McKnight met with some People First leaders in Ontario. The meeting started by telling stories about local groups, then figuring out what some of the common problems were. Here is a list of common problems:

1. Trying to organize chapters in big cities.
2. People are afraid to speak out and take action at the local group. They want out of their workshops and they are afraid to leave.
3. Getting people to meetings. Teaching people the transit in some cities.
4. People speaking for the group without the group approving.
5. Members acting on behalf of the group without the group approving.
6. Notifying members of meetings. Some people have trouble reading and some cannot use the phone freely.
7. Communication among members gets difficult.
8. People getting threatened by staff and agencies to make sure that they don't become People First members.
9. Agencies want to take over the whole show and control people's lives.
10. Leadership gets taken away from the People First local chapters by Associations.
11. It is difficult finding people who will act as advisors and make the commitment. Finding advisors who are not controlling. Some advisors seem overwhelmed by the work that needs to be done.
12. Members feel intimidated by advisors and find it difficult to accept them.
13. Members begin to fight among themselves instead of fighting the system.
14. Local groups are not connected with other groups that fight for their rights. (Sears, 1991.)

Both the National People First Project and People First leaders in Ontario came up with ideas about what will work to overcome the problems they described.

• We need to have strong leaders who understand People First and have ideas about how to put those ideas into action. When leaders understand how to do their job, that makes People First more independent. It means that People First doesn't have to depend on the advisors for everything...
• When groups don't know what to do or fall apart, it is often because they don't have new and fresh ideas from other groups about what People First is doing. When your group is cut off from other groups in other towns and cities, it is easy to get worn down and "run out of gas."
    When members from different places have a chance to meet each other, talk, share ideas, and make decisions, it can be very exciting. It is a way of

meeting new friends (or seeing old ones, and hearing our opinions. It makes People First stronger.

- An advisor can really help a group. They can also run a group... They have a lot of power. That is why it is important that the advisor really believe in the members. The advisor shouldn't tell the members what to do, or do things for the members. The advisor should help the members do things for themselves... (*National Organizer*, 1987)

- Realize that a group will make each person more powerful. A group helps you to reach and influence a lot more people.
- We must figure out why each member comes to the group meetings and what they want from the group.
- We must listen to each member to find out what each member is really angry about and what they want to see changed. This way we will keep each person involved in working for something they want to see changed.
- Must make each person feel powerful because they are a member of the group and make each person feel they have an important role in the group.
- Need to find ways to make members feel close to one another by getting to know one another and supporting one another to fight the system.
- We need to make sure that we do something and take action about the things that make our members angry.
- Be sure that when a group hears from members about the problems in their lives that they do something and not just give the person advice. This means group members getting involved in helping the person having problems take action.
- Need to think about how the group can make members feel courageous (brave) and will to take action. Need to spread stories of courageous things group members have done to change the system or other things in their lives.
- Need to develop allies that you can count on. Need to connect with powerful people in your community that will listen to our stories and that are not part of the service system. People like lawyers, women's leaders, civil rights leaders, reporters for local newspapers, politicians...
- Need to invite people in the community to meetings so that they find out more about what your group does and what it stands for.
- Need to find ways to get members out to meetings by organizing volunteer drivers or having people take transit together.
- Need to fight the agencies that run group homes and tell them that they cannot stop people from coming to People First meetings and becoming People First members and that this is against their right to freedom of association. (Sears, 1991)

The training workshops, conferences, newsletter, and books that the Project developed help groups deal with these issues.

People First members from across Canada have other ideas about what works.

- Gordon Fletcher advises new groups to start small. They should know why they are organizing. They need to have a plan of action with reasonable goals.
- Avril Van Pelt of the New Westminster (B.C.) Chapter wrote that groups should start on their own. Then, no other group can control them.
- David Reid from New Brunswick said that people want to deal with day-to-day concerns. They usually want to deal with something that affects them... "There is more to People First than just a name. There is work as well."

(*National Organizer*, 1987)

Peter Park thinks it is important for people to rally around a common concern.

> People First is a self-advocacy grass-roots organization. People rally round an issue with a common concern. It might be something so simple that at first it doesn't seem to matter to most people that have not been labelled. To a labelled person it is very important something tangible and winnable.... The work is only beginning let us not forget that. A few issues are sterilization, workshops, real jobs, Group Homes, the Association, and the Workshops, just to mention a few. (Park, undated)

Pat Worth has been thinking a lot about the question of what works. He has a number of things to say about democracy, keeping things personal, the style of meetings in People First groups, how to pick issues, and the need to celebrate.

- *Democracy.* I think it is important to never elect yourself as the spokesperson. You have to be identified as a leader by your group. People who have elected themselves as spokespersons in this movement have failed.

    There are too many decisions to be made by one person. They must be made democratically by a group. That is the only way you can make people feel they can make decisions.
- *Keep it Personal.* I think we have all got to be doing and participating in some thing that is personal to us. We have to make it personal to us. We cannot treat this just as a business. In People First, we call each other "brothers" and "sisters." That has to mean something. We are not "9 to 5" people and we are not resource people. We are more than just a civil rights movement. I think we establish ourselves as family to one another....
- *Style of Meetings.* Many of our local groups are still weak. There are lots of reasons for that. I think one of the reasons is that we have made our groups

feel they must come together to conduct business. We think we always have to make decisions in our groups. We think we cannot just meet to talk and make personal decisions. I think we expect too much from our local groups.

I think we have to bring, as leaders, our issues to groups and help them develop those issues themselves, and we have to understand that maybe sometimes people cannot come to decisions about things.

We should not have to meet in isolated places.... I have been to local group meetings where we meet in nearby and convenient places, But, there are other places where there is no bus transportation. There is no way for members to get there without having a ride. It is not accommodating to them. They expect the meetings to start on time. But if it is miles and miles away and there is no local transportation, then it is impossible to start the meeting on time.

I think it makes it more personal if people would be willing to share their homes with us, instead of going around trying to find a church hall or a college willing to rent out a place or something like that. I think we have made it just too much of a business with our local groups. We have made them feel like they have to come together to just discuss business.

• *Celebrate.* John McKnight says, and I think this is true, we should always celebrate our victories. Victories are never victories until we celebrate. I do not mean champagne and party all the time. I mean being able to hug one another, congratulate one another, and share the human spirit with one another.

We will never get the sense that *we did it together* if we do not celebrate.

• *Picking Issues.* The bad way to do it [pick issues] is to make people feel like their issue has to be theirs. I can pick on advisors for this. Sometimes People First members feel they have to go along with advisors. They think they cannot challenge advisors. Sometimes advisors feel their job is an issue. They will say to People First members that they cannot say anything about workshops, or my job, or service providers.

The bad thing that we have done is feel that we have to go along with it, because the advisor is our friend. The system is the enemy, but sometimes the service provider is our friend. We have made too many allowances over the years for service providers, and for advisors.

The good thing that we have done is to establish a very clear role for advisors in this whole movement. It becomes very clear to people after a while as to what kind of role they play as advisors. It is a very challenging and difficult role for people, but the name *advisor* becomes clear. [It means] a nonvoting member who has a role in helping groups and leaders develop their leadership, their issues and their plan of action, and becoming a friend. (Worth, 1992.)

Both Peter and Pat talked about how one provincial Association for Community Living really hurt People First in that province. It is an example of an Association thinking it knows best how to help self-advocates.

> One thing that was not good was the Rights Now Project in [one province]. The Rights Now people would identify the leaders, and would set up self-advocacy groups that would meet at the same times as People First. They would put them up in better hotels, and give them better meals. Most of the consumers went over that way... (Park, 1992)

> The [provincial] People First has never quite gotten the support that People First in Ontario has gotten, or the credit they deserve... They have had a long hard struggle with the [provincial] Association, especially the Executive Director, who did not believe in what they wanted to do... He did not believe in people labelled mentally handicapped organizing their own movement. He would hire People First movement members in the Rights Now project. It was done in competition with the People First movement. (Worth, 1992)

A number of People First groups have been started with the help of good supporters and advisors. Beth French (1992), a longtime advisor for People First, was talking to Peter Park about this. "While it seems there are these people [supporters and advisors] who helped you get together, it was your idea, Pat's idea, David Lincoln's idea. It was a solid core of people who thought People First was important."

Some groups have had trouble with their advisors and fired them, or made sure they did what they were supposed to do.

> At a meeting of the two groups from Brantford and Oakville, the advisor was talking a lot. A People First member told her either to shut up or he would leave. The advisor let the People First members do the work from then on. (Park, 1992)

> Powell River People First had to let their advisor go because she didn't understand what we wanted from her. She was nice, but that's not good enough. We wanted her to help us with decision making, not make decisions for us.... We would have liked to have the advisor take matters a bit slower, that we might understand better. She wasn't attending meetings regularly.... (McDonald, 1989)

> The [Saint John People First] group had a meeting to discuss how we should let our advisor go. One of the reasons we let her go was that she

wouldn't let us make our own decisions. She wouldn't let us spend our money the way we wanted.... Our advisor thought that People First didn't make the right decisions and that she should be the only one to make the decisions for the group... These are just a few of the reasons why we, as People First, had to let our advisor go... If you get an advisor, make sure he/she knows what People First is all about. (O'Donnell, 1989)

There are a lot of books, articles, films, and so on available from People First of Canada that have even more ideas about what works. For more information, contact People First of Canada, 489 College Street, Suite 308, Toronto, ON M6G 1A5, Canada.

We began this section with a song by Denis Laroche (see page 72). The last word also goes to Denis and another of his songs: "We Can Do It."

> We can do it.
> We can defend our rights.

References

Barnes, H. (1987, August). *National Organizer*.

Barnes, H. (1987, January). "An Interview with Harold Barnes." *National Organizer*.

Carpentier, R. (1989, January). *National Organizer*.

Consumer Advisory Committee (August 6, 1981). Minutes of CAC Meeting.

Fletcher, G. (1987, August). *National Organizer*.

French, B. (December 16, 1992). Personal Interview with Peter Park and Beth French by Bruce Kappel.

Goode, B. (1987). Letter to Editor, *entourage*, Spring.

Goode, B. (1991, January) The Eve Sterilization Case. *entourage*.

Heath, D.L., Schaaf, V., & Talkington, L.W. (1978, April). People First: Evolution Toward self-advocacy. *Canadian Journal on Mental Retardation*, *28*(2).

Juzenas, G. (1989, August). Discrimination at the Burnaby Inn. *National Organizer*.

Laroche, D. (undated). Lyrics to his songs, "Le National" and "We Can Do It."

Laroche, D. (1987, August). *National Organizer*.

Laroche, D. (1991, April). *National Organizer*.

McDonald, R. (1989, August). "Letter to Editor." *National Organizer*.

National Organizer (1987, August). "Building People First." *National Organizer*, pp. 6-7.

National Organizer (1987, August). Various submissions. *National Organizer*.

O'Donnell, C. (1989, August). "Letter to Editor." *National Organizer*.

Oulton, J. (1990-91). *Community development within a sheltered workshop: From personal self-help to political group-advocacy.* Paper for B.S.W. 4010 (r): Advanced Practice. Maritime School of Social Work. Fall and Spring 1990-91.

Park, P. (undated). Personal notes from Peter Park provided to the author.

Park, Peter (1985, July). *National Organizer*.

Park, Peter (1987). *National Organizer*. January, 1987.

Park, Peter (December 16, 1992). Personal interview with Peter Park and Beth French by Bruce Kappel.

People First of Canada (April 6-7, 1991). Minutes of the Annual General Meeting.

People First of Canada (1992). Autonomy Discussion Paper.

People First of Canada (1991, April). *People First of Ontario Newsletter*.

People First of Washington (1985). *Speaking up and speaking out: An international self-advocacy movement* (pp. 6-7). People First of Washington.

Reid, David (1987, August). *National Organizer*.

Sears, Norval (April, 1991). How to make our local groups stronger. *People First of Ontario Newsletter*.

West, Ann (1985). Letter to the Board of Directors of CAMR.

Worth, Pat (1990, February). "Message from the President." *National Organizer*.

Worth, Pat (December 30, 1992). Personal Interview with Pat Worth by Bruce Kappel.

Young, Paul (1991, April). *National Organizer*.

12

The Rise of Self-Advocacy
in Great Britain

John Hersov

Author/consultant JOHN HERSOV has been an advisor and friend to the self-advocacy movement in England for over a decade. A frequent visitor to the U.S., John often writes about the spread of ideas between the U.S. and England. We have asked John to focus here on the movement's early developments in England, leading up to the 1990s.

This chapter describes the ways in which the ideas of self-advocacy have gradually become established in Great Britain during the last decade. It will focus particularly on the establishment and the development of People First of London, as well as other similar groups. It also highlights some of the key issues arising from the concept of self-advocacy and from the growing popularity of the movement throughout the country.

In the Beginning: Help from CMH

Although the majority of developments in self-advocacy have occurred since the 1980s, some of the pioneering work in Great Britain was done by the Campaign for Mentally Handicapped People (CMH) in the early 1970s. Two publications, *Our Life* (1972) and *Listen* (1973), reported on two weekend conferences at which a majority of participants had a mental handicap. *Our Life* featured the views of several residents from long-stay hospitals, about where and how they would like to live. The opportunity to spend time with a mixture of people on this initial weekend was most important. As Ann Shearer wrote in *Our Life*, "They taught us just how much of their disability can be imposed by our own preconceptions of their capabilities, and the limits we deliberately set on their experience."

This theme was continued at the second weekend conference, held in 1973. In *Listen*, the participants discussed the issues of choice and independence, as well as the different sorts of relationships they had. Following this event, many of the participants from the previous two events came together for further discussions at a workshop on participation in June 1973. The feeling of "belonging" and responsibility for others was explored. This workshop also raised the notion of involving people with a mental handicap in the planning and running of the services which they utilized.

CMH continued to foster links with the USA, and Paul Williams went on an American study tour in 1979. The 1982 publication of *We Can Speak For Ourselves*, co-written by Williams and Bonnie Shoultz, was an important milestone in the development of self-advocacy awareness in Britain. Initially, the focus was on day center client committees or student councils — in other words, groups that met at their places of work, which were not therefore independently functioning. Bronach Crawley published her thesis on Adult Training Center committees a year later and returned to this theme with a follow-up survey, *The Growing Voice*, published five years later.

One of the first groups comprising people with learning difficulties to forge a national profile for itself was the MENCAP London Division Participation Forum. Originally invited to represent day center committees in the London area, the group developed its own identity when it hosted and videotaped its first conference, *Speaking For Ourselves*, in 1982 at MENCAP's National Center. By the time this group wound up in 1991, it had organized eight, one-day conferences, two more of which were recorded on video: "Have We A Future" in 1983 and "Let's Work Together" in 1986. These films continue to circulate throughout the country and have been seen by hundreds of different organizations. Members of the group and their advisor were invited to speak at professional conferences, and subsequently comprised part of the British representation for the first international conference in the USA in 1984.

Another influential place where individuals with learning difficulties could come and develop their potential was the city Literary Adult Education Institute in London (the City Lit, as it is more commonly known). The Creative Education program for students at the City Lit has been running since 1979. It is now called S.I.T.E. (the Section for Independence through Education) and is open to adults from throughout the Greater London area. Discussion groups have long been a feature of the program, as have music, dance, art, and drama workshops. Its basis for learning is that the individual student chooses the classes that he or she wishes to attend. Many of the students use public transportation to come into Central London and go to their classes. Over the last thirteen years, hundreds of students have attended the program. Some have become closely involved with People First of London. Others have used their educational opportunities as a springboard to make personal strides — like changing their daytime program of activities (i.e., leaving the day center) or moving their place of residence to a more independent setting (i.e., their own apartment). The City Lit students were also represented in the British contingent to the 1984 international conference.

CMH had been invited to be a co-sponsor of the first International Self-Advocacy Leadership Conference, held in Tacoma in 1984. Together with support from a number of organizations, notably London MENCAP, the King's Fund, and the City Lit, CMH was able to send a party of eighteen people from London and Essex. The conference itself had a momentous impact on all who attended.

The British representatives at the Tacoma conference returned home inspired by what they had experienced, and in October 1984 People First of London and Thames was formed. Initially, the group comprised those people with learning difficulties who had gone to the USA, and by January 1985 they had chosen two advisors, Andrea Whittaker and myself, John Hersov. Early plans included a newsletter to spread the word about People First, and a British self-advocacy conference for the summer of 1987. A proposed 1988 international conference in London was also on the agenda.

Right from the start, there was also a group of supporters (the Supporters Group) willing to shoulder the twin burdens of supporting the London People First members and letting more people know about self-advocacy throughout the country. These professionals who had accompanied the self-advocates to the USA continued to meet in support of People First, as well as attempting to influence policy and practice within their own organizations. Plans were also made to adapt some of the American training materials on self-advocacy.

Identifying Self-Advocacy Issues in Britain

The supporters of self-advocacy identified several important issues. Primarily, there was the need to help the People First members work out their own aims and goals, without professionals imposing their own views. A balance had to be found. It was important to enable self-advocates to learn and develop new skills, like running their own meetings and going out and giving talks to groups of service providers. On the one hand, it was as important to allow the People First members "time to be themselves." People First of London's difficulty in reconciling these aims was compounded by not having a full-time worker (like Bob Furman at People First of Washington) and, indeed, in not having their own funding. It would be more than four years before a People First of London office was formally established.

Self-advocate members of the London group were clear that, while they welcomed the administrative support from the King's Fund, CMH, and London MENCAP, they wanted to run their own meetings. They began to think of ways to raise money. While the tension between People First members and advisors/supporters was acknowledged early on (with the memories of Centers and previous staff/client relationships still very strong!), the moral and practical support being offered was also valued. As one People First member said, "**An airplane needs wings** [i.e., support] **and then a pilot/copilot** [i.e., members of the People First committee] **to fly**."

Increasing Formalization

In January 1985, at what was effectively the inaugural meeting of the London group, there were visitors from Holland — a mixed group from Zeeland. (My wife and I were able to pay a return visit later in the year.) It was instructive to realize that several of the Dutch self-advocates spoke very good English! Attendance at the monthly People First of London meetings grew steadily (mainly by word of mouth). The cafeteria at the City Lit was an invaluable communication network for the students attending its program, On a national scale, Gary Bourlet had begun sending out handwritten letters to people whose addresses he had compiled, and whom he felt would be interested in hearing about and supporting People First. (By June 1985 the letters numbered 136.) In June 1985, Eileen Carpenter, a People First of London member, and I were invited to run a workshop at St. Michael's House, Dublin, for staff and clients. Following this, Leslie Smart, a London member attended (with a supporter) the ILSMH European Congress in Hamburg during October 1985.

In May 1985, the first issue of the People First Newsletter was published. It listed the organization's aims and objectives. These included helping people to speak up for themselves and to support one another, along with speaking out about their rights. Another issue raised was getting more money — both through real jobs and more social security benefits. Other issues included putting a stop to negative labeling, improving living situations, and providing transportation assistance. At this time there were twenty-two self-advocate members of People First of London. The pace of development picked up; meetings were attended in the North West, the Midlands, and the South West of England. The advisors identified the need for occasions like the leaders' retreats organized by People First of Washington, where People First members could work on areas like committee skills away from the regular monthly business meetings.

In November 1985, members and supporters of People First of London (including the author) had a valuable day's meeting with John O'Brien, to reflect on the year's developments in Britain and to link these once again to the American experience. We discussed the growth of groups and when it would be a good time to split up into local borough "chapters" (as several states had done in the U.S.). In particular, we talked about how best to apply our energies, balancing the need to let influential professionals know about self-advocacy with helping new groups of self-advocates to start things up for themselves. Also, we discussed how to work together to achieve change, while stressing the importance of being able to say "No" to some invitations.

In January 1986, People First of London held elections for officers' jobs, and soon the officers were meeting prior to the monthly members' meetings. It was often said that all the work within People First was being done by just a few people (a familiar cry from many voluntary organizations). With hindsight, one way to have begun to combat these criticisms would have been to establish a routine whereby each officer could only serve for a year or two before they had to step down, so that someone else could be elected in their place. In fact, partly because of the advisors' desire not to be too directive, the status quo prevailed, until finally in the summer of 1991 there were new elections.

In June 1986, members were asked what People First meant to them. Comments included:

- "You meet friends and talk about things."
- "It is a good thing to come to because you get different ideas from other people."
- "People First helps me because we are helping each other."
- "It keeps me going."
- "It is a worthwhile organization. It should be maintained."
- "It is our future, to make a better life for the new generations; a better society for them to be living in — more freedom and independence."

During 1986 the Disabled Persons Representation Bill (sponsored by M.P. Tom Clarke) was being presented to Parliament. People First was consulted about its contents, and a "simple English" (jargon-free) version was produced. The bill was eventually passed into law, although some of its key sections were not fully implemented. There were also speaking engagements at the University of Kent and to the IDC (Independent Development Council), and a contribution made to the BBC program "People Like Us."

In 1986, *We Can Change The Future* was published. This staff training resource pack comprised of a book and video was written by Deborah Cooper and myself. It provided an introduction to the subject of self-advocacy, as well as practical suggestions of how professionals could support the development of these ideas and put them into practice. The authors ran a number of I- successful training workshops around the country to follow up the initial research. By 1991, the book was in its third edition.

THE NEED FOR A FULL-TIME ADVISOR AND AN OFFICE

During this time, the Supporters Group of People First of London recommended seeking funding for a full-time advisor for the organization. It had long been apparent that despite the generous administrative support of the King's Fund (which allowed Andrea Whittaker to spend some of her time on People First business), the workload needed to be put on a more permanent footing. In early 1987, I ceased to be an advisor due to the pressure of other commitments. The Supporters

Group continued to meet and offer guidance to People First members. In addition, supporters volunteered to work at the King's Fund and help whenever People First work needed to be done. This work included membership and treasurer's work, preparing the newsletter, and planning and preparing people to speak at meetings and workshops (invitations from around the country continued to pour in).

During 1988 the main focus of People First of London was on preparing for the second international conference. *A Voice of Our Own – Now and In the Future* was held September 3-10, 1988, at St. Mary's College, Twickenham. Nearly three hundred people attended from throughout the United Kingdom as well as parts of the USA and Canada, with some representation from Switzerland and Australia. The conference gave a great boost to all the groups already in existence throughout Britain, and helped to encourage other groups to get started. Helen Beckett, who was at Twickenham, was the prime mover behind the Bury St. Edmunds People First group in Suffolk (the Eastern Counties of England). She wrote that she "came away feeling more confident and more determined to do things." Her group soon developed a good local profile: fundraising in the weekend street market, advertising on the local radio station, and contacting the local Social Services Department about their concerns (especially access to the shops where the pavements were in a decayed condition).

In 1988, the Open University produced its first course specifically for people with learning difficulties, "Patterns for Living: Working Together." The course used audiocassette tapes and student workbooks to help students examine and debate issues related to the lives of people like themselves. This course has proved very successful and is being used throughout the country.

All the planning in preparation for a People First of London office came to fruition during 1989. Funding was received for a three-year period from the Joseph Rowantree Foundation, the Mental Health Foundation, and the King's Fund. As a new project, the office was to be evaluated by Paul Williams from CMH. The interviews for a full-time advisor and two part-time self-advocate office workers took place in July 1989. The interviewing panel included self-advocates representatives from outside as well as within London, plus supporters. Janet Wright was appointed as advisor. Gary Bourlet and Lily Samy became the office workers. Initially there still wasn't an office base, so for several months the workers had to operate out of different addresses. Eventually, in May 1990, the People First office moved to Oxford House, in East London.

The London office was not expected to act as a national advice and resource center. Its purpose was to concentrate on developing and supporting self-advocacy initiatives within the Greater London area. However, in its previous semiofficial status when based at the King's Fund, People First of London had published a newsletter which circulated nationally, and its membership embraced people from all over the country. A slight confusion of identity thus continued, and will probably remain until the time comes for the establishment of a national office which links with and represents all the various People First groups throughout Great Britain.

The People First Management Committee, comprised of both supporters and self-advocates, continued to exercise a strong influence over the direction that People First was taking. This was partly because of the responsibilities of overseeing such a new venture, and also due to the question of accountability to the funding organizations. Gradually, the professionals on the Management Committee began to dominate the proceedings, perhaps as a direct result of having to grapple with all the pressures (by the summer of 1991, the self-advocate representatives on the Management Committee had re-asserted their right to determine how things went). Once again, not having had regular elections within People First of London, and the delay in being able to agree on a constitution for the organization, contributed to the lack of focus.

The UK Self-Advocacy Conference took place in August 1990, and much of the year was spent in preparing for this event. During 1990, two of the office workers resigned from their jobs. Declan Treanor became the new advisor in December 1990, and in the following year Andrew Bright succeeded Gary Bourlet as the sole office worker.

During this whole period, People First's position in relation to other organizations in the field has gone through several phases. As already described, CMH/VIA's commitment to the participation approach, and then to self-advocacy principles, remained steadfast.

Continued Alliances

In 1988, VIA published the LAS pack (five booklets describing the processes by which groups of self-advocates get started and develop). Written in simple, straightforward English, these materials were ideal for use directly by self-advocates, themselves. VIA also published *The Growing Voice*, a survey of center and hospital committees/groups compiled by Bronach Crawley, which provided a useful update on progress around the country.

As an organization, CMH/VIA chose to campaign further in other areas, but they continued to be represented on the People First Supporters Group until mid 1991. Relations with MENCAP (the British counterpart to The Arc) have been somewhat stormier. Despite the active support for the original Tacoma conference by national and London MENCAP, attention soon focused on the vexed question of MENCAP's "Little Stephen" logo. This unfortunate depiction of a sad-faced boy remained the symbol of MENCAP until late 1991. Following their Open Day in June 1986, People First of London sent what would be the first of several petitions to MENCAP protesting the "Little Stephen" posters then widely publicizing MENCAP's 40th Anniversary. Further petitions followed the 1988 international conference and 1990 UK conferences at Twickenham. Despite initial rebuffs, it is reasonable for People First to claim a sizable part of the credit for pushing MENCAP gradually into the 1990s as regards changing their own logo. At the time of writing, there have been plans for MENCAP and People First to collaborate on producing a charter of rights for people with learning difficulties.

The King's Fund Center has also consistently offered People First of London moral and administrative support as well as providing the venue for the monthly meetings. During the last two years, Andrea Whittaker, Senior Project officer at the King Fund's Community Living Development Team, has been compiling a resource list of training materials about self-advocacy (with new publications and videos being added all the time). In November 1991, the Community Living Development Team also published the first issue of *Information Exchange on Self-Advocacy and User Participation* — comprised of contributions from different groups around the country — about their experiences.

Also in 1991, the organization BRIDGES (formerly called APMH) employed me to facilitate five regional workshops and a residential weekend, called "Talking Together," at which people with learning difficulties were asked for their views on services. A booklet describing this work was published in November 1991. Interestingly, APMH had invited four people with learning difficulties to address its annual group meeting at Roehampton in 1983 — one of the "firsts" in the self-advocacy movement.

Links have also been made with a number of different organizations representing disabled people. In January 1992, Gary Bourlet represented People First on the national council of the British Council of Disabled People. Later in 1992, People First, together with two progressive parents organizations — Parents in Partnership and Integration Alliance — organized a conference on how parents react to people speaking up for themselves.

It is important also to emphasize the national scope of developments. Day-long conferences on self-advocacy and related issues, at which people with learning difficulties themselves are strongly represented (and often the hosts), are now a feature of the work being done in Great Britain. Some parts of the country have now had several years of experience. In Coalville, Leicestershire, the Self-Advocacy in Action group have organized a number of annual conferences, as well as publishing their own newsletter. In the county of Oxfordshire, there are at least ten groups meeting locally, and there have been big conferences during the last two years. In the northwest of England, Skills for People (based in Newcastle) has run courses for a number of years and has developed a training package, *Speaking Up for Yourself*. The Belfast Self-Advocacy group in Northern Ireland made a video called "The Way We Are." A network of different organizations is also being actively built up in the Republic of Ireland.

People First of Wales has been in existence since 1989; in 1991 and 1992, it organized national conferences at Llandrindod Wells. Local groups have been meeting since 1984, and there is a strongly supported Welsh grass-roots movement, with a good opportunity to begin to influence the way that services are planned within the country. The Avon People First group, which meets in the Bristol area in the West of England, started in 1988 with five people; now there are other groups springing up throughout the county — thirteen at the last count, so that the Somerset network now meets four times a year to reflect the consumer demand. As Peter Stephens, one of the founder members, remarked, "It's very important to feel you're being noticed." He has recently been teaching in a local training course for doctors, nurses, and occupational therapists. The group has developed its credibility and is now being consulted by local health departments; they hope to get their own office soon.

1991: A Milestone Year

There were a number of significant milestones in 1991. The outreach work of the People First of London office paid off. Throughout the Greater London area, a substantial number of borough districts are supporting self-advocacy initiatives by running training courses for staff, developing training packages, and appointing development workers. A new constitution for People First of London was finally agreed upon. Elections for new offices were held on 16th November 1991; representatives were chosen from each London borough attending the monthly meetings. A People First Committee was elected, and chose its representatives to serve on the Management Committee. The latter now comprises seven self-advocate members (with voting powers) and supporters.

In July 1991, the book *Service Evaluation by People with Learning Difficulties*, by Andrea Whittaker, Simon Gardner, and Joyce Kershaw, was published. This described the evaluation of services provided in the London borough of Hillingdon in March 1990, and marked the first time that People First had been employed to undertake this type of work, which involved interviewing service users and reaching conclusions on the service provision. It is hoped that other agencies will follow a similar route.

In the latter part of the year, Gary Bourlet, Simon Gardner and Annette McDonald, representing People First, undertook ten successful staff training workshops in the borough of Haringey — with the prospect of offering more workshops to other groups of professionals. Work by groups of women with learning difficulties developed, and a national conference was held in Nottingham in March 1992. In October 1991, the first People First of London Annual General Meeting and Conference saw more than two hundred people attend the two day event. Policy statements were drawn up on education, abuse in institutions, ethnic minorities, labelling, employment, residents' rights, sex and personal relationships, transport, and women. John Sims, representing People First, addressed the International Down's Syndrome conference in Barcelona, Spain. In early 1992, British Telecom (the national telephone company) provided intensive training workshops on presentation skills for People First of London members. In May 1992, the People First of London office moved to larger premises at Instrument House, Kings Cross, London WC1.

The 1990s have been a very exciting period for the development of self-advocacy in Great Britain. Organizations like People First of London can take much of the credit for the increased awareness of self-advocacy. The parallel development of service provision has also created a climate in which the users or consumers of those services (namely people with learning difficulties) are increasingly being asked for their views on the way in which such services are provided.

Having managed to get self-advocacy issues on the agenda, the next step will be to ensure that service providers are not permitted to shift the forthcoming debate towards *their* concerns. The lengths to which people will go in order to preserve the status quo and protect their own interests are evident. Self-advocate representatives will continue to have an effect, by simply stating their case and making sure that their voice is still heard. But it is not a foregone conclusion that they will be listened to, or that changes will be made accordingly.

In the last decade, there have been important landmarks in the growth of self-advocacy throughout the country. Conferences have taken place which a few years earlier would have seemed unthinkable. Individuals with learning difficulties have met government ministers, hosted TV shows, questioned psychiatrists, written books, made videos, and helped to evaluate services. There is every reason to believe that the self-advocacy movement in Britain will continue to gain new members and widespread support, and that it will reach even greater heights in the future. It has proved to be one of the most significant developments in the British world of mental handicap/learning disability, as well as having an international impact.

References

BRIDGES (1991). *Talking Together.* BRIDGES (formerly APMH).

Cooper, D., & Hersov, J. (1986; reprinted 1991). *We Can Change the Future.* NBHS/SKILL.

Crawley, B. (1988). *The Growing Voice.* V.I.A. Publications.

MENCAP London Division Participation Forum (1982). *Speaking For Ourselves.* MENCAP Bookshop.

MENCAP London Division Participation Forum (1983). *Have We A Future?* MENCAP Bookshop.

MENCAP London Division Participation Forum (1986). *Let's Work Together.* MENCAP Bookshop.

Open University (1988). *Patterns for Living: Working Together.* Department of Health and Social Welfare, The Open University.

Shearer, A. (1972). *Our Life.* CMH/VIA Publications.

Shearer, A. (1973). *Listen.* CMH/VIA Publications.

V.I.A. (1988). *Learning About Self-Advocacy* (The LASA Pack). VIA Publications.

Wertheimer, A. (1989). *A Voice of Our Own: Now and in the Future.* Report of the 1988 People First International Conference.

Whittaker, A., Gardner, S., & Kershaw, J. (1991). *Service Education by People with Learning Difficulties.* King's Fund Centre.

Williams, P., & Shoultz, B. (1982; reprinted 1991). *We Can Speak For Ourselves.* Human Horizon Series, Souvenir Press.

13

The Wheels of Self-Advocacy in Australia

Lynn Romeo

LYNN ROMEO lives and works in the Australian state of Victoria, in southern Australia. This chapter traces the roots of self-advocacy "Down Under." Australian self-advocates — due to geographic distance — had less collaboration with the U.S. movement than Canadian or even European developments did. Yet their issues and progress are remarkably similar.

Introduction

As with most human rights movements, the development of self-advocacy in Australia has taken many paths and has many roots. Self-advocacy in Australia is shaped by the unique nature of the country.

THE COUNTRY AND PEOPLE

Australia is a large island-continent with a vast, dry and relatively uninhabited inland but more fertile coastal areas. Two-thirds of Australia's population of about seventeen and a quarter million people live in the seven cities, which are spread around the vast coastline

Kooris (or Aborigines, as they are commonly known by whites) had lived on the continent for about forty thousand years when European settlement began two hundred years ago. Now only 1.5 percent of the population are of Koori origin. Until the wave of post-World War II migration, the remainder of the population were mainly of English, Irish, Scottish, and German origins. Since that time, Australian society has become a more multicultural mix with significant numbers of Italian, Yugoslav, Greek, Asian and Eastern European citizens.

Australia has its own national government, but is still a member of the British

Commonwealth. The national or federal government was formed in 1901 and is responsible for such things as income tax collection, Social/Income Security, defense, employment, allocation of monies to the states, and funding and provision of some community services.

There are six states and two territories in Australia, each with its well-known capital city: Australian Capital Territory, or ACT (Canberra); New South Wales (Sydney); Northern Territory (Darwin); Queensland (Brisbane); South Australia (Adelaide); Tasmania (Hobart); Victoria (Melbourne); and Western Australia (Perth). Each state has its own state government, with unique legislative and service systems (both government and non-government) in areas such as health, education, transport, housing, and community services.

SERVICES AND LAWS IN THE DISABILITY FIELD

Funding and services for people with disabilities come from a complex array of state and federal government departments, non-government groups, and philanthropic trust funds. Legislation is equally complex, but new, significant and progressive laws have been enacted in some states (for example the "Intellectually Disabled Persons Services Act," Victoria, 1986). The National Disability Services Act (1986) is an attempt to facilitate the growth of more progressive, developmental and rights-oriented services around the nation. (You will note that the term *intellectual disability* is used in Australia, rather than *mental retardation*.)

SELF-ADVOCACY IN AUSTRALIA

Self-advocacy in Australia is not a coordinated or cohesive movement. This could be due to the distance between groups, or to the vast differences in services and funding among the states, or maybe it is simply because the movement is only about twelve years old. Some groups have developed from the bottom up, others from the top down. Varying social and economic circumstances have also created differences between the groups. However, the self-advocacy groups do have a lot in common, and the movement is strong and growing, as noted in a couple of national reports (*People First Resource Unit*, 1989; Bramley & Elkins, 1988).

In this chapter we will look at the various self-advocacy groups that are currently active in Australia, in order to explore how and why they developed and what they've been doing. People from within the movement describe their experiences and views about self-advocacy. Self-advocates and other workers discuss how governments, professionals, and families have responded to the movement. Finally, the chapter discusses the critical lessons that the Australian self-advocacy movement has learned and self-advocates' hopes and dreams for the future.

Here are some of the things that self-advocacy means to self-advocates in Australia (taken from *People First Magazine* and group interviews conducted in Melbourne):

Self-advocacy is about getting a fair deal, knowing and standing up for your rights, getting the same rights as everyone else and having the right to know what your rights are. It is learning to be assertive and standing up and speaking up for yourself. Self-advocacy is also learning new skills and meeting new people. It's getting the information you need and understanding the issues. It is being independent and making your own choices.

Self-advocacy in Australia is also joint action and support, lobbying and networking. Some people within the movement see it as a universal thing that covers everyone and everything. It's also about doing something about your problems and sometimes it means "standing on other people's toes" and "talking back" (that's a big part of self-advocacy for people who are in institutions).

So self-advocacy is much more than self-help, although it is that too. Some people think self-advocacy is encouragement, some think it is experience or a stepping-stone.

The other side to self-advocacy which some people stress is that it means taking responsibility for yourself, it means being committed and involved, getting to know the group or organization and taking responsibility for your actions.

What Self-Advocacy Groups Are There in Australia?

NATIONAL

There is a loose, national coalition called People First Australia (PFA), which is made up of representatives from most states and territories. PFA meets about two times each year so state representatives can share information and experiences, support each other, lobby together, and take ideas back to their state (*People First Magazine*, 3rd edition).

STATEWIDE

In each state and territory, except the Northern Territory, there is at least one group with a statewide focus. Some of these groups are made up of representatives of local self-advocacy groups. Some act as umbrella or resource groups. Some take an active role in research, lobbying and community education about issues that affect people all over the state. Others are involved in providing specific services like housing, training, social events, and conferences.

LOCAL

There are at least four different types of local self-advocacy groups.

1. *Workers' committees in sheltered workshops.* Many sheltered workshops have workers' committees that aim to give people a say and improve wages,

working conditions and workers' rights. In 1986, a national research project found that this was the most common type of self-advocacy group in Australia at the time (*People First Magazine*, 2nd edition).

2. *Active participation in services.* Some organizations that provide housing options and support services involve the people who use the services in management and decision-making. These include tenant/resident committees, women's groups, consumer units, and management committees which are made up of a majority of consumers.

3. *Creative groups.* Other exciting developments in self-advocacy involve radio, music and drama. There is a regular radio show on community radio [called *Raising Our Voices*] which is run by people with intellectual disabilities. *Back-To-Back Theatre* is an innovative community theater project that enables people with intellectual disabilities to perform theatre and music which deal with issues about institutions, rights, etc.

4. *Local branches and speak-out groups.* Lastly, there are numerous local or regional branches of state self-advocacy groups and a growing number of independent groups. Some of these call themselves "Speaking-Up" or "Speaking-Out" groups. Most of them are community-based, but there are some located in institutions.

Clearly, self-advocacy is a widespread, varied and growing movement in Australia. In the words of one self-advocate, "The wheel of self-advocacy in Australia certainly has many spokes!!"

How the Wheels of Self-Advocacy
Started Turning in Australia

A range of events and factors contributed to the beginnings of self-advocacy in Australia. Changes in community attitudes and social policy towards more humane, rights-based approaches certainly laid the ground work. Although not a well-documented factor, the growing discontent of people who had been segregated and discriminated against — and their individual attempts to regain power over their lives — must have provided a major push. As one self-advocacy group says, self-advocacy started because

> ... people with an intellectual disability wanted to speak for themselves. They wanted to make their own choices and to live as members of the towns, cities and country where they live. (*People First Magazine*)

Developments in self-advocacy, normalization, and deinstitutionalization in other parts of the world had both direct and subtle influences on the whole of the disability field in Australia. The first big steps towards self-advocacy in Australia were two conference/camps held in Victoria in 1980 and 1981 for people who lived in state-run institutions, hostels, halfway houses, and the community. These were organized by support workers and members of a social club from one of Melbourne's inner suburbs. The outcome of the conferences was the formation of a union of intellectually disadvantaged citizens, originally called Force-Ten and then later re-named Reinforce.

In 1981, the International Year of the Disabled, the South Pacific Regional Conference on Mental Retardation was held in Melbourne. At that conference, Reinforce and members of the Fifth Strand Campaign presented the "Code of Rights" (see box, facing page) which, together with the video *Don't Think I Don't Think*, became major resources which stimulated the development of self-advocacy around Australia.

The History in Brief

It is not easy to give a quick sketch of how self-advocacy has spread. There have been so many different groups it is difficult to trace all of the threads. The information in this chapter comes from the national or local reports and papers that are available, plus some Victoria and interstate networks.

Self-advocacy started in Australia in 1980–1981, and by 1984 there were self-advocacy groups or efforts in each state (I could not find any record of any groups in either of the territories at this time). Between 1986 and 1990 a great growth spurt of self-advocacy occurred. There was a national resource project and federal funding for various state and local groups and projects. By 1988 there was a statewide self-advocacy group in each state. During 1986-1990 attempts were made to establish an interstate network and a national group.

This national group, People First Australia (PFA), still meets, and there was an interstate conference in 1991 in Tasmania. However, PFA and other national networking efforts still struggle against a lack of funds and resources and the fact that many groups need to be preoccupied with issues and survival struggles in their own states. All of this hampers the development of a national focus for the self-advocacy movement in Australia.

On the local level, by contrast, there are an ever-increasing number of self-advocacy groups, speaking-out groups, and workshop workers' committees. Some of these seem to come and go; still, many are strong and active and seem like they'll be around for a long time.

The People in Self-Advocacy:
Where Have They Come From? Where Are They Going?

How do people get involved in the self-advocacy movement in the first place? Has being involved in self-advocacy changed them or their lives? What have they achieved?

THE CODE OF RIGHTS
AUGUST 1981

- We want more training for jobs outside.
- We want to see more people out of institutions.
- We want better transport and lower fares and better service.
- We are humans first and disadvantaged second.
- All theatres to have concessions for each session.
- We need more access to community facilities.
- Everybody living in institutions has the right to community living, to be trained for jobs and to education.
- We want more group homes to be built and more half-way houses.
- Each pension should be above the poverty line and increased quarterly.
- We want the right to have our own choice of medical insurance and our own doctor.
- We have the right to have our rights protected, to be protected from violence and crime.
- We have a right to information about marriage and relationships.
- We have the right to live in our own home.
- We have the right to spend our own money.
- We demand all discrimination to cease.
- We have the right to live with whom we want.
- We have a right to know where our money is going.
- Intellectually disadvantaged citizens should have access to low-rent flats and houses in the community.
- We demand the closing of all institutions for intellectually disadvantaged people.
- We have a right to education.
- We have a right to privacy.
- We have a right to private ownership.
- We have the right to equal day's pay for a fair day's work.
- We have a right to workers' compensation.

— from Reinforce, Victoria

The following information is taken from five group interviews conducted in Melbourne. Fifteen people, in groups of one to four, each gave about two hours of their time. We began with broad questions and then the discussion usually flowed as people talked about their experiences, feelings and opinions about self-advocacy. These people came from a cross section of self-advocacy groups in Victoria: two statewide groups (People First Victoria, relatively new, and Reinforce, the original group in the state); two from outer suburban areas; and one from a large traditional institution in a Melbourne suburb. It is by no means a representative sample. (For example, no rural groups were involved.) However, this selection of groups represent a variety of different approaches to self-advocacy and have members with a wide range of experiences and backgrounds.

Some of the people had lived in institutions for a large part of their lives; some were still living there. Others had moved out of institutions and had been living in the community for some time. Still others had moved from family homes or community residences and were living, independently or with support, in the community. A couple of the younger people (late teens, early twenties) were living with their parents.

How Have People Become Involved in Self-Advocacy?

It seems that quite a few people have become involved in self-advocacy while attending sheltered workshops or day training centers. Those who became involved in the early 1980s were not approached directly but became involved through camps or conferences. Others were approached by workers or members of self-advocacy groups who visited their centers.

> The person who was setting up the self-advocacy group came to the Day Training Centre and explained what they wanted to do — so I joined... because I wasn't doing nothing except sitting at home and watching TV... and I thought it would be a good idea. At the time I was in a relationship and it was good, but I thought I wanted something for myself.

One of the big events that a few people identified from the early days of self-advocacy was the International Year of the Disabled Conference on Mental Retardation in Melbourne. It seems that it was through this conference that a few people became involved in Reinforce, the first self-advocacy group in Australia. The people who referred to this spoke of it as a major turning point in their lives.

> At the time I was attending a workshop. Five of us were chosen to attend the big conference in Melbourne, the South Pacific Regional Conference on Mental Retardation. I was going to give the conference a miss... but in the meantime... I met one of the organizers on a tram.... He said "good — you can get yourself there."

Funny how you turn corners, and look at me today.... I'm pretty involved. I didn't think I'd ever be public speaking... but there you go... who knows what's around the corner.

Another way people became involved is through social clubs. One such club in Melbourne was instrumental in helping to set up the first self-advocacy group, Reinforce. AMIDA (Accommodation for Mildly Intellectually Disadvantaged Adults), which is a group that develops and housing and support options with an emphasis on consumer participation and control, also began as a social club. Around Australia, social groups/activities seem to have been a common pathway to self-advocacy groups.

It also seems that people became involved in self-advocacy groups through their involvement with progressive housing and support services and groups that take specific action to ensure consumer participation.

How did you get involved with this self-advocacy group?
It was through another organization where they help look for flats.... I went to see them and I told them I wanted to get out. I was living in a group house and having a rough time.... I also told them about my other problems. I got out and before I got out they put me onto.... I got a letter from this other person who was running a self-advocacy group... and it was in the same building, so that's how I got involved.

I started living in one of the houses and developed my confidence, once I could change from living with my parents. I'm glad I did that change, I can't depend on my parents, because they will die one day. I can do my own thing.... From there I got involved in the committee and so on....
What changes does self-advocacy bring to your life?
Oh boy, that's a so-many-pronged question. Since I've been involved... well... you pick up new skills and new friends and you're outside doing something, not getting bored out of your head. You're out going places; you're playing an active, active part in the movement which is sort of like a PR [public relations] exercise. Because as well as being involved in the disabled movement, I have some other outside interests that get me out into the eyes of the public and I've been able to learn, sort of transfer those skills from the [self-advocacy] group and just turn them around and fit them to my outside interests.

And I've made friends there and I have done a few courses to try to teach myself to better certain skills and that. And I've even written a couple of songs that have been recorded.... I am sort of reaching out apart from the disabled movement. I have this leg out here, this one out there and another somewhere else. So I am heavily involved in the disabled movement and I've managed to pick up outside interests.

> Having a mixture of interests is a bit like this… putting these skills [from
> self-advocacy] and turning them around to fit other outside interests, and
> I have been able to do that quite successfully, and I have support too."

Another longtime self-advocate agrees that self-advocacy gives you skills that change
your life.

> Self-advocacy is the biggest stepping stone that has helped me learn things
> Things that I hadn't been taught in the past, like public speaking…. I didn't
> think I'd ever see the day I would come as far as I've come today, with the
> self-advocacy groups.

These quotes speak for themselves, but it is interesting to note the significant
changes in these peoples' lives, the skills learned and transferred to other parts of
their lives. Other people also refer to self-advocacy as creating "movement" in their
lives, such as the woman who said self-advocacy had taken her "a long way."

Some of the changes. When people talked about specific changes that had occurred
in their lives one of the most common things was developing *confidence* and overcoming shyness. As one woman put it:

> [I've learned about] standing up for myself and having confidence in my-
> self that I can do things as good as other people.

Another woman said quite emphatically:

> I was sort of a shy person and since I got involved [in self-advocacy], I can
> speak for myself and if people walk all over me I put them back in their place.

The other change that quite a few people had noticed was that since they had been
involved in self-advocacy, they were getting more *respect* from other people.

> I've got respect from people who I didn't think I would ever get it from…
> that's the biggest thing… you're half way there if you get respect.

(During this conversation there was talk of how politicians, parents, famous figures, and others with power/status had shown or voiced their respect during meetings, events, etc.)
Another person talked about respect in these terms:

> I'm getting respect from other people. People are treating me like an
> adult… and I notice it more now when they treat me as an adult.

One of the other changes that was mentioned by a few people was having more *independence*. One woman explained that she had "found a life of my own" and wasn't just depending on her family. Another young woman talked about how her family were even starting to ask her now when she was going to move out.

Becoming involved with other people, *meeting people*, and making friends are also things that self-advocacy brings to people's lives. Some people added that helping and supporting other people was a new dimension that self-advocacy gave them. One person's story' about his first few months in a self-advocacy group explains how important contact with other people is.

> The first time I came I felt different to other people....Then I kept going back and back... because it was a nice place to go, I felt quite happy and things started to change for me, slowly, in 3 or 4 months maybe. Before, I was on my own, no one to talk to, no one to share. When I went there it started to change.

On another level, self-advocacy has led some people to meaningful *employment*. There are quite a few instances in Australia where self-advocates have been employed in self-advocacy groups or other projects.

> Since I've been in self-advocacy groups I've had a couple of jobs, like a project worker. I've found self-advocacy has done a lot for me and where I was beforehand. Because I was working in an office and only getting $2.50. I thought that was crummy. Now I'm earning a proper wage.

It seems, then, that self-advocacy can result in major changes in people's lives, especially in terms of confidence, independence, respect from others, contact with others, and employment.

Self-Advocates Learn Skills

In our discussions, people talked about a great range of skills they had learned or developed through their involvement in self-advocacy groups.

Personal skills. Most of the personal skills people thought they had learned were about relating to other people. These skills included being able to share ideas with others; knowing how to make a point and get a message across; and respecting oneself and others. Developing money skills, shopping skills and other daily living skills were also mentioned. Taking responsibility for themselves and meeting their commitments were other skills that people thought they had developed.

Group skills. A second area of skills are those involved in being a part of a group or organization. Almost everyone talked about the fact that they had learned how to be part of meetings, how to input their ideas, how to chair a meeting, how to make and follow an agenda, and how to fill other roles such as president, secretary and minute-taker. Some people had also learned administrative skills such as typing, photocopying, and writing letters.

Community work skills. At a broader level, it seems that many self-advocates have developed skills that are essential for community development workers. Specific skills people mentioned include public speaking, networking with other groups, learning from other groups, having a good knowledge of the field, learning how to support others, learning how to produce and use videos and other publications.

Some of the Problems With Self-Advocacy: Views From Self-Advocates and Workers

Much of what the self-advocacy movement does involves breaking new ground, challenging very entrenched patterns and attitudes, at a broader social level as well as in the lives of individuals. It is understandable that it is a movement that has been surrounded by debate, controversy, ups and downs, and dilemmas.

While people are quick to highlight the positives, they are also not shy about the negative side — the problems they have experienced with self-advocacy. The overall picture was a positive one. As people were talking about the issues and problems, they often offered examples of how these issues had been or could be overcome.

The problems or issues that were identified in the interviews and discussions fall into four main areas:

- personal issues for self-advocates
- issues within & between groups
- support workers: self-advocates' concerns and workers' dilemmas
- broader issues: money, voluntary labor/exploitation, power, people with high support needs, poverty/homelessness.

PERSONAL ISSUES FOR SELF-ADVOCATES

The personal issues people had experienced were mainly to do with others not showing respect or not wanting to listen.

People don't want to listen to you, don't respect you...

(This was raised especially in relation to being a woman and a volunteer in groups.)

One person said that sometimes, **"People haven't got faith in what you say...."** However, this, he explained, was more in the early days of self-advocacy, not so much today.

Someone else felt that one big problem was that in her work everyone was giving advice and that she didn't know what to do, who to listen to.

A couple of other people who were relatively new to self-advocacy said that when they were asked questions they didn't know the answers to, they felt bad. Others noticed that problems came about because some people didn't have some of the necessary basic skills (e.g., how to use videos, how to use public transport).

ISSUES WITHIN GROUPS AND BETWEEN GROUPS

Self-advocates felt that sometimes groups struggle a bit because some people lack skills, or don't 'pull their weight' and do their share of work.

A current issue for some women was the experience of discrimination and lack of respect within some self-advocacy groups. There was a concern that there were no ways to address this problem within the groups. It was felt that there is a lack of information, and that it is hard to find help to deal with issues of sexual discrimination and learn about your legal rights. Some felt there wasn't enough briefing and training for members of self-advocacy groups to learn about overcoming discrimination against women. This leads us to the issue of general prejudices, and sexist and racist attitudes. It is my observation that these are often as evident in self-advocacy groups as they are in the broader community. However, it does seem that sometimes their expression and impact can be more exaggerated in self-advocacy groups.

Another issue raised by both workers and self-advocates was that of the relationship between different self-advocacy groups. Some people were concerned about conflict and jealousy between some groups. This conflict seemed to stem from different styles of working and funding, and from feelings of ownership of issues or activities. One worker felt that people can be easily upset and rumors and conflict often can divide groups and create "in-groups." As we discussed this, we acknowledged that it happens in *all* groups and committees. But we began to wonder if it might be more of an issue for self-advocacy groups because people sometimes have limited experience with friendships and relationships. In addition, it seems that self-advocacy is often the main source of people's social life.

Some self-advocates were also concerned that people outside the movement seem to get confused about the different self-advocacy groups and what they do.

A big concern for one worker is that the main self-advocacy groups get sidetracked and respond to others' demands on them. It's not easy for the groups to be clear about their *own* agenda and to stick to it, to respond to their own issues. Some may say that the groups get trapped in to being *reactive* rather than *pro*active.

One point that could be made about all of these issues within and between groups is that all groups and fields experience these sort of things. As with any movement, different groups handle or resolve these conflicts in different ways.

The important thing to note is that these issues do not apply to every part of the movement. The movement feels very dynamic; it is growing and adjusting and learning all the time. This I know from my personal experience since first starting to work alongside self-advocacy groups in Victoria, seven years ago. One of the most rewarding things about doing the research for this chapter was the opportunity to sit and talk in depth to people from the movement. It was very clear to me that individuals and groups with whom I was then involved have developed to an amazing level of sophistication, political awareness and ability. This is true despite the ups and downs, the tightening economic climate and continuing battles that the movement is facing. In my opinion the movement has also developed depth and variety, with a great range of groups that function in different ways, with a range of people, and with many different aims.

SUPPORT WORKERS

Self-advocates' concerns about support workers. Support workers — their styles, attitudes and approaches — have become one of the hottest issues when self-advocates raise their concerns about self-advocacy. However, everyone who took part in this discussion stressed that the problems are only with *some* support workers *some* of the time.

It seems the biggest issue with support workers is when they are seen to be overpowering, telling people what to do all the time, running the show themselves, trying to run people's lives and/or work. One person referred to it as the "ultimate power of support workers."

One group's experience was summed up in these words:

> We were like a self-advocacy group, [but] they were running our project, telling us what to do *all the time*.... We should have been telling them what to do... and that wasn't very nice. But it's all changed now... we're the bosses.

Another person said:

> I just feel they want to run the show themselves....They think they should run it their way.... But some of the other support workers, they play it fair and help us and try and do it evenly. What really frightens me... people like that have too much power over disabled people. When you've got someone like that, it's taking away independence from people with an intellectual disability. I think you have to be careful. Not all of them are bad, but some are.

Another issue about support workers is that they sometimes don't have enough time. One person sensitively explained,

> People like me feel a bit lost, because people who work in the office have got too much work these days because of the hours [and funds] being

cut down... so they haven't got time to train us to do other [new] things... which they like to do....

Support workers' dilemmas. Many of the support workers acknowledge these concerns and agree with them. However, they have their own set of pressures and dilemmas.

This is one support worker's view, in response to the question, "What are the particular issues for support workers?"

> Oh, so many....
>
> We get such a hard time. It's very tricky. You tread a very thin line all the time. For example, a person has been told all their lives they can't do things, then the movement tells them they have rights and can do things It's like self-advocacy sets up a situation where people are told they can do *everything*, when sometimes in reality they can't. People can have inflated and unrealistic ideas about what is involved and what they can do.
>
> So people have a love/hate relationship with support workers. At times they want support from you, and at other times they hate you because you are there.
>
> Sometimes people are happy being token and aren't interested in putting time in with support workers to understand more about meetings they are involved in and follow-up.
>
> In some cases people are happy to sit back and let the support worker do the hard thinking stuff.... You really have to work hard to get people really involved and doing it themselves, sometimes. Maybe it's because people are lazy, but often it is because they have other priorities (like maybe they are just after social involvement).

These dilemmas over how much support and when, how much direction and when are echoed by many support workers.

Another issue for some workers is how to handle situations in which they disagree with self-advocates. Another way of putting this dilemma is how much a supporter should put across his or her own work or personal philosophies in supporting the groups, and how much the supporter becomes simply a vehicle for what the group wants to do. One worker believes that many support workers have made the mistake of thinking that to support self-advocacy means agreeing with everything the movement and individuals say.

Some workers discuss the fact they often slip into the role of an advocate in their work, when really their intention or job is to support self-advocates. Given that most support workers are fully committed to people's rights, it is understandable how difficult it is to hold back and not speak up, but support the *people* to speak up.

Accountability is another big issue for support workers. Most workers would support the notion that they are, first and foremost, accountable to the self-advocates in the group. However, there is often a lot of pressure on the workers to be responsible to the funding bodies or other interested powers. Workers some times feel torn between the direction the committee wants to take and the direction that is being dictated by other players.

BROADER ISSUES

Money. As you have probably already gathered, getting and keeping funding has been an ongoing concern for most self-advocacy groups. The other side to this dilemma is the time and energy it takes to continually fight to survive financially. It seems that, especially with government funding, there is also that familiar issue of the "strings attached" — the requirements, regulations and expectations that don't always fit with the work, aims or philosophy of the movement.

One worker noted that there wasn't enough funding around to start self-advocacy in rural areas and the many other areas where the was a need and a demand. This same worker also talked about the inadequate level of funding that many groups receive, so they are unable to pay all of their workers or are unable to employ the best possible workers.

Poverty, homelessness, decreasing access to services. Related to the issues around money, is the reality that there is a general increase in homelessness, poverty and a decrease in funding and access to services for all people. People who have an intellectual disability are, as we know, certainly not exempt or protected from these trends. One worker's experience tells that these factors are affecting the movement. People are less able to afford to be involved in self-advocacy groups and activities (in terms of time, money, support, skills etc.)

Time to learn vs. getting things done. This seems to be a continual dilemma for the movement and specific groups: how to balance the need to get things done, with the need to allow the time it takes for everyone in the group to develop their skills and be involved in the decisions. One worker described the exceptional length of time that it had taken to form a committee, employ workers, and set up the office of a new group. In the same way, meetings can seem very slow affairs, as can using the phones, etc. This can place pressure on the group when funding bodies and other outsiders want to see action and results and demand responses and reactions. In a video entitled *Support Workers Talk*, made by the National People First Project around 1989, support workers from each state discussed this issue in depth.

Voluntary labor and exploitation. The issue of the voluntary labor that is so common in the movement is often discussed in Victoria. Many support workers have given a lot of their own time over the years. Some people argue that this helps to ensure that workers do not manipulate self-advocacy groups, but many are concerned that this does not allow for long-term or substantial support of the groups.

For me, the most alarming thing about the voluntary labor that keeps the movement going is that many self-advocates are giving their time, sometimes as full-time workers, without receiving any money or even reimbursement for expenses. Many of the people I have worked alongside are living in uncomfortable circumstances — sometimes with not enough money to see them through the week — and yet we all (i.e., the government, paid workers, services, etc.) have high expectations of them as workers and representatives. Now that self-advocates have begun to be employed as paid workers in some self-advocacy groups, I am hoping that this exploitation will stop.

Self-advocates talk about the broader issues. These are the issues that have confronted people as they and the movement have dealt with the community and society in general. Some self-advocates and supporters commented that some people in the community don't seem to want to know about their group or learn about disability. Others talked about the barriers that society's attitudes still create:

> Society is saying we can't do stuff most times... like people who want to go out into groups, like gyms and that.... If you've got a disability, they say no, you can't.

Problems in getting access to public transport was another issue that was identified.

A big issue for one group at the moment is *jargon*, particularly at meetings and in conferences.

> If consumers don't understand the words, they're just there as tokens. We won't get anywhere until people who talk this jargon change their attitude and talk the basics... and give others a chance to understand what they're talking about.

Another issue the movement faces is the reaction from some parents. It was thought that some parents reacted angrily to self-advocacy groups, especially if they had strong ideas about what was best for their son or daughter. On the other hand, there were people who talked about how supportive of self-advocacy their families were.

Successes for the Movement

THE CLOSING OF CALOOLA

The biggest success story on everyone's minds at the moment is the closing of one of Australia's most notorious, old, state-run institutions on the outskirts of Melbourne. This institution is known as Caloola or Sunbury. After years of fighting, debate, controversy, promises and broken promises, this institution is now closed. While some people were concerned and skeptical about the process of the closing and the alternatives being provided, everyone saw the closing as a success. A number of self-advocacy groups in Victoria have been actively lobbying and demonstrating for years to have the institution closed.

> We're getting Sunbury closed down, which was a great effort. We've been fighting to get Sunbury shut for years.... Finally it is happening... and then after Sunbury we're trying to close down other institutions.

Another major success is the funding of a self-advocacy group for Caloola.

CHANGES IN INSTITUTIONS

One Melbourne institution, Janefield, has a well-established self-advocacy group which has had many successes. This group has developed a complaints process that residents can have easy access to and confidence in: the *"I've Got A Problem" Form*. Other restrictive practices, such as having to fill out a leave-of-absence form to leave the institution's grounds, have also been stopped.

In past years, self-advocacy groups have drawn attention to a variety of inhumane conditions in institutions, such as mixed bathing, and abuse. Self-advocates feel that these have been successful efforts because authorities have acted upon the issues and the general community awareness has been raised.

SERVICES AND GROUPS HAVE BEEN FUNDED AND HAVE SURVIVED

Some people pointed out that the fact that self-advocacy groups had gained funding and recognition and had survived some tough times was itself a major success. Those who had been involved for a while sat back and thought of how much the movement had grown since 1981. One person felt that being invited to the Queen's Garden Party showed the recognition that their group had. Some had many stories to tell about positive feedback they had received over the years which showed the great impact that self-advocacy had on individuals, the government, and other services.

SUCCESS STORIES

The following are some of the specific achievements that people thought were successes for self-advocacy.

- Completing projects such as the Reinforce De-institutionalization Project, which interviewed residents of institutions about what sort of places they would like to live in.
- Successfully lobbying the state government to produce a consumers' version of the Ten Year Plan (a major plan for redeveloping Victoria's services for

people with an intellectual disability). This version of the plan attempts to use simple language and photographs.

- Getting children into ordinary schools was seen to be a major achievement. As one person put it: **"If we do that, people are going to think 'they're just like us,' and they will understand that 'because they're slow doesn't mean they can't learn,' and then they'll change."**
- One person thought that public transportation campaigns had been successful because the new and confusing ticket system had been changed and conductors had been kept on some trams.
- The Code of Rights presented to the International Conference on Mental Retardation in Melbourne in 1981 (see p. 145) was one of the early successes that some people remembered.

As most of us who have been involved in social movements such as self-advocacy can understand, it is not easy to stand back from the day-to-day work and struggles and see or remember the successes. I have offered quite a substantial list of achievements, but I'm sure others in the self-advocacy movement could identify many more successes, both for individuals and the field as a whole.

Responses to the Self-Advocacy Movement in Australia

When it began in Australia in 1981, it is reported that the prevailing attitude towards self-advocacy was one of "hostility, rejection and disbelief that people with an intellectual disability could speak for themselves or that they would say anything useful or sensible." By 1986 the climate had changed considerably. A lot of organizations by then were beginning to involve consumers and allow them to have a say. Legislation and policies were being developed to encourage this.

One of the most interesting measures of the success and impact of a social movement such as self-advocacy is the response it receives from major players in the In this case we have considered the major players to be family; workers; organizations and services; and the government.

THE RESPONSE FROM FAMILIES

Self-advocates talk about a full range of responses from their own families and parents in general. On the positive side, they say that their families often become more aware, more informed, more understanding and give them more respect once they have become involved in self-advocacy. Families also seem to acknowledge their experience and what they know, when they stand up for themselves. As one woman puts it:

> It has made my friends and family... aware of me being involved. I find that my friends and family understand what I go through, and they don't give

> me a hard time... or else I tell them if they stand on my wrong foot...
> because then they know that I have got my experience and knowledge,
> and they know I should be able to say what I think.
>
>   It has given them a new area to be aware of and think of, and when
> they see me they can ask questions. It's like... educating them through my
> involvement, my rights, words and actions.... It has given a new lease to
> my family... they can see what I can do. I've been able to get out and do
> things, and my family and friends treat me with respect. And they want to
> talk to me about this.

A few people noted that members of their family are now more interested in what
they do. On the other hand, some people say that, although their family think it's
good that they are involved in the self-advocacy group, family members are more
interested in other parts of their lives. One persons explains that "this is because
self-advocacy is for me and not for them."

These comments, and others from self-advocates, show how families can be
empowered as a son or daughter becomes more powerful and in control of his or
her life. It seems that self-advocacy can give a whole new basis for relationships and
conversations, a whole new positive area of life to talk about. On the other hand, it
can also become a whole area of life that the family feels it does *not* need to be
involved in.

On the not-so-positive side, self-advocates talk about families being scared,
shocked, or even irate about self-advocacy groups in general or about their daughter or son being involved in the movement. One woman described the fear some
parents seem to experience:

> The parents are scared... because they don't want their son or daughter
> to grow up. They're scared that "out there" is an evil place and they [the
> daughter or son] will get hurt by having self-advocacy. For example, we
> had a member who was adult age and she had to do what her mother
> asked her to do. There was friction in the home because her mother
> didn't want her to work with us, and she left.
>   Do *you* think it is an evil place "out there"?
>   It can be... but it can be *very* beautiful.

Some people explained that parents are sometimes not happy about their involvement in self-advocacy because parents feel that other parts of their life are
more important. Sometimes self-advocates feel that parents don't realize that they
can manage. One person said that his parents were shocked when he started working with the self-advocacy group because it was not a paid job.

Some self-advocates had been in situations where they had been confronted by
what they termed "irate parents." They thought that the parents were angry about

self-advocacy groups talking about rights and choices for all people with disabilities and about closing down institutions. Some people .thought that parents reacted like this because they believed they were the ones who knew what was best for their son or daughter.

A worker who has worked in and supported the self-advocacy movement summed up his experience of parents' responses as follows:

> I guess it is unfair to put parents into one group because they're obviously all very different; but I reckon that it's nevertheless true to say that parents have *generally* reacted to the self-advocacy movement with a sort of friendly cynicism. A lot of parents who are themselves active in the disability movement, I think, see the people who are involved in self-advocacy as rather "unrepresentative" of people with disabilities — and certainly unlike their own daughters and sons. They see them as people who are much more articulate — much less disabled — than the "average" person with an intellectual disability. In this sense, I think that a lot of parents tend to tolerate the self-advocacy movement, as long as it is kept in its place. Some do not think that what it has to say should be taken too seriously.

Unfortunately, in writing this chapter, there has not been the time or scope to talk directly to everyone or every group who have a right to have their views recorded. However, my experience working with parents suggests that most would discuss the difficulties of allowing and encouraging a son or daughter to become independent and become involved in self-advocacy. Many parents have spent years of intensive time and energy caring for their child, fighting for services and struggling through the maze of advice, theories, and policies offered by professionals and organizations. Some also seem to have put a lot of energy into protecting the child from the world and the world from the child (a world that has so often been hostile towards people with disabilities). It must be very difficult to withdraw that investment of energy and to challenge the advice and beliefs that over the years have said "Your child will never...." The examples of positive, supportive reactions from parents at the beginning of this section show how many families have managed to deal with these hurdles.

The Response From the Government

There has been a range of different responses from different areas of government. First, we will hear self-advocates' views about politicians, the government's intentions, money, and policies. Then there will be a summary of the efforts that the federal and Victoria governments have actually made towards self-advocacy before we discuss some critical comments on Governments' responses to the self-advocacy movement.

Representatives from a few self-advocacy groups say that they have had good responses from individual politicians. They have found, in these cases, that the politician listens, keeps his or her word and gets some things done. Others have stories about politicians ignoring, dismissing or blocking their efforts and ideas. Some people have felt that some politicians have come to discredit them or fear them after they've been vocal or persistent.

Some self-advocates, especially those who have been around for a while, are frustrated that there's still a lot of debate about new policies and plans. Some people feel like there are always "debates, then stalemates, and then we're back where we started, going over the same old stuff." When people discussed this, there was a sense that there *were* some good plans and intentions, but that these don't seem to get off the ground.

Quite a few self-advocates mentioned the recession and acknowledged that the government does not seem to have much money. One young self-advocate talked about the funding cut her group had suffered and the possibility the group may have to close. She questioned the government's commitment to self-advocacy groups:

> I'm probably wrong... but what I think is that the government doesn't want any advocacy groups... so they're taking the money away....
>
> The government hasn't got a lot of money, but it's getting new buildings and trains and... they've got to pay for them.... That's probably why they're taking the money away from us.
>
> The government probably doesn't realize what is happening to the group... they probably don't care.

These, I think, are important grass-roots observations that reflect the realities in tight economic climates and the reality of how slow *real* change can be. These sorts of views and experiences need to balance the enthusiasm that a lot of us have had for the government's developments such as new legislation, funding and projects.

Especially in the last few years, state and federal governments have made some concrete efforts towards the self-advocacy movement. The following are some of those efforts that I have observed or that have been documented or referred to by self-advocates or workers in the field.

Federal government. At a federal or national level, the government has made significant contributions in funding and legislation that support and foster self-advocacy. Some examples of the services funded are the National Self-Advocacy Kit Project, a number of statewide or local self-advocacy groups, and a number of innovative demonstration projects, such as the AMIDA Consumer Participation Project.

One of the purposes of the Federal Disability Services Act of 1986 is to ensure that provisions are made for more flexible responses to the needs and aspirations of people with disabilities. The act is based on seven major principles, one of which relates directly to consumer participation and self-advocacy: *"People with disabilities have the same right as other members of Australian society to participate in the decisions which affect their lives."*

There are a number of objectives which are specified by the Government in order to put this principle into practice:

- Services providing assistance to people with disabilities should be account-able to consumers.
- People with disabilities should have access to advocacy support where nec-essary to ensure adequate participation in decision-making about the ser-vices they receive.
- Services should provide appropriate avenues for people with disabilities to air and resolve any grievances about the services they receive.
- People with disabilities should be provided with avenues for participating in the planning and operation of individual services and opportunities for consultation relating to major policy development and program changes.

The federal government now expects the range of service providers which receive federal funds to follow these objectives. Currently, these include both well-estab-lished and new services in the areas of accommodation, support, employment and advocacy. The federal government is also working closely with each state govern-ment, encouraging them to adopt progressive legislation and principles such as giving everyone the right to have a say.

State governments. It is unfortunate that it is not possible, here, to detail the responses of each state government toward self-advocacy. Each state would prob-ably present quite a different picture. However, it is interesting to look at Victoria as a case study, especially since it was the site of the first Australian self-advocacy group.

Victoria's Intellectually Disabled Persons' Services Act (IDPS Act) of 1986 sets out 14 principles for the development and provision of services to people with an intellectual disability. There are two of those principles which relate to self-advo-cacy:

- Every intellectually disabled person is entitled to exercise maximum con-trol over every aspect of his or her life.
- Intellectually disabled persons have a legitimate and major role to play in planning and evaluating services.

Thus, there are principles in Victoria law that support and promote self-advocacy and consumer participation. One of the Victoria government's efforts towards putting this into practice was to consult with consumers about the Ten Year Plan for redeveloping state services and to produce a consumer version of the report. Members of self-advocacy groups and individuals with disabilities have also been involved in government advisory committees and reference groups, such as the Ministerial Advisory Committee (MAC).

The Victoria government, through the department of Community Services Victoria (CSV), has also funded one statewide self-advocacy group. From 1981 until 1990 this was Reinforce; since then, CSV has chosen to fund People First Victoria instead of Reinforce. In some regions of the state, CSV has also funded and helped to initiate some local self-advocacy groups.

One worker sums up the history of the relationship between the government and the self-advocacy movement in Victoria as one of apparent support but in reality a relationship of convenience and shallow commitment.

> I think that the self-advocacy movement was really starting to grow and to make a noise at a time when there was considerable movement from the government towards reforms in laws, services and policies — that is, in the early to mid-eighties. It was at this time that the government was proclaiming the need for services that were community-based and which provided people with disabilities with opportunities to have more control over their own lives and to be real participating members of the ordinary community.

> Obviously this sort of thrust in the Government rhetoric was quite consistent with a lot of what the self-advocacy movement was saying, too. The government reacted quite favorably, even enthusiastically, to the self-advocacy movement at that time.

> The problem, however, was that this enthusiasm was probably a bit misplaced. It was enthusiasm simply because the self-advocacy movement appeared to be supporting what the government wanted to do anyway. Government was therefore supporting self-advocacy because it was an ally, not really because of any deeper commitment to the principles of self-advocacy.

> So this meant that as soon as the self-advocacy movement ceased to be seen as, or needed as, a supporter of Government initiatives, then the Government either lost interest in self-advocacy or became antagonistic towards it.

This worker and another both discussed the two-sided and varied responses from the government. One argues that:

> It is difficult for the Government to grapple with — they have the idea that people have rights to have a say and be involved in decisions... but

they haven't really taken it on board... don't really take what people say seriously.

At a statewide level the Government recognizes the power and importance of the self-advocacy groups, but they expect too much without giving enough support. They expect people to get involved in meetings and committees (like the Ministerial Advisory Committees) but give them no support or resources in return.

As the first worker adds:

We are now left in a situation where the government has to at least appear to be supporting self-advocacy because it made such a fuss about it in the early days. But given that the self-advocacy movement doesn't serve any really useful purpose for the government, that support is minimal.

It also means that the government is forced to continue to involve people with intellectual disabilities on all of its working groups and committees, not because there is any real interest in what they have to say, but rather because they are obliged to *appear* to be listening.

Another worker agreed:

It's like the government goes into plan B — now that they have to accept self-advocacy, they work out how to minimize the influence.... There is still the game of token representatives who get done over in decisions.

This worker gave the following example of how self-advocates' involvement is often not taken seriously.

Self-advocates who were involved in one government advisory committee were recently unhappy about the way the meetings were run, about the jargon used and how the committee was handled. They felt they weren't getting a real chance to have a say, understand the issues, or have their views listened to. One of the self-advocacy groups involved wrote a letter about the concerns. The senior bureaucrat involved convinced these people that there was no need to take the matter to higher authorities as they had intended. The bureaucrat assured the self-advocates that the situation would be rectified. However, months later, nothing has changed, and people are still complaining about their treatment at the committee.

The are quite a few of us who also believe that if the government had a real commitment to self-advocacy, it would have supported the movement in Victoria to organize itself and resolve the issues it has been experiencing in the last few years. Instead, the government's reactions (such as taking funding away from one group and giving it to another) seem to have divided rather than supported the movement.

A simple measure of respect, I think, if the Government had seriously listened to the self-advocacy movement, would be for the official terminology to reflect the movements' call to be seen as "People First." However, official documents, such as annual reports, still refer to "intellectually disabled people." It is also interesting to note that self-advocacy is not mentioned as a goal or a specific interest to the department in its work.

Although there are significant efforts by the Victoria Government toward staff training and development, there have not been formalized staff development activities around self-advocacy (nor are there plans for this, from what I have been told). The curriculum of the training courses for new or untrained workers does include a single three-hour session on advocacy. Not only is this insufficient time to do the topic justice, but this small session is meant to cover a list of areas, the *last* of which is self-advocacy.

Each region within Victoria is, according to legislation, developing a regional planning committee. These were intended to provide the opportunity for people to become actively involved in the planning and development of services. However, it seems that some are not providing opportunities for people with an intellectual disability or self-advocacy groups, or are having difficulty involving them.

All of these examples show how minimal the government's response to self-advocacy in the intellectual disability field has been. It seems that self-advocacy remains a marginal consideration — at times an afterthought or a token gesture, at other times totally ignored.

It is interesting to note that the Victoria government has a much better track record supporting self-advocacy efforts for other groups of people. For example, tenants in most areas in the government's public housing system receive funding and support to have a say in their housing and the policies and services that affect them. This is seen as a major and important part of the housing department's work.

This marginal government response to self-advocacy would explain why some self-advocates have had difficult experiences trying to work with the government department. One woman reported:

> They're not too helpful. It's really hard... hard to break down the barriers....
>
> What sort of barriers?
>
> Getting people to listen *really* properly....There's political things that go on behind closed doors and we never see or hear about it.

Another person characterized the relationship between her group and the government as a "fighting" one. She felt that the department was telling the group what to do all the time, pushing and pushing the workers and applying a lot of rules and regulations that, to her, didn't seem necessary.

THE RESPONSES OF WORKERS AND ORGANIZATIONS

Representatives from one self-advocacy group in an institution summed up the sort of responses there have been from workers and organizations in the field. They thought there was a scale of reactions, from very negative, to no response, to very positive.

A small percentage of workers and organizations are *very* responsive in a positive way. They are supportive; they understand the need for self-advocacy and the ways it works. In addition to the support workers employed by the movement, there is a collection of workers who in different ways have attempted to support self-advocacy from the outside. Some workers are also active in trying to incorporate self-advocacy or consumer participation in their work and organization.

On the other hand, a small percentage are very responsive in a *negative* way. Sometimes workers or organizations discount what self-advocacy groups say, discredit individual self-advocates, or degrade their activities. Some argue that groups should not and cannot be run by people with intellectual disabilities. One self-advocate adds that some workers and organizations are scared about self-advocacy.

> Some workers... not all — some — are very frightened of self-advocacy because they see self-advocacy as real riff-raff. But it's not like that....

The same person related a particular experience she had after speaking out about an organization she had been involved in.

> I was asked to give a talk and I spoke about my experience where I worked, in a certain organization. I spoke my opinion about what I thought of it, and apparently I got a nasty response back by the organization. The thing is, when you do something like that you sometimes have to walk on people's toes, but you have to be careful about how you go about it.... It's good in some ways because it helps you overcome and it tells other people what you have been through. A lot of organizations mightn't like people telling about their experiences... but sometimes they have to be told. The thing is, I had a rough time when I saw workers from that certain organization. I wasn't too popular.

A worker in the field agrees that this often happens if people are vocal. She believes that people get labelled as "ratbags" or "stirrers" if they are vocal. According to this worker, there is still an attitude that people with disabilities should be grateful and submissive — "Assertive people with disabilities are a real shock!"

And then there are shades of grey in between the very positive and very negative reactions. A lot of workers and organizations do not seem to be really interested in or see the relevance of self-advocacy to their work. One worker in the field had the impression that self-advocacy is, in some areas, "at best ignored, at worst degraded." As one self-advocate said, "they don't *really* listen." Another thinks some "only listen 50/50."

This leads us to the frequently made claim that often only token efforts and responses are made towards self-advocacy. One worker in the field believes that many service providers embrace consumer participation in their services in ways that create token involvement, without real self-advocacy.

> I think that service providers were initially quite resistant, or at least quite skeptical, about the prospect of having people with intellectual disabilities participating in their committees of management. But now we are finding that it is now more and more common for service providers to have consumers on their committees. Many service providers are finding out that these consumers are not creating the big hassle that was anticipated, usually because so many of them just sit there and don't say anything for the whole meeting.
>
> I think this has led a lot of service providers to believe they have a commitment to self-advocacy. Of course, we know that the two — consumer participation and self-advocacy — are by no means synonymous. The trouble is... that a lot of service providers... and consumers do not realize this. So we now have the situation where legislation has forced services to adopt a particular structural model for involving consumers which will, in many cases, lull both service providers and consumers into a false sense of "everything is fine."

As mentioned earlier, many self-advocates also argue that their involvement in some committees and meetings is token. This is especially so when the language and jargon that is used prevents them from understanding what is being said, and when their opinions are not listened to, acted upon or are thought to be irrelevant. Many self-advocates believe (rightly, I think) that the big words and jargon that seem so common in this field are unnecessary. Some talk about how workers and professionals can sometimes use big words to trick people, or hide things. One self-advocate related this story with more than a touch of irony and humor in his voice.

> I was at a Consultative Council meeting as a [self-advocacy group] rep., sitting next to this man who used this big word, I can't get my tongue around. I had to stop him and ask him to explain the meaning of that word... and he said he didn't really know the meaning!!

Hopes and Dreams

In the discussions I have had with self-advocates and support workers about self-advocacy, it has been difficult to be disciplined enough to move from the specific issues, ideas and events and talk about dreams for the future. However, we have come up with quite a few hopes and some broad dreams. Some of these are individuals' dreams for themselves; some are hopes for the movement or all people labelled as having a disability; some are dreams about the community, the government, and professionals.

PERSONAL HOPES

Some self-advocates who had been involved in the movement for some time had hopes of moving on and doing something else; some wanted to have more opportunities to teach others what they had learned. One woman said that she would like to run part of the movement one day, further explaining that this meant managing or coordinating a group on her own.

In very straightforward terms, some self-advocates simply expressed a hope that one day they would be *really* accepted, respected and listened to. Some people talked about the day they would *really* have their rights and choices, when they could speak from their own minds and feelings, without being scared.

Others talked about how much they enjoyed making and being in videos and hoped they could make more. It also seems, for some of the people living in institutions whom I met, that many of their hopes and dreams still revolve around the day-to-day things we take for granted. Things like visiting old friends who had moved on, living in a house, smoking when and how much they wanted, making a cup of tea for themselves, learning to go out to the shops, and crossing the road on their own were some of the things that came up in our discussions.

HOPES AND DREAMS FOR SELF-ADVOCACY GROUPS AND THE MOVEMENT

"There are so many goals out there, I hope the movement can keep going and meet those goals." This was one self-advocate's response when asked what hopes and dreams he had for the movement. This was a hope for a lot of people: that the movement would be able to continue. Perhaps this reflects the uncertain times and economic climate at the moment.

Some self-advocates said they hoped that new groups would keep developing and that, as one put it, "I hope that one day we can all work together with the same goals." Other, more specific hopes for the movement and individual groups revolved around people getting a fair opportunity at meetings and committees, and having real input.

I wish that everyone could input to committees to tell the government what's right and what's wrong. People should be a part of the committee, but they can't [at the moment] because the jargon stops them.

I hope that people could represent their group at meetings without having to go back to the group and say they didn't understand.

HOPES AND DREAMS FOR THE COMMUNITY, GOVERNMENT AND SERVICES

Many self-advocates talked about the sort of changes they would like to see in the community and the sorts of things that this would mean for all people with disabilities.

All levels of the community would be educated, one person said. *There would be more support for people to be independent,* another added. *Everyone would use plain English and every person would be treated like other people. Then all people would be accepted and respected, all would have their rights and choices and dignity. All people would speak up about their feelings and would be heard.* These are the hopes shared by many of the self-advocates who contributed to this chapter.

Some of the most clear, dearly held and definite dreams that self-advocates voiced were visions of what an ideal world might look like.

- All institutions are closed
- Everyone is sharing community living
- Everyone is living in houses in the community
- All institutions buried and more community places for people.
  (Who knows it might only be a dream!)

Section IV

Self-Advocacy in the United States

I do not stand here alone! There are generations of disabled people behind me. They were subject to physical and educational barriers. They were prejudged by the rest of society and otherwise made to feel less than human because of the circumstances that were given to them at birth or later by fate. No one noticed that they were people first. I come this way with respect to those I follow, whether they be developmentally disabled, physically disabled, or cognitively disabled. I am their brother. I have the same pain! And we are people first. I am here to teach, but I am also here to learn. I am here to take, but I am also here to give. For I am the voice of generations past and an advocate for the voice of the future. I am here to pass the torch from advantaged hand to disadvantaged hand. For we are all people first!

— Kenneth Lee Heral
People First of Illinois

14

People First of Oregon

An Organizational History and Personal Perspective

Valerie Schaaf
with Hank Bersani, Jr.

We are especially happy to have this report on the origins of People First in Oregon. All of our research indicates that this was the first group to incorporate as People First, and they continue to be a vital organization today. VALERIE SCHAAF has been involved from the start and offers a deeply personal reflection on the history of the movement.

Our History

People First was started in 1973, by those of us who were former residents of a state institution called Fairview Training Center. Our advisor, Dennis Heath, took a group of former residents with him to Vancouver, B.C., to a convention for people with disabilities. At that time, individuals up there who were disabled did not speak for themselves; their advisor did all the talking for them, or else the advisors wrote down what they wanted certain individuals to say to those in the audience. The group came back to Salem, Oregon and told us what they saw and heard while they were there. During this time most of us were living in either a group home or what were called "satellite apartments." In some ways the news from the conference made us feel as though we were a toy or a robot run by remote control. We realized that if we were to continue in this way, we would not be able to have any freedom to live our own lives; we would be like slaves.

This is why People First was brought together; we wanted to let those in authority know that we are just like them and would like to be treated in the same way. How would you like it if someone did all your talking for you? We wanted to speak for ourselves and show the world and our communities that we can do many things for ourselves.

We are more alike than different. The things that we need are the same things that other people need: to hold jobs, to get married and raise a family, to vote, to be able to choose what kind of church to belong to, and to be self-supporting some day. Is that too much to ask?

People First started small. People First does not thrive on state funds. We are a non-profit organization. We don't ask for charity, but donations are always welcome. When People First initially began 25 years ago, we started as true beginners. We had to do some research in how do we elect our officers; many questions were raised during this time. Some of these were like, Where are we going to hold our meetings and how often? Are we going to use *Robert's Rules of Order* and what is the correct way to have our meetings?

Local People First chapters can now be found in almost every county in Oregon. We have also spread ourselves into other states. Each state has different laws and rights for people with developmental disabilities. Many times I have been asked, is it all right to let people get married and raise a family? My response has always been "yes!"

There are groups forming to help the disabled and his/her neighbor as much as possible. And along the same lines be open and honest towards them and you may find something unique about them that you didn't know before.

Since then, most of our people are living in their own apartments and more people are becoming *former* residents of Fairview, which is good to see.

Our first conference. We decided to split into two small groups with each taking a task that had to be completed before we could even have a convention. One group had to decide where we were going to hold our convention. Here are some of the ideas that were listed: to hold tent meetings, or to use the county or state fairgrounds and sleep in sleeping bags. (No one could come up with a solution on how we would eat our meals.) Other ideas or suggestions were to have it at the beach, or at a hotel and spend the night and eat their food. We decided to have our first convention at the Inn at Otter Crest, located on the coast of Oregon, in Lincoln County. Then, the public relations committee went to work at getting the word out about our first convention. These people visited all the sheltered workshops, training centers, and activity centers in the area, putting most of their time in the three counties around the state capitol Salem (Marion, Polk and Yamhill Counties). They traveled to other counties in Oregon, when called upon to come. We thought it would be better to spread the word by mouth, to save money, and to have a little fun exploring and seeing what some of our state looks like. We figured we could get more people interested in the plans that we made and what was on the verge of happening. We also put an ad on TV on the "Calendar of Events." I also put an ad over the radio.

Another reason we selected the Inn at Otter Crest (a small resort hotel) was because we were only expecting a small number to show up! But we were taken by surprise because we had over 500 people with disabilities who came to our first convention. We were on the news on TV that evening, and made the headlines in the local papers the next morning. Many a times I have often wondered if it was really that easy back then, because it seems like a lot of work now. Maybe it's because I am a lot older now than I was more than 20 years ago. And prices have increased since then too!

Annual Meetings. In 1975, we had over 750 in attendance at our second convention. This is also where we had the movie of "People First" filmed on location, as well as spots detailing where some of us lived, work, and have our fun, like watching the World Series. In 1976, our third convention was held at the Sheraton Hotel in Portland, Oregon. Our attendance was over 900 people. In 1977, we decided to have a small regional convention, for this we went back to Otter Crest and our attendance there was 350. The reason for this convention was because there were many states who wanted to start their own People First group. A People First group does not have to be called as such. Some do copy our methods or they do things a little different to satisfy themselves, and that's okay just as long as they don't take our history away from us! But first and foremost the group must be for and by people with developmental disabilities.

The year 1978 marked our fourth year as an organization. We had our convention again in Portland at the Sheraton and it was attended by more than 1000 people. 1979 was our 5th annual convention and had another attendance of more than 1000. It was held at the Hilton Hotel. In 1980 we had our 6th annual convention and had another 1000 in attendance.

1981 was very special for the mentally handicapped because President Reagan declared 1981 as the "International Year of Disabled People." People First held an international convention at Memorial Coliseum in Portland, Oregon. We had people come from all across our country, Canada and other countries. It was a great privilege to hold the first international conference in the birth state of People First. It was a great happiness for me to be International Board President at that time, a time that I will never forget as it was done with great joy.

During 1982, 1983 and 1984, People First met in Eugene, Oregon. In 1985 People First moved back to Portland. The 1986 conference was also held in Portland, and in 1987 and 1988 People First returned to the Eugene/Springfield area. In 1989, People First was in Portland at the Red Lions Inn on September 2 and 3.

Self-advocates need to speak up. I would like to tell you what happens if we don't speak out. If I don't say what's on my mind, if I don't talk about what bothers me, I won't be understood because I will have said nothing. I won't be communicating to anyone. I will feel less than a person. I will feel like I have nothing to offer. I won't think much of myself as a person. I will be uncomfortable, shy, insecure, helpless, and become nothing much more than a vegetable. I become angry and hurt. My temper gets out of control and I would not be able to cool down very quickly. I also feel people won't listen or try to understand me. I would feel alone and not wanted. When I talk, I can let people know what's on my mind. I would tell them what's bothering me. I want to get my feelings to be known, so I can talk freely without feeling down about myself. I want to be a person who has something to offer or give of myself. I want to be helpful; I want to have friends that would understand me. I want to overcome my shyness and to feel secure with myself and my feelings. I do not want to be a vegetable. I want to be known for what I can do and not for what I cannot do. I am a person just like you all are.

I need to let my weak and strong feelings be known. When you show your strong feelings you tend to be mad, angry and hurt. Your crying also shows how you feel. Tempers may be lost. At times, when you have lost a loved one, you can sense strong feelings during this period of your life. Some people, when they get mad or angry, also tend to dislike things like people which could bring about hate. In my opinion we should not dislike or hate anyone. We can dislike the wrong things that people do, but not the person themself. I can truthfully say it took me a long time to learn to dislike the wrong in people instead of disliking the person themself. But now I can separate my dislike between people and their natures, especially if they act out of ignorance.

Another area of feeling is love. Love can be shown in many ways. The excitement of love is shown in quietness, and its genuine softness. There are many different ways of showing love to another person or animal. Fondness is caring. If you do not love yourself, then how can you want to love or care about anyone else? Love is mostly when two people want to share their lives together. Love is not only seen on special dates and times of the year such as Christmas and Easter, but also at times of loss such as funerals. *Happiness is Love!* We should always have love in us and with us everyday through everything that happens to us. Self-advocates need to love.

Self-advocates communicate in many ways. Different people use different communication styles. Let me talk about a few of them here. For instance, a person who is blind uses Braille to communicate in writing to another blind person. They are able to talk as plainly as you and I. Usually they have people or guide dogs to get them around. I am sure you all have seen some blind folks who use white canes. And then there are those who are deaf and they use sign language with their hands and the finger alphabet to do their talking for them. There are others who are known as deaf interpreters that translate for the person who is talking. Some people have hearing dogs who let them know when certain noises occur, such as door bells, alarm clocks, timers, a knock on the door, plus other things that I do not even know about. Some can also read the lips of those who are speaking, and this is helpful to those who have learned that skill. Some use hearing devices. There are a wide variety of ways to choose from to help them to communicate. I have a hearing loss which I am not ashamed of. I am deaf in my right ear. This is one of the reasons I tend to talk loud.

I have a friend named Judy and she has cerebral palsy and she has trouble talking. Her words are scrambled. I could not understand her speech pattern when I first came to know her. I have been around her enough now to understand her when she speaks. If I am not sure of what she is saying, then I tell her what I think she said and she will tell me whether I was right or not. She told me she does not mind repeating herself when I am confused. Now she sometimes uses a computer to speak.

There are those who are physically unable to talk, so they use communication boards to help them do their talking. There are others who use letter boards with either their hands or their feet. I know of a fellow who uses a letter board with his feet. He also feeds himself and smokes a cigarette with the help of his feet. I was truly impressed with his talent. We also receive communication through the media which is the newspaper, radio, T.V., and the telephone. All that I have just mentioned are things which aid us in letting each one know what is happening and what is being done in problem areas of our everyday lives as well as in the world we live in. Knowing what is happening around us tends to help us in our own feelings and planning for the future.

Another way to get to speak is at various places, like your Arc, local chamber of commerce, state legislature, your church, club organizations, your city council, or your governor. All of these places are excellent to let your feelings be heard regarding problems that need to be brought to their attention. This is the most sure and best way of getting problem issues solved. Self-advocates must communicate!

We are people first. People First means that we are seen as a person first before we are seen as different.

One of the most widely talked about issues is regarding labeling people. People do not like to be labeled as "MR's," "retarded," "idiots," "dummies," "stupid," "trouble makers," "slow pokes," "lazy bums," etc. None of these labels should be given to anyone. Most people cannot help it if they have trouble in learning or that they cannot read or write, cannot talk, walk, or hear, or that they are slow in getting their tasks or duties done. Name calling is not for humans to use on humans, but maybe for jars, packages, or other objects that need labeling. But when you want to talk about a certain subject or topic, that is where the labeling should be used. Just like you have a name you are called by. Self-advocates shouldn't label another person just because they labeled you. They do not understand themselves like we do our own selves.

It does help us if we realize that we have a disability and need to work to make the best of our lives. Then we have to overcome the hurt that can cause us to not see ourselves as valuable people. Some people may never be able to learn quickly. There is nothing wrong in being slow which is better than learning too fast. Who would ever want to be a speedball in learning, not me! So do not be scared or afraid when a person calls you names.

We want to have jobs. Some of us work like everyone else does. We do not just sit around and let others do the work for us. If we did, how could we ever learn to do many things which were once thought impossible for us to do? We work in sheltered workshops, activity centers, some even hold down regular jobs. Let me say again that labeling is for things and not to be used on people. There have been many different issues which have been talked about. There have been many different ideas and/or arguments given to each topic of issues. Everyone has different feelings and should make them be known. Every state is different with rules or regulations to follow or made to be changes at a later time in life. Other issues that have been brought to our attention were: dating, marriage, voting, getting an education, living independently, having a family, budgeting, using the city buses and how to do so, etc. Posters, signs and billboards are another way of announcing events in a silent form of communication. They also advertise upcoming events that are happening or that are going to take place in the near future. That is why there are so many ways to be communicative. Let everyone speak up and speak out and make ourselves heard to all those who are around us every day. You should be heard, not ignored!

We want to make decisions. If you don't speak up and let yourself be known, you can let people override you and make plans for your life for you. If you want something, ask for it. You can't gain anything if you keep silent. People may think you don't know how to speak.

Being able to speak is a very big part of your life. Because it enables you to say what is on your mind, how you feel about yourself or others, and it also enables you to get a job, which is very important to all of us.

How do you get people to speak up and to speak out? If you live in a group home and have group home meetings, this is where you as individuals have an excellent opportunity to speak and say what you want. Other places where you can speak to others are at work, at church, and with friends and neighbors. Most people use the telephone a lot. I suppose all of you know how to telephone someone who lives somewhere. You talk to lots of different people year around. When you hear of a friend that's in the hospital you go to visit them. When you do so, you talk to them. All people talk to someone, like their doctor, barber, or hairdresser. You also communicate with your family.

I can remember when we first started to encourage other members to speak up and say something. We had an open microphone where everyone who came had a chance to say something, even if it was just their name; it also shows people that they can trust you to be patient.

We want to lead. Try your hand at being a leading officer of a small group and work at being president, or vice-president, secretary, treasurer, or even sergeant-of-arms for at least two years. Being an oficer will help you learn all the skills you will need to have as a leader and for any other position you may want. Being a leader of a small group will give you a chance to be a leader in local, state or national organizations or even a chance to be an international leader.

I am confident that all of you can do the same as we did in Oregon. It will take time. It took US time, and look where People First is at NOW!!!

Leadership development. As you learn to speak up, have confidence in yourself in whatever you desire to do. If pressure builds up while you are speaking, wait until you are done, then take a break. If you feel bad about something, or something is bothering you, talk it over with someone you know; not with a crowd or even a stranger, because they could make you feel worse than you did in the beginning by embarrassing or even hurting you in some way.

When you speak, let yourself be known, and you can let others know how you feel about anything. Whether you agree or disagree, this is one of the most important abilities you have. You are a valuable person because there are NO TWO people alike living in this world and you can be glad of that! If you don't express your thoughts or feelings, how else can you communicate with another person? Be open with yourself at all times and you can see what a difference it could make in your growth and in your personality.

Some were shy and scared, but after the first few times they forgot about being scared or shy. In fact it became fun. Some couldn't wait for their turn to say something into the microphone again!

Being able to speak about myself tells me that I have a right to talk just as much as anyone else. I don't have to be as quiet as a mouse, I can make a lot of noise. But I can work quiet as a mouse, like most people, and I can make a plan for myself and make my own decisions.

How does someone learn to talk to a gathering of people, no matter what size the crowd? You should start with a small group of people like a 4-H Club or a class of students. Then gradually involve yourself in larger groups. One of the most important things to remember about speaking with one or more people is to wait your turn, as this is the polite thing to do.

Basic Assumptions

First: We Need Each Other. My friends and I do find special and important meaning in our relationships with each other. We need each other; we like to be around each other; we have something to offer each other. We don't like to be lonely or isolated in the institution or the community.

Second: We Love. Consumers have emotions, feelings, desires, passions. We love and hate. We get happy; we get angry. We like to be seen as people who care and are concerned about people around us. We want to be intimate. We want to love and be loved.

Third: We Speak Up and Speak Out. When I was at the institution, one of the best ways we found to talk is in group. Consumers need to learn how to talk to each other. When we lived at the institution, we always went to the aide or staff when we wanted something. We were never encouraged to use each other, or to ask each other to help solve problems. One of the best ways we have found to talk to each other is to talk in groups. Small groups all over Oregon keep getting together to talk, share, feel, and think. We are learning to speak about what is on our minds. As long as we use the professional person, the aide, the staff, to meet our needs, we will never think it is important enough to talk to each other. We need to know we have common experiences, and common concerns, and common needs.

Fourth: We Meet. We need to get together in groups so that we can learn things like talking to each other, listening to each other, making decisions, developing action plans, and feeling like we have some say in our lives. This will take some time, but it is critical we learn how to do this. As we learn how to talk in smaller groups, we then feel more comfortable talking in larger groups and eventually we can act like we know what is going on. These groups are our time: The agendas are ours. We need this opportunity. Without it we have no chance to become a group.

Fifth: We Have An Identity. Consumers need a group identity, a culture, a history, and heroes. We need each other so that we are able to develop what the rest of society has. You all came from someplace. You all belong to special groups which give special meaning. Without developing a history we will have nothing to look back on — we won't know where we came from. Without a history and background we will then have a difficult time knowing where we are now in society, which, of course, means we will have no ideas or input about our future.

It is also very important as we develop a history, a present and a future, that we become the heroes and superstars. We need to feel good about ourselves. We need to feel important about our accomplishments. We want that feeling of being noticed and important. Agencies' attempts at normalization to date have not met our needs. It just hasn't gone far enough. Services will have to change or they won't be meaningful to the people they are supposed to affect.

I can talk pretty clear but some of my friends cannot. They use sign boards, sign language, and their bodies. Many of my friends have a difficult time getting in front of a group and talking. They want me to communicate to you what needs to happen regarding normalization.

First of all:

1. I want you to understand that I am a person who has something to offer others, and that I have needs to be met.
2. I want to have a say in my life and my friends want a say in their lives.
3. We want to be part of any plans made about us.

4. We want to talk to you professionals, but you will need to slow down and use simpler words.

5. My friends and I want to get together to do more than bowl, dance, run a race, or watch T.V. We want to talk about our lives and what we need. We want to feel close to each other. We want to make decisions that effect our lives. (When rules are made and programs are being run on us, we want input.)

6. We need to be able to get together but there are some problems:
   Transportation: There is no evening bus service in my town and no Sunday bus services. Most of us can't drive cars. Some of us are in wheelchairs and it's hard to get around. If we can ride a bike, there are hardly any bike lanes. We have to walk or hitch a ride.
   Money: We are poor people; we don't have enough money. We don't have jobs that pay good money. If we make too much on our jobs, SSI and Social Security are cut back or cut off.
   Communication: Our people have some problems with reading, writing, and understanding. Even though most of the people don't have phones, if they did, they wouldn't know how to use them. Also phones cost money. It would be helpful if we knew where everyone was. It's hard to call a meeting if you don't know where the people are.

I used to ask permission from my aides or my group home staff or my parents when I wanted to do something. My friends in Oregon and other states forgot to ask permission to meet, so we've been meeting together in groups from 10 to 1,000 for the past 20 years. We are helping each other make it as members of the community in spite of the system — and by the way, is it OK if we keep meeting???

15

The History of People First of Washington State

Bob Furman

As an advisor first to People First International in Oregon and later to People First of Washington State, Bob Furman has been involved with self-advocacy since the beginning. His chapter offers insight into the early days, blended with an analysis of the political forces affecting those years.

Setting the Stage: Fertile Ground for Self-Advocacy

Americans of all ages, all stations in life, and all types of disposition are forever forming associations. They are not only commercial and industrial associations in which all take part, but others of a thousand different types — religious, moral, serious, futile, immensely large and very minute.... In every case, at the head of any new undertaking, where in France you would find the government or in England some territorial magnate, in the United States you are sure to find an association. — Alexis de Tocqueville, *Democracy in America*, 1835

If you think you are handicapped, you might as well stay indoors. If you think you are a person, come out and tell the world.
— Ray Loomis, Project Two, Nebraska

The stage was set for self-advocacy by people with developmental disabilities in the state of Washington by four major factors: (1) the "pioneer spirit" of the Pacific Northwest, (2) the early history of parents' organizations and parent advocacy in the state, (3) the general civil rights movement of the 1960s and 1970s, and (4) changing public perceptions and attitudes about people with disabilities.

The history of the United States is filled with stories of individuals and groups moving ever farther westward to pursue individual and collective freedoms of association, religion, and lifestyle. The Pacific Northwest, which includes the state of Washington, was one of the last places where individual pioneers traveled to establish better lives and personal freedoms. This pioneer spirit remains evident in the state government, which allows citizen-led initiatives and referenda on political issues, and in the electorate, which supports individual choice and innovative programs.

Washington was one of the earliest states to create special education, accessibility, and nondiscrimination laws, years ahead of federal mandates. Several parts of the federal laws concerning Education for All (the original P.L. 94-142), section 504 of the Vocational Rehabilitation Act, and the Americans with Disabilities Act are based on Washington state laws. This pioneer spirit helped to set the stage for self-advocacy by citizens with disabilities.

In 1935, the Children's Benevolent League (CBL) was formed by Washington State parents, "for the purpose of organizing a group of citizens who will cooperate with the officials of the State Custodial School for the mentally deficient at Medical Lake, Washington" (Jones & Barnes, 1987). The Children's Benevolent League of Washington State, formed to improve the lives of people with mental retardation, was the first large association of its type. It played a leading role in the emergence of the national parents' group, first known as the National Association of Parents and Friends of Mentally Retarded Children, later as the National Association for Retarded Citizens, and now simply as The Arc. The CBL/ARC/Arc has a long history of advocacy for people with developmental disabilities in Washington. During the late 1940s, as parents were forming their national organization, a crucial decision was made to be separate from the professional organization, the American Association on Mental Deficiency (AAMD, which had formed in 1876 as the Association of Medical Officers of American Institutions of Idiotic and Feeble-minded Persons). This decision was based on the unique needs and perspectives of parents, a fear of being co-opted by professionals, and a belief that a separate parent organization would be stronger on its own.

During the 1960s and 1970s, the civil rights movement took hold in the United States. People with disabilities learned from this movement, and people with physical and sensory disabilities began the Independent Living Movement in the late 1960s and early 1970s. The 1960 White House Conference on Children and Youth, the election of John F. Kennedy who had a family member with disabilities, the demands and expectations of a rising middle class, and the increasing wealth and power in the United States following World War II all contributed to a national environment that sought to empower all citizens. The publication of *The Principle of Normalization* by Wolf Wolfensberger in 1972, the federal Rehabilitation Act in 1973, the Developmental Disabilities Assistance and Bill of Rights Act of 1975, and the Education for All Handicapped Children Act of 1975 are all indices of a growing national awareness and advocacy for and by people with disabilities for civil rights, independent community living, and justice. They also represented a movement away from the myths and stereotypes of people with disabilities perpetuated by the mythical "Kallikak family" and eugenics movement advocated by Goddard and others during the first half of the 20th century.*

The pioneer spirit of the Pacific Northwest, the rich history of parent organizing and advocacy there, the general civil rights movement, and the increased national awareness, debate and focus on people with disabilities set the stage and provided the fertile grounds for self-advocacy by people with developmental disabilities in Washington. The ground was fertile; all that was needed was the seed. This seed came with the creation of People First in Salem, Oregon, in 1973.

Many organizations and associations had historically spoken for people with developmental disabilities. These organizations included the American Association on Mental Deficiency and the Association for Retarded Citizens. There was a growing national debate about public policy and people with developmental disabilities. The very fact that these organizations have been "on" or "for" people with developmental disabilities demonstrates the extent to which people with developmental disabilities had been dependent on others to advocate on their behalf. People First, and the self-advocacy movement by people with developmental disabilities, would change all of this. People with developmental disabilities were no longer willing to let others speak for, by and about them... it was time to *speak for yourself*.

People First: Salem, Oregon, 1973

In November, 1973, two staff workers and three residents from one of Oregon's institutions, Fairview Hospital and Training Center, attended a meeting billed as the "First Convention for the Mentally Handicapped in North America," in Parksville, Victoria Island, British Columbia, Canada. The convention, sponsored by the Bevan Lodge Association and the British Columbia Association for Retarded Citizens, carried the theme "May We Have A Choice?" Conference participants spoke out firmly about their frustrations at being called "retarded" and being treated as though they were children their entire lives. This Canadian meeting was organized and directed by professionals, and the Oregon group returned home determined to build a self-advocacy organization that at long last would release them from the intentions of professionals, organizations, and agencies and allow them to advocate for themselves. They dreamed of holding a convention that was organized and directed by themselves, with assistance from non-disabled helpers only when requested.

---

* Material in this section was adapted from: *The Last Civil Rights Movement; Disabled Peoples International;* American Association on Mental Deficiency (1976); President's Committee on Mental Retardation (1977); Jones, L., & Barnes, P. (1987); Scheerenberger, R.C. (1983); Gould, S.J. (1981).

January 8, 1974, marks the official birth of the People First movement, as eight residents and former residents of Fairview met, officially initiated their organization, and began planning for their own convention. In many ways, the development of this self-advocacy group and organization was an outgrowth of ongoing follow-up programs for people leaving Fairview on their way to community placement. Social workers had been meeting with groups of people leaving Fairview on a weekly or monthly basis, teaching people how to listen to others, how to make decisions and solve problems, and how to develop self-assertion skills. Group homes provided natural settings for these resident's meetings and peer support groups. This "quiet revolution" had a subtle but powerful impact. These regular group meetings became the first organizational meetings for People First. Members learned decision making, organizing, the roles of officers and committees, and other organizational skills. In May, 1974, the name *People First* was born, as members planned for the upcoming convention and decided they needed a name for themselves. The name People First reflected what the members were, and how they wanted to be seen and treated. On October 12-13, 1974, the first People First convention was held at Otter Crest, a resort convention center on the Oregon coast. Over 550 people attended. People attending the convention shared powerful messages about their personal lives, their hopes and dreams. The seed for People First, planted by Oregonians, was to multiply and divide to Washington State and eventually around the world.*

A Model for Organizational Development

Alfred Katz, in his article "Self-Help Organizations and Volunteer Participation in Social Welfare" (1970), describes a model of five stages of organizational development. The history of People First of Washington closely follows these five stages:

1. *Origin:* Origin is two or more people getting together to work on a common problem. For People First of Washington, *origin* was attending the People First conference in Oregon, and returning to Washington state dedicated to start a similar organization.
2. *Informal Organizational Stage:* During this stage, ideas begin to spread among friends and other interested parties through an informal exchange of information and personal contacts.
3. *Emergence of Leadership:* During this stage, the informal group develops leaders who begin to take on the task of spreading the word and assisting the organization or concept to grow.
4. *Beginnings of Formal Operations:* During this stage, the organization develops and formalizes rules, develops goals, creates a constitution and bylaws,

* The above history of People First was taken almost in its entirety from Edwards (1982).

incorporates itself, etc.
5. *Professionalization:* During this stage, the organization obtains funding, opens an office, hires employees, and begins to use "professional methods" of operation.

People First of Washington has chosen to add a sixth stage to Katz's model:

6. *Keeping the People In Charge:* During this stage, it is important that the origin — the non-paid, "non-professional" leadership and grass-roots element of the organization — be preserved. The nature of self-advocacy demands that people with developmental disabilities speak for themselves and be in charge of their own organization.

Self-advocates must take care to insure that their organization is controlled by self-advocates and not by well-meaning professionals. The use of professional methods for fundraising, public relations, and agency operations and accountability is not totally understood or accepted by self-advocates. Using professional methods is viewed at times as a potential loss of control by self-advocates. Questions continue about self-advocates as professionals and executive directors of their own organizations, about the role of the non-disabled advisor or helper within the self-advocacy movement, and about the effectiveness of systems to insure informed choice and self-advocate control (People First of Washington, 1985, 1989).

The Early Years (1975–1980) of People First of Washington

In the late 1960s and early 1970s, Washington was like many other states in that services for people with developmental disabilities were rapidly expanding. Support for community services, as opposed to institutions, was coordinated by the Bureau of Developmental Disabilities, later to become the Division of Developmental Disabilities. In 1969, the state legislature passed the small group home law to assist people to live in the community. The Kennedy Foundation and the Special Olympics were held in 1973. The definition of mental retardation changed, abolishing the category *borderline*, and the large-scale movement of people from institutions to community living began. By 1976, the expenditures for group homes in the state of Washington was $1,952,960 for 660 residents in 48 group homes. An additional 3,500 infants and adults with developmental disabilities were supported through developmental and activity centers utilizing $4,000,000 in public funds (Tolle, 1969; Department of Social and Health Services, Bureau of Developmental Disabilities, 1976).

Federal Title XX funds were used by the Bureau of Developmental Disabilities to support community recreation and other programs. One such program was the Handicapped Adult Recreation Program in Puyallup, Washington, sponsored by the Valley School of Special Education. In 1975, Melba Grau — the administrator of Valley School of Special Education, an ARC activist, and the parent of a person with developmental disabilities — drove a van provided by the Bureau of Developmental Disabilities to the second Oregon People First Convention in Bend, Oregon, at the Inn of the Seventh Mountain. In the van was John Reid, future president of Puyallup [WA] People First, along with other future Washington People First members. This second Oregon People First convention was the origin of People First in Washington, and the seed for the development of the first People First group in Puyallup. The first group in Puyallup was closely followed by a group in Tacoma.

In Tacoma at this time, many local civil rights activities revolved around St. Leo's Catholic Church. When the church was approached as a possible meeting place for People First, support and facilities were eagerly provided. An initial meeting was planned. The Women's Auxiliary of the ARC provided a free spaghetti dinner. Employees of the Bureau of Developmental Disabilities contacted potential members. Parents and local services providers helped pass out meeting flyers and spread the word. Over 40 potential members attended this introductory meeting, and the Tacoma Chapter of People First was born. The development of the Tacoma Chapter of People First provides an excellent example of a local environment that reflected the "pioneer spirit" of the Pacific Northwest, parent advocacy, the general civil rights movement, and changing perceptions (by service providers, professionals and others) of people with disabilities, all of which created fertile ground for People First to develop and grow.

In Washington, recreation clubs served as the natural gathering places for adults with disabilities, just as the peer support groups and residents' meetings had provided the organizational groups for People First in Oregon. The first People First groups in Washington were a combination self-advocacy group/recreation club. In 1976, the Puyallup Handicapped Recreation Club changed its name to People First. A September 8, 1976, newspaper article in the *Pierce County Herald* describes the group:

> A band of Valley area developmentally disadvantaged adults have banded together to stick up for what could be called "rights for the retarded".... Some of the developmental disability rights discussed include the right to vote, to live independently, to handle money privately and to marry.... People First has been a busy club this summer. They went on a weekend camping trip to Lake Cushman State Park, fished at Westport, and camped at Cougar Rock in Mt. Rainier National Park. (1976)

Many members who became involved with People First in the self-advocacy/ recreation club era still refer to any recreation/leisure activity as a People First program. Differentiating the People First self-advocacy and business meetings, and holding the People First meetings on separate days and in different locations from other ongoing recreation/leisure activities, has helped to define more clearly what People First and self-advocacy are all about.

Meeting in a recreation setting, away from where people lived and worked, provided a good forum for people to talk about the things that were really important in their daily lives. Recreation staff were not responsible for residential or employment care or training, worked for separate agencies, and were less encumbered with potential conflicts of interest regarding people's daily lives.

Regardless of the focus of these early People First meetings, the process of people working together, sharing, speaking up for themselves, making decisions, solving problems, learning to lead, and supporting each other became the essence of what self-advocacy and People First were all about. Learning, practicing, and implementing these self-advocacy skills became the focus, whether the group was planning a recreational outing, registering people to vote, or talking about better employment and wages.

The loose network of adult recreation clubs, funded by the Bureau of Developmental Disabilities, provided the *Informal Organizational Stage* for People First (the second stage in Katz's [1970] model of organizational development). By 1977, an informal exchange of information and personal contacts between recreation club members and staff (now called *helpers* or *advisors*) quickly led to the development of People First groups in Tacoma and Olympia, Washington, which are within 30 miles of each other.

People First members continued to receive advice and information from the Oregon group, who by now had established a statewide network and organization. The People First groups in Washington had elected officers, and these officers began to meet together to discuss and plan for a statewide organization in Washington. This became the third stage in organizational development: *Emergence of Leadership.*

By now, People First in Oregon had published a handbook entitled *People First*, which was a how-to book about support groups, meetings, election of officers, seminars and workshops, conventions and core groups. The handbook describes the core group as "a combination of handicapped persons and helpers who are the foundation for the movement.... They are responsible for helping the development of local chapters and coordinating statewide activities" (People First of Oregon, 1977).

The Washington core group of leaders began to meet regularly in July of 1977. The members included Gail Maddox from Puyallup, Polly Christian from Ellensburg, Jodi Robleski from Yakima, Jack Phillips from Olympia, and Mary Hart, Mary Tyburski, and Mary Harrison from Tacoma. The agenda from the core group meeting of July 11, 1977, with Jack Phillips from Olympia as Pro-tem Chair of Washington State People First, included:

1. goals of People First
2. purpose of People First
3. what our state committee should be called
4. the regional meeting in Oregon
5. how to organize a local People First

The Washington core group continued to meet regularly and carry out its stated goals of organizing a state chapter. It communicated with other communities to help get People First groups going, used the radio, newspaper, and TV to inform the public about People First, and organized a state convention (People First of Washington, 1977). A listing of actual and potential People First chapters now numbered 10.

The fourth stage of organizational development, *Beginnings of Formal Operations*, was now taking place. Clearly stated goals were developed, rules for working together were established, agendas were published and minutes of meetings kept. The Puyallup chapter established bylaws for themselves to include purpose, goals, officers, duties of officers, and general club rules. The core group was now called the Executive Committee.

After over a year of planning, the first People First of Washington State Convention was held August 25-26, 1978, in Olympia, Washington. Convention workshops included "We've Got Something to Offer" and "What is People First?" This convention was informational in nature. Although discussions were held about forming a statewide group, there was no formal action taken and no election of officers, since the core group/executive committee felt strongly about the process of developing more local chapters and grass-roots participation before the establishment of a statewide organization.

People First of Washington was now gaining recognition and status within the state. Other groups began to take notice. A letter from the President of the King County [Seattle] ARC, dated August 14, 1978, states, "King County ARC feels strongly that the time has come when the ARC movement must look to developmentally disabled consumers for input concerning programs and services which affect their lives." The letter goes on to suggest that designating a spot on the ARC board of directors is not the best method for accomplishing this goal, since consumers would "...be forced into the position of not being able to follow the line of reasoning, being asked to or being expected to make input on issues they have not understood, or having to vote on issues that pertain to fiscal, governmental, community relations or other related matters." Although the State ARC ultimately did designate a position on its board of directors, People First declined and responded to the ARC by stating that "...while People First was concerned about consumer representation, we feel that we must first develop and strengthen our own organization before determining our relationship with other organizations." People First members and advisors were right to be concerned with their own organizational development and autonomy — and concerned about tokenism and co-option by the ARC. The ARC had made a similar decision many years ago when deciding to establish their own organization as opposed to being a division of the American Association on Mental Deficiency.

During 1979, People First of Washington held its second convention. State officers were elected and formally charged with developing a state organization with incorporation, bylaws, and funding. Jim Novak, from Tacoma, was the first State President for People First of Washington. The officers elected were President, Vice-President, Secretary, Treasurer, Western Washington Representative, and Eastern Washington Representative. The representative positions were established to ensure that rural eastern Washington had a voice in People First and would not be outvoted by the large cities in western Washington.

In April of 1979, People First of Washington held a Learning Workshop (Leadership Retreat). This was to become an annual event where each local chapter sent representatives to develop leadership skills and leaders from across the state could meet to discuss and plan the business and future of the organization. Still coupled with the self-advocacy/recreation club model, the Learning Workshop included organizational business and seminars on equal rights, public speaking, dressing for success, interpersonal relationships, beginning camping and hiking, and a forest and beach walk. The workshop was held in a state park with cabins where participants as a group cooked meals, cleaned up, held evening campfires, and engaged in other group activities that fostered friendship, cooperation, unity, and *esprit de corps*.

As the organization grew, it became increasingly difficult for volunteers to manage its affairs, answer all the requests for assistance and information, and coordinate statewide activities. People First of Washington submitted a grant proposal to the state's Developmental Disabilities Planning Council (DDPC) for funding to open an office and hire an employee to assist in conducting the affairs of the organization. State DDPCs had been established through federal legislation and funding, and among other things were charged with providing seed money for innovative programs, model program development, and other activities. This same federal legislation also authorized state Protection and Advocacy agencies to provide individual and systems advocacy for people with developmental disabilities and their families. The director of the state Protection and Advocacy agency felt that self-advocacy was a logical extension of the agency's mandate, and that funding and coordination of self-advocacy should run through the agency. The Protection and Advocacy agency was successful in blocking funding from the state DDPC for one year, until these politics could be worked out. Once again, the autonomy and self-control of self-advocacy by people with developmental disabilities had been threatened. People First persisted and submitted a second grant proposal to the DDPC during 1980. This grant was funded. People First was able to control its own future, the stage was set to open a People First office, and the beginnings of the *Use of Professional Methods* (Katz's fifth stage of organizational development) began.

Coming of Age: People First of Washington, 1981

In January, 1981, People First of Washington opened its office in Tacoma, Washington, using funds from the state Developmental Disabilities Planning Council. A committee composed of Mike Raymond, who was now the State President, hired a paid state advisor to assist the organization to grow and develop. Bob Furman, who was an advisor with People First of Oregon, was hired for this position. A *Washington People First Newsletter* was started to increase communication between chapters and provide information on state activities. The People First state officers and the newly hired state advisor began to actively organize People First chapters across the state. By the end of 1981, there were 17 active local chapters. The opening of a state office, a paid employee, and formal operations made 1981 a very significant year in the history of People First of Washington. It had taken seven years of slow growth with membership and leadership development to reach this stage. The organization was a grass-roots movement that was coming of age.

That year also marked the United Nations International Year of Disabled Persons — later the International Decade of Disabled Persons. People First leaders from Oregon, Washington and British Columbia had been meeting for over a year to plan for an international convention to celebrate the United Nations Year and the growth of People First. Meetings to plan the convention were held in Salem, Oregon; Tacoma, Washington; and Vancouver, British Columbia. A Pacific Northwest network of People First activists was formed. As the only organization with paid staff, People First of Washington played a major role in putting this convention together.

A pre-convention retreat was held before the 1981 People First International Convention. People First leaders from California, Colorado, Michigan, Montana, Oregon, Washington, and British Columbia met for 3 days to share ideas and develop strategies and goals. Nine goals were developed at this pre-convention retreat, and ratified by the over 1,200 People First members who attended the International Convention on July 4-6, 1981, in Portland, Oregon. These nine goals marked a significant increase in the civil rights and social justice aspects of the People First Movement. While retaining the support group and recreation club aspects, People First became formally involved in the civil rights movement and politics.

The nine goals developed by People First leaders in 1981 were:

1. making local chapters stronger
2. officer and leadership training
3. reaching out to people with severe or multiple disabilities
4. getting People First members on boards, committees, and other positions of power where decisions are made
5. public awareness

6. to react to and fight state and federal budget cuts [Ronald Reagan had recently been elected]
7. getting real jobs with real wages
8. community housing and closing the state institutions
9. communication and information-sharing

These nine goals continue to define the People First movement and reflect a realistic concern for strong local chapters, leadership development, sharing information, and political activity as the ways to achieve the human and civil rights goals of the People First movement. The 1981 People First International Convention also marked the true international development of People First. The theme for the convention was "International Independence for All."

In an article entitled "Growing is Green," Charlotte Clark, who attended the pre-convention retreat from Denver, Colorado, wrote:

> I love green. Green reminds me of growth. I love plants. I love to watch plants grow, to watch them develop, and to see them reach their full potential when they bloom.... The convention and the retreat were incredible, once-in-a-lifetime experiences. For me and for People First, there will be other conventions, and hopefully other retreats. This one will always stand out as special. People First as an organization grew. I saw other individuals growing before my very eyes. It was definitely a growing experience for me.... If I appear to be slightly green these days, I'm not jealous, I'm growing!

During 1981, Maxine Crocker, a People First member from Olympia, was appointed to the Governor's Committee on Employment of the Handicapped. Maxine was the first person with a developmental disability to be so honored. Maxine reported back to the Washington core group that the Governor's Committee was getting involved in proposed legislation and that People First should get involved as well. Later that year, Paul Johnson, from Olympia People First, and Mike Raymond, from Tacoma People First, testified at the state legislature. People First was involved politically.

Paul Johnson was appointed as a consumer representative to the state Developmental Disabilities Planning Council at the end of 1981, and Susan Teague from Tacoma was appointed to the County Developmental Disabilities Administrative Board. People First members were becoming involved on decision-making bodies.

Robert Bouton and Janice Marker of People First in Tacoma spoke with elementary school students about People First and people with disabilities during 1981. People First was getting involved with public and community awareness.

The grant from the state Developmental Disabilities Planning Council also allowed People First of Washington to develop a People First Handbook during

1981. This handbook included the following chapters: Introduction to People First, Self-Advocacy and How People First Works, How to Start a People First Group, How to Be a Good People First Officer, How to Have Successful Meetings, How to Handle the Chapter's Money, How to Set Goals and Get Things Done, Public Relations/Public Awareness, and Hints for Helpers. This handbook expanded and formalized materials developed by People First of Oregon. The handbook and revisions have been used by self-advocacy groups around the world.

During 1981, People First of Washington formally incorporated and received IRS tax-exempt status. The Board of Directors established rules for chartering chapters to be official and legal parts of People First of Washington. People First received an award from the ARC of King County (Seattle) during 1981 in recognition of its outstanding work. During 1981, People First of Washington, and the People First Movement, formally came of age.

The Maturation of People First of Washington, 1982-1990

We're Handicapable, Not Handicapped
We're handicapable, not handicapped.
Is there anyone out there really listening to what we've got to say?
We're handicapable, not handicapped.
We are capable of living on our own or get married if we choose.
We're handicapable, not handicapped.
Is anyone out there really listening to what we've got to say?
— Terrie Erwin, Seattle People First, 1982

Having come of age during 1981, the self-advocacy movement, People First of Washington, and indeed self-advocacy organizations across the United States, Canada, England, and other countries, matured and continued to implement and institutionalize self-advocacy. In the state of Washington, this maturation took several forms: (1) developing a stable and diversified funding base, (2) building support for local chapters, (3) impacting decision makers, (4) developing self-advocacy materials, and (5) organizing the national and international movement.

DEVELOPING A STABLE AND DIVERSIFIED FUNDING BASE
The initial state Developmental Disabilities Planning Council Grant for 1981 had been for $9,000. The council, heartened by the success of People First, agreed to include $30,000 for each of the next three years for People First as part of the council's three-year plan. The State DD Planning Council had historically funded projects at much higher rates ($75,000 to $150,000) for much shorter periods of time (12 to 18 months). People First convinced the council that a smaller amount of stable funding over a longer period of time would allow People First more time

to mature and access other sources of funding. During 1982, People First obtained a three-year grant from the Campaign for Human Development (CHD), an action-education program, sponsored by the Catholic Bishops of the United States. Since its inception, CHD has funded projects throughout the country which attack the basic causes of poverty and empower the poor. CHD realized that the self-advocacy movement and empowerment of people with developmental disabilities was similar to the more traditional civil rights and anti-poverty projects they funded. CHD believed in grass-roots community organizing and gave People First a free hand to use funding for this purpose. CHD provided funding of $50,000 during 1982-1983, $45,000 during 1984-1985, and $40,000 during 1986-1987. The CHD funds, combined with State DD Planning Council funds, grass-root fundraising of $15,000 per year, and small grants from local United Way and other organizations, provided a stable and more diversified funding base during 1982-1990.

BUILDING SUPPORT FOR LOCAL CHAPTERS AND THE PEOPLE FIRST MODEL OF SELF-ADVOCACY

> Reaching a hand out in friendship.
> Helping someone along the way.
> Saying you can do it,
> Give it a try.
> By helping others, I help myself,
> It's a feeling I just can't explain.
> Seeing the person hidden way down beneath,
> Reaching out for someone to hold.
> Looking beyond the handicap
> To a person whose willing to learn
> And understand why.
> I give my hand out in friendship
> And help whenever I can
> To help others stand up for their rights
> And beliefs
> And shout out with a great big
> HURRAH
> We are PEOPLE FIRST!
>
> — Carol Bonson, Clarkston People First, 1983

While the state office continued to coordinate statewide events, such as the Leadership Retreat, State Convention, Newsletter, support for members who served on statewide decision-making bodies, and so on, People First used its increased funding base to open regional offices in Spokane and Seattle.

The regional offices brought increased supports for self-advocacy closer to the local level. The People First model for self-advocacy was implemented. This model focused attention on the local chapter as the forum for individual and group self-advocacy. Local chapters elected their own officers and set their own chapter goals and agendas. Regional meetings provided a forum for chapters close to one another to share ideas and information, and attend education and leadership seminars. State leadership retreats and conventions provided the forum for local leaders and members from across the state to meet. National conferences and conventions provided a national forum for "speaking up and speaking out." People First believed in developing leadership and ideas from the grass-roots up, and in the importance of the local chapter for a strong statewide organization. By 1990, there were 32 local chapters in the state of Washington.

A significant step in organizing Washington People First occurred in 1982 with the development of the United Cerebral Palsy (UCP) chapter. People First has always stated that it is a self-advocacy organization of people with *developmental disabilities*. The UCP chapter was indeed composed of people with developmental disabilities — in the form of severe physical disabilities, but not necessarily people with mental retardation. The UCP group wanted to make sure People First was comprised of people with developmental disabilities, and set about educating the rest of the membership who thought that people who used wheelchairs were the ones with handicaps. This slow education process continues, and it continues to open the doors for cross-disability cooperation. The inclusion of the UCP chapter and other chapters composed of people with physical or multiple developmental disabilities made People First stronger and truly an organization comprised of people with a variety of developmental disabilities. Good cooperation and coordination across disability groups remains an incomplete dream.

IMPACTING DECISION MAKERS

> Speaking up and speaking out is self-advocacy. Making your own decisions, being more independent. Standing up on your own two feet and sticking up for your rights is self-advocacy.... Just being good citizens in our communities, people will learn to respect us and our ideas. People will see us as more important and maybe they will let us become friends. This will help us make our voices count as real people.... Don't be afraid to stand up and speak up, and tell people what you really think about things. Be strong and proud for each other.... Keep your chin up, your eyes straight ahead, stand tall....
>
> — Betty Sutton, Walla Walla People First, 1984

The funding from the Campaign for Human Development was also used to hire several members to work for the organization, including Paul Johnson who was hired as the People First legislative analyst. Over the next three years, Paul organized voter education workshops and represented and facilitated the involvement of local chapter members of People First at the state legislature. People First began to have an annual Legislative Rally and invite politicians to local, regional and statewide meetings. People First also joined several legislative advocacy coalitions covering a broad range of advocacy concerns from Section 8 housing, welfare reform, and fair budget action to programs and services for people with developmental disabilities.

People First members became involved with local, regional, state, and national decision-making bodies, conferences, and conventions. Members attended PASS (Program Analysis of Service Systems) workshops facilitated by John O'Brien and Connie Lyle O'Brien. Betty Sutton, from Walla Walla, joined the state ARC board in 1982, as People First was now strong enough to support relationships with other organizations. Ginny Sellman, from Seattle, and Susan Teague, from Tacoma, presented at the 6th World Congress of the International League of Societies for Persons with Mental Handicaps in Toronto, Canada.

People First joined in several *amicus* ("friend of the court") briefs before the Supreme Court of the United States on issues such as zoning laws for group homes, the right to medical treatment (Baby Doe), and others. People First members participated on the State DD Planning Council, the Governor's Committee on Employment of the Handicapped, the Disabilities Research and Information Coalition, the Washington Assembly for Citizens with Disabilities, and numerous other local and state organization decision-making bodies. Almost every conference about people with disabilities included representation and presentations by People First members. People First members from Washington continued to attend the Oregon, British Columbia, and other states' People First conventions to share ideas and information.

DEVELOPING SELF-ADVOCACY MATERIALS

What People First Means To Alot Of Us

People First lets us get out more, and make friends, so we don't get lonely. We learn alot from our organization. We get over being shy, we learn to make speeches and to speak out more. We learn about being on different boards of directors. We learn to help each other and to get along with others. People First has done alot for me. I have learned alot being on the board of directors and the personnel policies committee. It has made me not to be afraid to speak up and speak out. People First has helped me to grow alot. In People First I have been able to help another chapter and their problems. In People First I have learned how to be three different kinds of officers. Our State President, Kyle Matheson is going to teach me about being a President.

— Ginny Sellman, State Vice-President, 1984-86,

State President 1986-88

To support the growth and development of self-advocacy and local chapters, People

First expanded materials developed under the 1981 state DD Planning Grant. During 1982-1990, People First of Washington completely revised and published the People First Handbook on how to start and support self-advocacy groups. Self-advocacy materials on **Assertiveness, Voter Education, Participation in Your Individual Service Plan (ISP), What We Want From Residential Programs, The Worker's Handbook, How To Rent An Apartment, The Role of the People First Advisor,** and other materials were developed. The materials were shared with other self-advocacy groups around the world and became the best information available about self-advocacy. People First of Washington actively sought information and materials about self-advocacy from other groups and became the informal national self-advocacy clearinghouse of information. The Washington People First files contain letters from all 50 states and over 25 different countries who requested and received information about People First.

Seminars from the 10th Washington People First Convention, 1987
- People First & Citizenship
- Residential Programs — What You Need To Know
- Employment — What You Need To Know: Real Jobs and Real Wages
- Leadership Development
- Resident's Rights Video & Discussion
- The Art of Fundraising
- What People First Means to Me: Open Microphone
- Exploding the Myths about People with Disabilities

Organizing the National and International Movement

Following the successful 1981 International Independence for All conference in Portland, the continued expansion of the People First movement around the world, and the increasing role of People First of Washington as the informal national/international clearinghouse on self-advocacy, a dream began of organizing a truly international People First convention. *Speaking Up and Speaking Out: The International Self-Advocacy Leadership Conference* was held July 23-29, 1984, in Tacoma, Washington. People First of Washington began to plan the conference in the fall of 1982. Eight conference co-sponsors were recruited: the Campaign for Mentally Handicapped People, London, England; the Massachusetts Coalition of Citizens with Disabilities; People First of Oregon; People First of Nebraska; Reinforce — The Australian Union of Intellectually Disadvantaged Citizens; United Together; and People First of Washington. During the summer of 1983, questionnaires were sent and received from all the co-sponsors to decide on the conference theme, date, costs, location, and other details. Questionnaires were also sent to every self-advocacy group that was known, to get their ideas and willingness to lead seminars, etc.

After 18 months of planning, self-advocates from Australia, New Zealand, Canada, England and 21 states arrived in Tacoma. The conference covered self-advocacy from A to Z and included information and presentations for people who were just learning about self-advocacy, as well as groups who had already established statewide organizations. John O'Brien and Connie Lyle led a seminar for self-advocates on evaluating services, while information was translated into French for Denis LaRoche, who would eventually become the President of People First of Canada.

A book (now out of print) entitled *Speaking Up and Speaking Out* was written by People First of Washington (1985) with assistance from the Research and Training Center at the University of Oregon. This conference and the conference book were the impetus for the development of many self-advocacy groups around the world. During the conference, People First of Washington received the first Award for Self-Advocacy from the International League of Societies for Persons with Mental Handicaps, presented by Rosemary Dybwad. The International League has been very helpful and supportive of self-advocacy around the world.

At the end of the conference, people voted to meet again in four years in London, England. This conference was held in 1988 with the involvement of more countries. The Third International People First Conference was held in June 1993 in Toronto, Ontario, and was attended by 1,300 self-advocates representing 33 countries. What was born in Oregon has truly become an International Movement.

On the national level, People First of Washington was working with many other organizations to form a national self-advocacy organization in the United States. Leaders from the key self-advocacy organizations met in Atlanta, Georgia, in May 1990 to talk about effective self-advocacy and the dream of a national organization. Speaking For Ourselves of Colorado took the lead in organizing the First North American People First and Self-Advocacy Conference, in Estes Park, Colorado, in September 1990. The theme for this conference was "A Voice In The Community." A framework for a national self-advocacy organization was worked out at this conference. A Second Annual North American People First Conference was held in Nashville in September 1991, where other details were voted upon. Members of People First of Washington played important roles in both of these conferences and in the development of what is now called Self-Advocates Becoming Empowered. The birth of this national self-advocacy organization is described in detail elsewhere in this book.

The period from 1982 to 1990 was a time of maturation for People First of Washington. Members were speaking up and speaking out, and participating in ways that were not dreamed of a few short years before. As an organization, People First of Washington had come of age, matured, stabilized, and participated in the development of self-advocacy around the world. During this time period, People First of Washington was widely held up as the international model for self-advocacy. This period of maturity and stability was to be tested with the coming of the 1990s.

Growing Pains: People First of Washington, 1990+

The first signs of growing pains had developed in 1986, with a change of staff in the state advisor's position. The first paid state advisor had been with the organization for over five years and had guided People First through its "coming of age" and the first half of its "maturation period." The board of People First was hesitant to hire someone who was unknown to the organization, even a person with good backgrounds and skills. Having developed a personal and trusting relationship with board members appeared to be more important than having the skills for administering complex organizational needs. The board was divided between two candidates. One was an advisor for a local chapter; the other was the director of the Seattle Regional People First office. An outside consultant was called in. Eventually, Karen Ritter, the local chapter advisor, was selected. Karen guided People First through four good years of growth and maturation. Hard feelings remained, however, over the selection process. These hard feelings spilled over from the board to other members and local chapters. It became increasingly difficult to manage the complex affairs of People First. There were over 30 local chapters, a state office and two regional offices, constant efforts to maintain and expand funding, and increasing requests and demands from People First members and local chapters placed on the organization. The organization was being stretched to the limits. By 1990, the dream of a self-advocacy organization was now coping with the real-world realities of funding, differing opinions, a large and geographically dispersed constituency, accountability, and increasing demands on the organization.

In 1990, after four relatively stable years, Karen Ritter left People First in good shape to pursue other employment. A new paid state advisor was hired. This advisor also had been a local chapter advisor. He resigned after less than six months on the job. In the interim period, funding was lost for the Seattle Regional Office and the employees there formed a new self-advocacy organization, further polarizing the board and membership. Another new paid state advisor was hired. He resigned after less than a year on the job. The rapid change in paid state advisors was taking its toll. The board of directors was having to spend most of its time hiring and transitioning from one employee to another, while other important business languished. Funding became tighter — not because of the difficulties being experienced by People First, but by the general recession in the United States: cutbacks in federal and state budgets and competing priorities for funding. Funding sources lost interest in funding ongoing grass-roots self-advocacy organizing and local chapter development, and instead became more interested in more specific time-limited projects. The third paid state advisor in less than two years was hired in December 1991, and continues as the state advisor today. Currently, the board of directors is divided over the performance of the paid state advisor, and a great deal of time and energy is again being diverted from the ongoing business of self-advocacy to resolving this situation.

The difficulties experienced by People First may be typical for any organization that experiences rapid growth in a short period of time. As more and more people become involved, greater differences of opinion emerge. Members can become dependent on paid staff for functions that were once performed by the volunteers. As organizations grow, the complex realities of maintaining an organization can weigh down the original dream. The use of professional methods can make members feel unneeded or incapable of managing the affairs of the organization, or make members feel less in control of the one organization that is truly theirs. A large and geographically diverse membership strains organizational resources, especially in times of increasing competition for funding. Change is difficult, and People First was having to adapt to change.

SUCCESSFUL CHAPTERS IN THE 1990S

Most of the difficulties experienced by People First of Washington during the 1990s were confined to the board of directors, the paid state advisors and a dozen or so members interested in state office politics. Local chapters just kept on meeting. At this time, the strength of most local chapters was not based on having a strong state office. Many local chapters had now been meeting for 10-15 years, and continued to conduct their business. In fact, many members and local chapters grew stronger as a result of the difficulties experienced by the state organization. Members began to speak up more strongly than ever, to support each other, and to discuss different options and strategies to solve the problems. Members were not going to give up on People First because of the difficulties being experienced at the state level. Some chapters in King County (Seattle) who had left the organization over disputes about past paid state advisors rejoined the organization. People First had always believed that the strength of the organization lay in strong local chapters, and many local chapters are showing their own internal strength.

Tacoma, Puyallup, and Bremerton are good examples of strong local chapters that have grown and thrived for over 15 years and continue to thrive today. The success of these and other strong local chapters is based upon:

1. A core of members who have remained involved for 15 or more years and developed leadership and self-advocacy skills.
2. The ability of new members to be recognized as leaders and join with the core members.
3. The stability and reliability of advisors, many of whom have been involved for 15 or more years.
4. The development of a community of friends who support People First — who don't regularly attend local chapter meetings, but are available to support members or chapters when needed.
5. A communication network between the three chapters — in essence, there is a core group composed of members, advisors, and friends from the three

chapters. This core group call each other regularly to share ideas and information and meet 3 or 4 times a year to plan and organize regional meetings and other regional activities.

6. The availability of transportation and local grass-roots fundraising to support chapter activities.

7. A trusting relationship between members, advisors, and others, where debate can occur, and *the members remain in charge*.

ACCOMPLISHMENTS DURING THE 1990S

During the 1990s, People First of Washington members have been very involved in
two programs: Informed Choice, and Quality Assurances. Informed Choice involved a grant to People First from the state Division of Developmental Disabilities. This grant paid People First to provide informed choice for people who were
moving out of the state institutions. People First members, each paired with a
volunteer recruited and trained by People First, met with people who wanted to
leave the state institutions, and advocated with the person for the development of
the community supports that the person desired and needed for success. Quality
Assurances involved teams composed of People First members and others who
visited with people who had left the state institutions, to insure they were receiving
the quality of supports they desired and needed. In essence, one group of People
First member was advocating with people to move out of institutions, and another
group of members was assuring that these people were receiving the supports they
needed to thrive and grow in the community after leaving the institution. Informed
Choice and Quality Assurances, along with legislative advocacy, are ways that People
First of Washington is working to slowly close the state institutions and provide
choices and quality in community living.

During the 1990s, People First of Washington continues to have regional meetings, a newsletter, an annual leadership retreat, and a state convention. The State Developmental Disabilities Planning Council continues to fund People First of Washington, although the funding is now used by People First to provide technical
assistance and support to people with disabilities who serve on the DD Council
and other decision-making bodies, as opposed to developing and supporting local
chapters. Obtaining funding for the ongoing development and support of local
chapters remains difficult.

GRANTS OF NATIONAL SIGNIFICANCE

In September, 1990, People First of Washington received a two-year grant of na-
tional significance from the federal Administration on Developmental Disabilities
(ADD). To our knowledge, this is the first direct U.S. government funding for self-
advocacy. This grant was co-sponsored by People First of Nebraska; Speaking for
Ourselves of Philadelphia, PA; People First of Tennessee; the Center on Human
Policy in Syracuse, NY; the Institute on Community Living in Minneapolis, MN;

and the national ARC. This ADD grant researched self-advocacy "best practices" across the United States. Each of the grant co-sponsors received a subcontract from People First of Washington to research self-advocacy best practices in their geographic area. A mailing list of all known self-advocacy groups and self-advocacy materials was developed. Technical assistance about self-advocacy was provided to over 200 organizations and individuals across the United States. This grant allowed People First of Washington to truly become the national clearinghouse of information about self-advocacy and to assist in the growth and development of many self-advocacy groups. The book *No More B.S.! – A Realistic Survival Guide for Disability Rights Activists* was published at the conclusion of the grant. (This excellent book is available for $10 from People First of Washington, P.O. Box 648, Clarkston, WA 99403.)

Following completion of the ADD grant, People First of Washington was awarded a three-year grant from the federal Department of Education to develop self-advocacy materials and training for people with disabilities in high school. This grant has just begun and is helping to fulfill a People First dream of reaching out to high school students. Self-advocacy skills are needed by all people, regardless of whether they choose to join a self-advocacy group. This grant will also allow for the development of new young leadership within the self-advocacy movement. A similar grant was awarded to People First of Tennessee. These grants signify that People First members are now being recognized as good teachers for others!

Epilogue

People First of Washington is proud of its role in fostering self-advocacy in the state of Washington and, indeed, around the world. Since the beginnings of People First in Salem, Oregon, in 1973, the self-advocacy movement has spread around the world. The 3rd International People First Conference, held in Toronto, Ontario, in June 1993 was attended by self-advocates from 33 different countries. A self-advocacy "United Nations" was held, where self-advocates described similar struggles to gain recognition, respect, and the opportunity to live, work, participate, and contribute in the community. No one who attended will forget this "United Nations" of self-advocacy, the Parade of Nations during the Opening Ceremonies, or the opportunity to share struggles and successes. A 1998 International People First Conference has already been scheduled for April 23–28, in Anchorage, Alaska. For information, write to People First International, P.O. Box 143062, Anchorage, AK 99514.

Self-advocacy has come a long way, but there is an equally long – if not longer – way to go. Besides overcoming negative community perceptions about people with disabilities, an awesome task in its own right, some self-advocacy groups continue to face organizational and growth problems. People First of Washington has faced serious difficulties during the '90s, leading some Board members to sue the organization over policy and control issues. One quarter of the membership left People First of Washington over this issue in 1993 and formed a new organization, Self Advocates of Washington. Managing a large organization was proving difficult. Some self-advocacy groups, such as Speaking for Ourselves in Pennsylvania and Advocating Change Together (ACT) in Minnesota, have purposely stayed small to insure local control and involvement and keep their organizations manageable. Small may indeed be "beautiful."

Recruiting new and younger membership is also an issue for the future. The majority of self-advocates are "fortysomething," as with the general population. A new generation of people with disabilities, who have not been exposed to institutionalization and who have received far better educational and other services, is coming of age. Their issues and expectations are different.

Real power and control for self-advocates remains elusive. In most instances, self-advocates have not achieved the "Degrees of Citizen Participation" (citizen control, delegated power, partnership) described by Sherry R. Arnstein (1969) and remain under "Degrees of Tokenism" (placation, consultation, informing). Changing society's perceptions of people with disabilities is a long-term struggle, as other civil rights movements have discovered. It is to be expected that as self-advocates begin to change perceptions and increase their power base, other groups will fight back to maintain the status quo. Dennis Heath, the founding advisor with People First of Oregon, has described self-advocacy as "an evolutionary movement." The movement continues to evolve, and self-advocates continue on the long road toward acceptance and full participation as contributing citizens.

Being a part of People First of Washington, Self-Advocates of Washington, and the civil rights movement by people with developmental disabilities has been — and continues to be — one of the most exciting and inspirational events in my life. I have received so much from people who have historically been given so little. Self-advocacy is a movement for civil and human rights, for equal opportunity, for a chance to be present, participate, and contribute. I urge all people to get involved. If you can't be involved with a self-advocacy group, just help to welcome our citizens with disabilities in the communities where they live and work.

References

American Association on Mental Deficiency (1976). *A Century of Concern: A History of the American Association on Mental Deficiency 1876-1976.*

Arnstein, S.R. (1969). The right rungs on a ladder of citizen participation. *AIP Journal*, July, pp. 216-224.

Department of Social and Health Services, Bu-

reau of Developmental Disabilities (1976). Proviso #17, Group Home and Developmental Centers Programs.

Edwards, J.P. (1982). *We are people first: Our handicaps are secondary.* Ednick, Inc.

Gould, S.J. (1981). *The mismeasure of man.* Norton & Co.

Jones, L., & Barnes, P. (1987). *Doing justice: A his-*

tory of the Association for Retarded Citizens of Washington (p. 2). Seattle: The Arc of Washington.

Katz, A. (1970). Self-help organizations and volunteer participation in social welfare. *Social Work, 15*(1), 51-60.

People First of Oregon (1977). *People first.* Portland, OR: Author.

People First of Washington (1977). Minutes from August 4, 1977, core group meeting.

People First of Washington (1985). *Speaking up and speaking out: An international self-advocacy movement.* Seattle: Author.

People First of Washington (1990). *A short history of People First of Washington.* Seattle: Author.

Pierce County Herald, September 8, 1976.

President's Committee on Mental Retardation (1977). *MR 76: Mental Retardation: Past and Present.*

Scheerenberger, R.C. (1983). *A history of mental retardation.* Brooks Publishing.

Tolle, M. (1969). *A brief history of the development of programs for the care and treatment of the mentally retarded in Washington.*

16

People First of Nebraska

8 Years of Accomplishments

Nancy Ward & Bonnie Shoultz

NANCY WARD has had a long involvement with self-advocacy. She is the paid staff person (Self-Advocacy Organizer) for People First of Nebraska, and gives presentations nationally on self-advocacy. BONNIE SHOULTZ was a state advisor of People First of Nebraska until she moved to Syracuse. Nancy and Bonnie worked together, along with many other people, to create People First of Nebraska. This chapter* is an interview that is also a dialogue between them. In some cases, names of people and places mentioned by Nancy were removed from the final transcript, and in a few places minor changes were made in the order in which statements appeared. Other than that, this is a transcript of their discussion.

BS: What do you remember about the early history of the Nebraska self-advocacy movement?

NW: I remember that it was started in Omaha by a gentleman whose name was Ray Loomis, and he had been in Beatrice, which is our institution, and he wanted to have a way to get support. I think it was 1975. So he and some of his friends formed a "rap group," and they called it Project Two. Should I say why?

* Preparation of this chapter was supported in part by the U.S. Department of Education, Office of Special Education and Rehabilitative Services, National Institute on Disability and Rehabilitation Research (NIDRR) under Cooperative Agreement No. H133B00003-90 awarded to the Center on Human Policy, School of Education, Syracuse University and Cooperative Agreement No. H133B80048 under a subcontract from the Research and Training Center on Community Living at the University of Minnesota. The opinions expressed herein are those solely of the authors, and no official endorsement by the U.S. Department of Education should be inferred.

BS: Yes, if you want to.

NW: Well, it was called Project Two because ENCOR, which is the Eastern Nebraska Community Office of Retardation, was "Project One" in Ray's mind. Then they had this group, but they didn't know they were doing self-advocacy until they saw a film that was done by People First of Oregon about People First. Then they decided that Nebraska should have a People First also. So that's how it came into being. Does that answer your question?

BS: Yes. At first People First was an idea in their mind, that they wanted something statewide, and then it became a reality. Do you remember how it became a reality? Were you involved when it was decided that there should be a statewide organization and it should incorporate and write bylaws? When a group of people met to do the bylaws and the incorporation? Wasn't that when it became a reality?

NW: Yes. Because we had had conventions before that, but they were really conventions of local groups getting together. It wasn't a statewide organization until later. I think you're right, that that was when it became a statewide organization. I remember I was really excited, because David Finkelstein and Steve Richards and I were the ones who signed the incorporation papers. We were all involved in doing the first bylaws and we were on the first Board of Directors. That was in 1985.

BS: What do you remember about those days?

NW: People were trying real hard to be able to work with all the chapters, and to learn how to network, and to work together as a team. Because people had never been part of a statewide organization before. All we ever had to worry about before was our own chapter.

BS: Let's back up a little. Would you tell us about your chapter and how your chapter fit in with all this, and how you fit in with your chapter?

NW: This is going to be hard, because it's my own perspective.

BS: That's okay, this is your chapter.

NW: Okay. Well, I think Advocacy First of Lincoln has always been a strong chapter, and has always been a strong link for People First of Nebraska. One year, while we were forming, all four of the officers were from Advocacy First of Lincoln. That's why we have in our bylaws now that there can only be two from any specific chapter. Advocacy First of Lincoln has bylaws, and People First of Nebraska used our bylaws for ideas.

BS: I remember sitting in those meetings with the lawyer from Nebraska Advocacy Services and all of you, and all of us trying to figure out what you wanted to say.

NW: Yes, and that was hard. It's hard because even though our bylaws are written so that we can understand them, and I think most People First bylaws are written so you can understand them, they're still complicated because of all the different things you have to put in them. So if you don't know what you need to put in bylaws, that makes it hard, working out what we needed to have in there. Like how we were going to handle the voting, because at first people didn't know about doing motions and all that stuff. Or what officers we would have and how long their terms would be. And then plug all that stuff in where it's supposed to go.

So you kind of do it piece by piece, and that makes it hard because you don't have the end result yet. You don't see it completed until it is completed, so when you are doing it it's like you are piecing it together. That makes it real difficult, because you don't know how it's going to go into the next thing.

BS: And have you changed the bylaws since then?

NW: Yes. Our officers now do two years. I shouldn't say just officers, it's the whole board. Before it was one year.

BS: Was that something you learned by experience you needed to have?

NW: Yes. I really feel it's made a difference. Because people are just learning the first year. In the second year, people know how to contribute, and they don't feel intimidated about saying how they feel.

BS: Can you tell me some things that People First of Nebraska has done?

NW: Yes. One year, we didn't get to have a convention because the person who had always helped us do the convention went to Australia with a member of Project Two. Since she had always organized the whole convention for us, we didn't have one that year. That was 1981. A lot of us were really upset, because we wanted to be able to have a convention, so then we decided that we should be able to do this ourselves. So that's one of the things that People First of Nebraska is real proud of, because I don't think there is any other state where the convention is completely planned by the members.

BS: How does the convention planning go?

NW: Our conventions are in October. In May every year the board does the convention planning. The hotel that we are going to have the convention at will give us rooms to stay overnight in and a room to meet in, and we plan. We plan the theme for the convention, and then we plan who the keynote speakers are going to be, and that's changed over the years because now we have three plenary sessions. And then we decide what other sessions we want, and who the speakers will be. Each of the chapters is responsible for at least one session, and some chapters do two, depending on what they want. We work all that out, and then we do the menu, and who we're going to have for the DJ, and the lifeguards. The lifeguards are for the pool, because hotels don't provide lifeguards, and one year somebody had a seizure in the pool.

We also decide how we're going to do the business meeting. We have President's Report and Secretary's Report and Treasurer's Report, and any other business that we want to discuss. We have what we call "Open Mike" at the business meeting. The business meeting is also where we have elections. I should go back and say that the way we do elections is, we send nomination forms out ahead of time, and people nominate people, and put down why they think the person would be a good person for the office. Their chapter nominates them. The four officers are all from different places. That represents four chapters, and then each of the other chapters has a representative on the Board. That makes it hard, because if your chapter has someone running for an office, you have to take that into consideration. Like, if you have somebody running for an office, you don't know that they will get that office, and you might want to have someone as an alternate running for a place on the board.

BS: So how many people might run from an individual chapter for the board?

NW: You could potentially have somebody for each office, and then since the President is elected first, if the person that your chapter nominated got the President position, that would knock out the other three. It's the highest office on down.

BS: Would that also knock out the person from that chapter who was just running for a board slot?

NW: Yes. And that way, because we're getting so many chapters, we don't have such a big board. And it was also done for fairness. If you have more than one person from a chapter on the board, they could have three votes. The way we did it before, your chapter could have two officers and one representative, so they could have three votes. Now it's just one, and that makes it more fair to everybody.

BS: Once the officers are elected at the conference, are the other board members pretty well set because they are selected by their chapter?

NW: Right, because who better knows the person than their chapter?

BS: Well, that is a big change from the old days, because I remember when people got nominated right at the convention.

NW: We do have nominations from the floor for the officers, too. I forgot to say that, but we do. What we do is we allow everyone two minutes for their nominating speech, and then they get their pictures taken with a Polaroid camera, and we put their picture on a shoebox, one box for each picture. Then everyone gets four pieces of paper (one piece for each officer position), and they drop a piece of paper in the box for who they want to vote for. That way people who don't know how to read can vote without help, and people can vote only once. People can vote for themselves if they want. When you vote by raising hands, some people vote too many times, and the candidates can't vote for themselves.

BS: What do you think the convention does for the organization?

NW: I think it does a whole bunch of things. I think it gives us more confidence in ourselves, because we see we can do something for ourselves. That's what I think it does for the Board. I think for individual members it does that, too, because a lot of times people have never done a workshop or a session before. That gives them a lot of confidence. The one thing that we haven't talked about yet is that we also have "Open Mike," and that's where people can talk about anything and everything that they want, but they're given a two-minute limit. That's where People First gets our goals. Most generally, people talk about wanting to get people out of Beatrice, wanting to get a real job, wanting to live on their own, have their own checkbook. Stuff like that. So that determines what we have for our goals.

BS: That's really an interesting process. Does somebody record that, and then the Board thinks about it afterwards?

NW: Yes. And I'm not sure that everybody in People First knows we do that.

BS: Let's talk about the chapters. How many are there now? When I left there were about six.

NW: There are two things that have made a big difference in that. When we had John Murphy [from Nebraska Advocacy Services (NAS), the Nebraska Protection and Advocacy agency and the first external funder of People First of Nebraska] working with us, that made a big difference, because it enabled us to have transportation. We were able to go out and develop chapters. Steve Richards, who was president then, and I developed a training packet, and we each had a part that we did. And we got about five chapters that way. The other thing that made a difference was by having a staff position.

BS: And that's you?

NW: Yes.

BS: What do you do to develop chapters or keep them going once they've started?

NW: I go out to the different towns and try to organize people or help them out after they are organized. Do you want me to tell you what our goals are? I have to read them, because we recently changed them.

Personal development is the first one. Each member will learn to use self-advocacy skills.

The second one is *local chapter development*. People First will develop, support, and strengthen local chapters.

The third one is *the state convention*. People First will plan, organize and support a statewide convention.

The fourth one is *systems advocacy*. People First will work together toward commonly-agreed-upon goals. We don't like how that's worded because not everyone can understand it. We're going to have to work on that.

Public education is the fifth one. People First members will teach others about the purpose, beliefs, goals, and needs of People First.

The sixth one is *stable state structure*. People First will provide for a stable state administrative structure, and funds to carry out the plans for People First.

BS: Which goals are the new ones?

NW: Before, to strengthen local chapters was the first one. We didn't have a goal for personal development. And then the second one was to work with the Board of Directors. And the third one was to start new chapters where there weren't any. The fourth one was to do public education. And the fifth one was the administrative part. And those were the goals we had under the contract with Nebraska Advocacy Services.

BS: Are the new goals your internal goals, or do you use them for writing grants?

NW: Both. They're goals that we use to write our grants by. We also tell them what our beliefs are. Basically, the DD [Developmental Disabilities] Council gave us some money to have a retreat. The Board put together a plan for the next year, which includes our goals and our beliefs. We already have one grant to take over after the contract with NAS ended, and we are applying for other grants, too.

BS: What other accomplishments has People First of Nebraska done, for example in the area of systems advocacy?

NW: One of the things that People First of Nebraska is real proud of is, and this really blows my mind, because you would think that since Nebraska is one of the leading states for community services for people that have disabilities, we would have done this a long time ago. It took People First of Nebraska to notice that we had a lot of obsolete language in our state statutes, like "moron," "idiot," "imbecile," and to do something about it. We got the legislature to get rid of the language. It was a compromise, because we had to replace it with "people who have mental retardation," but at least it's better than nothing.

BS: In what way is that a compromise?

NW: We didn't want any label at all. We only agreed to a label because the state said there had to be one. Now they have changed it to "developmental disabilities." I like that better, but we didn't see why there had to be any label at all.

BS: That's really a big accomplishment, to get that changed.

NW: Yes, because David [Powell, then the Executive Director of ARC-Nebraska] had to walk us through step by step by step, because we knew how to testify, but we didn't know how to do anything else. And sometimes he had to push us to get us to do it, because we didn't think we could do some of the stuff he was asking. Like, talking to Senator Sieck to sponsor it. People First didn't think we would be able to do that, because we didn't know how. So each step that we did, David had to teach us. And the thing I liked about that was that he *taught* us, he didn't do it *for* us.

Another big accomplishment of People First of Nebraska is Baby Doe, and the lawsuit that Ohio's Protection and Advocacy agency did against Kentucky, the one where people with mental retardation are put in institutions just because someone says they should be there, but people with mental illness are treated different and can defend themselves against it. Do you know the one I'm talking about?

BS: Yes. You mean this recent lawsuit that is just going to the Supreme Court now?

NW: Yes, except they got the results back and it didn't pass, but yes, that's the one I mean.

BS: What was the Baby Doe case?

NW: That was a long time ago, when a baby was born with a whole bunch of different disabilities and the parents just let the baby die. People First of Nebraska was a friend of the court, like they were on the lawsuit against Kentucky. We also did the one in Texas, the Cleburne case, about allowing a group home in a neighborhood. We were a friend of the court on that, too.

BS: What is involved in being a friend of the court?

NW: You have to give your testimony on how you feel about the case, and that you support it or you don't support it, depending on what the issues are. Our Board goes over the case so they all understand it, and then they decide if they want to do it or not. If they do, the executive committee does the testimony. Because you know, you don't have enough time to have everybody do it.

And then, I'm not going to remember what this is called, but you know when they had the community living legislation that Senator Chaffee was supporting?

BS: You mean the Medicaid reform legislation, when they were trying to change Medicaid so more would be spent in the community and less in the institutions?

NW: Correct, that one. I testified on that, to that committee. I flew to Washington and testified.

BS: Can you think of some other achievements?

NW: Just — and I don't know how to say this — just watching people grow within themselves and gain confidence in themselves, to be able to speak out at their IPPs, for example, or maybe just to staff in general, or maybe to their parents.

BS: It would be interesting for you to give an example, maybe you could change the person's name, where you've actually seen this happen because of People First.

NW: I can give a bunch of examples, where it's because of self-advocacy and learning and gaining confidence in yourself and learning that it's okay to tell people how you feel, and that you're not going to get in trouble for saying that.

One example is when I was working with people in one town. A couple years ago in July, their advisors helped people get their checkbooks, because people wanted to have control of their own checkbooks. Well, they bounced checks, because nobody taught them how to *manage* their checkbooks. And so, rather than teach them, the staff took their checkbooks back. People worked on getting their check-books again, but they lost their advisor, so they lost the support they needed to do it. It was real frustrating for me, because I'd go when I could and I'd help them, but then it would all fall apart again. Now, they are working on it again because they have an advisor. I also think it's made a big difference to have a new director of services for their area program, because he believes in people. So far, there's just one person who has stuck with the issue and didn't give up on it, but it's still one person.

BS: That's a good example, and you never know what might happen if that one person is successful. Other people might want to try again.

NW: Another example would be that we have a member, we'll say his name is John, who needs to learn how to share things and not be on an ego trip. He tries to dominate. And at our last board meeting, the person who's from that particular chapter got real fed up and said that she's not going to listen to John any more and she's going to make decisions for herself. And that's another example, because John was telling her that he needed to be the board rep, and was really discouraging her. It was real hard, because I had to do all this over the phone — this was during the time a few months ago when I couldn't go to chapters because we didn't have funding. So I had to give her all this encouragement over the phone, and tell John to bug off, and to explain to him that he needs to give other people a chance, and let other people grow. It doesn't always need to be him.

BS: Could you also talk more about the transition between when People First of Nebraska didn't have funding and when you did? Before I left, you had a Board that met, and a little money that you raised in various ways, and then you got funding. You were on that board, weren't you? Could you talk about that time?

NW: Yes, and I'll give you two perspectives. My personal perspective and then the perspective of People First. Before we got the funding is when John Murphy would take Steve and I around the state. When we got the funding from NAS [Nebraska Advocacy Services], we lost John, because they gave us the $9000 instead of having John. It made it nice when John was able to take us places.

BS: Were you doing that as a volunteer, on your own time?

NW: Yes, and Steve did it on his own time, as President. We started People First of Holdredge, and People First of Kearney, and People First of Dawson County, and People First of Hastings.

BS: What was your role with that, if Steve was President?

NW: Just being on the Board, and people saw me as being real responsible. I just believe in People First, and so I did it. And so John would take us to the meetings, and Steve and I would talk about People First. Then groups would form. That was right before we got staff. What made it hard when we got staff is that the guy I was dating and I were the only people that applied for the position. And I got the position, and that made it hard to work through all that, because to give him the support that he needed when he didn't get the position was difficult. Because I was excited for myself, and that made it hard.

My job is like having your cake and eating it, too, because I love talking about self-advocacy and doing People First, and I get paid for that now.

BS: When did it start? Was it a full-time position?

NW: 1988, and no, it's always been part-time.

BS: Did you have an office and lots of support from the different agencies?

NW: No, my office is in my apartment. The support part was difficult, too, because NAS [Nebraska Advocacy Services] wanted us to be independent of any other agency. NAS has done a lot for us, really a lot, but that made it real hard. Because this had never been done before, it had never been done where it was set up with just the person with the disability. Always before, in other states, it was set up with the support. Like, for example, they might have a paid advisor working full time for them, or even more than one. But NAS didn't want us to be influenced by the other agencies, even by themselves. That's why they didn't want me to have an office in their office. And that's why the money went to People First, not some other agency. After that, I had to go to the other chapters by myself, like on the bus.

BS: How did you get the support that you needed?

NW: I have an advisory committee, and that's made up of two people that have disabilities, and a chairperson, and a secretary and a financial person, and then, because I wanted the support of our state advisor, I asked her. And my mentor, who is the chairperson. And it was originally supposed to have a community organizer person, but it doesn't. That would be somebody that we thought would be a good idea, but we've never found somebody. They would show me how to go into a community and show me how to organize the community to have a People First chapter. We don't have that, so I had to learn how to do that myself, which is hard.

BS: What's your mentor's role?

NW: Her job is to show me the ropes, because I didn't know how to do this stuff, when I was first learning. Like organizing myself. That's a big issue for me. I now use a calendar, you know, and I know that sounds silly, but that was something I had to learn how to do. So that I was to meetings on time, and I didn't forget about them, and that kind of stuff. And that took a long time for me to learn how to do. And she gives me support when I'm frustrated.

BS: And now that funding has ended, and you have another grant?

NW: Yes, and NAS helps us write grants. The director does.

BS: It sounds like now you have a relationship with the Arc, where you can go in and get things typed, or have someone fax things to you. Is that correct?

NW: Yes. We started that when the contract with NAS ended. For example, now our money is in one account, and is managed by ARC-Nebraska. We did that because the contract was over, and asking people to volunteer their time to do the finances wasn't working. We ran into a whole bunch of problems doing that.

BS: Well, one of the good parts about it was that when their contract ended you had things set up so that you could go and seek funding elsewhere.

NW: Yes, that helped out a lot. We were out of funds for a while, and I wasn't getting paid, and that was real scary. But now we have a new grant, and we are applying for others.

BS: What about the advisors and their role with the group, both the local chapters and the state? Do you think they're important?

NW: Yes! I think the advisors are important because they give the individual members support. I can't be every place at once and all the time, so the advisors are what hold the chapters together. Because the advisors are the ones that give the support to people and encourage them and keep them going. At the same time, I think the advisors get a lot from the members, because they learn how to work with people that have a disability. How do I say that? People with a disability have a different perspective about life. You know what I'm trying to say?

BS: Yes. Do you think the advisors get something different out of it than if they were staff members in programs and worked with people that way?

NW: Yes! Because people can be themselves, and people can say how they honestly feel about issues. And they don't have to be afraid that they're going to be jumped on. And if they have issues, they know that they'll have the support that they need. And that's why People First is so important, because when people are first learning how to speak out for themselves, it's real difficult to go and tell staff that they're doing something wrong, if they don't have the support. The advisors get to see this side of people, and they have to be open to hearing they are doing something wrong. That's one way they get so much from the members.

BS: You must have some really good advisors there, who aren't controlling and dominating.

NW: Yes, we do. And then we also have some who *are* controlling and dominating. I think that there are four things you need to have to have a People First chapter.

The first one is that the members want to have the chapter, because I think we get used sometimes for tokens. Because it looks good to have a People First chapter in your agency. The second thing is that the advisor not be paid, because we have enough paid people in our lives. We want friends. And I also feel that if the advisor works for the agency that's sponsoring the chapter, then if there's a conflict of interest, where's the advisor going to lie? And we've had that happen. With one of our advisors, it happens sometimes, that we are in conflict with the agency she works for. This advisor contradicts what I'm saying, because we know her well enough, and we trust her enough, and she believes in People First enough, that her job wouldn't be an issue. If it was something she believed in, she'd stand by it, even if it threatened her job. But there's a lot of people where that isn't the case.

So that's the second and the third thing, and the fourth is, for the above reason, that you don't have it at the workshop. Because how are people going to be able to talk about issues if they're afraid? The perfect example of that is that I went and talked to an Arc chapter, and I said these four things. So the president asked if I would go and talk to the potential members by myself, and I said I would. [In Nebraska, the Arc doesn't provide services.] I went to the meeting, and you can't always tell who has a disability, and staff [of the provider agency] came in there. And it's real difficult to get people to talk when staff are there, and they finally did, and staff went back and told the director of this particular program, and we had 60 people signed up for convention from this agency, and nobody came!

BS: That's terrible. What about at the state level? What role does the advisor play there?

NW: Well, since I don't have a support person except the state advisor and my mentor, they play big roles. They are both my support. The state advisor helps me go over the agenda for the board meeting, and if we need to add stuff, we do. We do all the preparation for the board meetings together. She helps me with preparation for the advisory committee, also. She's also my personal support for when I'm real frustrated with chapters. Because we have one chapter in particular that I'm real excited about. This Saturday when we have our board meeting, this chapter has been a chapter for 3 years and this is the first time they're coming to a board meeting. So I'm pretty excited about that.

BS: Great!

NW: So I get real frustrated about one of the chapters, because their advisors are staff. So she's my personal support for that, and she's just my personal support for everything.

BS: To change the subject, Nancy, is the part-time work for People First enough to pay your bills, or do you have to do other work?

NW: Other work, in that I do personal care for some of my friends, and I also used to work with kids who had problems with alcohol and drugs.

BS: Is there anything else you want to tell me about People First of Nebraska and how it functions?

NW: Maybe this is too personal, but I just feel that some form of self-advocacy is real important to people because that's how they gain their confidence in themselves and learn about their rights — but along with that, learn about our responsibilities. Because if we expect to be treated the same as everybody else, then we need to know the consequences for those responsibilities if we don't live up to them. I feel People First of Nebraska provides that opportunity for people. Obviously, I am really proud of People First of Nebraska.

Self-Advocates Becoming Empowered

The Birth of a National Organization in the U.S.

Bonnie Shoultz & Nancy Ward

NANCY WARD is Chairperson of Self-Advocates Becoming Empowered, a grass-roots national organization of self-advocates that began to form in 1990. BONNIE SHOULTZ has been a self-advocacy advisor in Nebraska and New York since 1975. She is a national advisor for the new organization. This chapter* is broken into sections, each of which ends with Nancy's thoughts about the events discussed in that section.

Since its beginnings in the United States with the formation of People First of Oregon in the early 1970s, the self-advocacy movement has been a grass-roots effort. That is, the idea of self-advocacy spread, but most of the early work to carry out the idea and establish groups took place in local settings, as individual people with developmental disabilities and their supporters heard about the idea and wanted to get involved. Other chapters in this book describe the many ways in which individuals and groups of people became self-advocates and began to make a difference in their own lives and the lives of others. It was evident to many of those involved that self-advocacy was a powerful force. Many of us felt, however, that the movement needed to grow slowly, person by person and group by group, and that the power of the self-advocacy idea — that people could speak for themselves and make changes in their own lives — would best make itself felt that way.

* Preparation of this chapter was supported in part by the U.S. Department of Education, Office of Special Education and Rehabilitative Services, National Institute on Disability and Rehabilitation Research (NIDRR) under Cooperative Agreement No. H133B00003-90 awarded to the Center on Human Policy, School of Education, Syracuse University and Cooperative Agreement No. H133B80048 under a subcontract from the Research and Training Center on Community Living at the University of Minnesota. The opinions expressed herein are those solely of the authors, and no official endorsement by the U.S. Department of Education should be inferred.

By the late 1970s and early 1980s, state organizations developed. Many of the state organizations that flourished came into being through the efforts of people in local groups who wanted to band together for greater strength. Others were started by a central group who formed a state organization first and then worked to establish local chapters. More than a decade was spent, in many of the states, in strengthening and diversifying the state organizations. By 1993, there were about 37 state organizations, some having as many as 75 local chapters and others with as few as two or three. No one seems to have exact information on all the organizations that exist, or on which are to be counted as statewide organizations, but this is a good estimate.

Late in 1989, people working at two universities with federal funding to study community living and community integration for people with developmental disabilities* decided to sponsor a meeting of leaders in the self-advocacy movement at the annual conference of the American Association on Mental Retardation (AAMR) in May, 1990. This meeting was facilitated by John O'Brien, a well-known consultant who had spent time with a number of self-advocacy groups. O'Brien's ideas about the meeting helped to shape its outcome. The invited participants included leaders who have developmental disabilities and advisors from several states that have strong organizations. The meeting also included leaders and advisors who were attending the AAMR conference and who wanted to join the group. One of the meeting's questions was "What will strengthen self-advocacy?" The participants proposed that it was time to band together nationally. No one knew what this national coming together would look like, but they agreed that they would try to take it further at the next available opportunity. A report on that meeting, *Effective Self-Advocacy*, was prepared by John O'Brien and disseminated widely by the University of Minnesota's Research and Training Center on Community Living.

NANCY:

I became involved in self-advocacy when Advocacy First of Lincoln started its chapter in 1979. I wanted a way to direct my feelings in a positive way. I knew real well how to direct my feelings in a negative way. What happened was this: They had a Special Olympics commercial on TV where they were parading kids across the stage. I felt the worst thing you can do for people who have a disability is feel sorry for them, because you don't give them the opportunity to grow then. You're going to see them as little kids for the rest of their lives, and some of us *do* happen to be adults! So it made me mad, and I yelled at the TV. But a lot of good it's going to do to yell at a TV! So some of my friends talked to me about becoming a member of Advocacy First of Lincoln, so I did, and we wrote a letter about how we felt about it. We had a

---

* The Research and Training Center on Community Living, Institute on Community Integration, University of Minnesota, and the Research and Training Center on Community Integration at The Center on Human Policy, School of Education, Syracuse University. Both are funded by the National Institute on Disability and Rehabilitation Research, Office of Special Education and Rehabilitative Services, U.S. Department of Education.

petition attached to it, and we sent the letter to the Joseph P. Kennedy Foundation, and also to President Carter. And they took the commercial off the air. I don't think it was just because of our one letter, I think it was because a bunch of people wrote, but they took it off! And that taught me how to direct my feelings in a positive way. My self-advocacy skills are real important to me. They taught me how to deal with my feelings about having a disability, the anger and hurt and being made fun of. Now I can explain to people about having a disability and not get mad about it.

Once I learned how to direct my feelings, I wanted to learn how to deal with the fact of having a disability, so that was one thing I did to get more involved. I started going to the ARC conventions and our own self-advocacy conferences. I learned about how to gain confidence in myself, and how to tell people how I feel about things. Then I got more active as a leader, because by then I had confidence in myself to do that.

Finally, we had the Atlanta meeting, and I thought it was really good, and a lot of good things came out of that. Because people talked about wanting to have a national organization, and we put our ideas together. We knew what we wanted to do next, which was to ask people whether they wanted it. I really like working with John O'Brien because he lets us have the time that we need to figure out the issues for ourselves. He doesn't try to rush us. So we got a lot out of it because it was all work that we did. Learning how to fight through conflict is hard, and there was some conflict. It was frustrating, in everybody having a turn and saying how they felt about things, but learning how to do that was really good.

The Colorado Conference: Debating Whether to Begin

All during 1990, the statewide organization, Speaking for Ourselves of Colorado, planned for and publicized the first North American self-advocacy convention, which was held in Estes Park in September, 1990. Several members of Speaking for Ourselves had been present in Atlanta for the meeting at AAMR (American Association on Mental Retardation), as had people from other organizations who had already planned to go to the Estes Park convention. The report *Effective Self-Advocacy* reached many other people who were saving their money for Estes Park. By the time the conference was held, people all over the country were beginning to wonder whether they could put together something that would represent self-advocates at the national level.

The Estes Park conference planners had developed a full program for the four days of the conference, but had not allocated the time that would be needed to discuss development of something at a national level. The topic was on people's minds, but was not formulated well enough or early enough to be given a prominent place on the program. No one knew what it might mean, or who would lead the discussion, or how decisions would get made. On the first day in Estes Park, people spread the word among the 400 people present that there would be a meeting after supper in the lounge of one of the dormitories. About 50 people came to that meeting, and stayed till nearly midnight discussing the possibilities. Debbie Robinson, president of Speaking for Ourselves of Pennsylvania, facilitated the meeting. An advisor took notes while people talked.

Opinions were varied, and the discussion became very heated at times. Several people cautioned that there was no money for a venture of this type, and others cautioned that it would fail because no one knew how to do it. Some felt that since the meeting to discuss forming a national organization was chaotic and confusing, further efforts would be even more so.

However, many people felt that they and other people with developmental disabilities were ready to take this step. They pointed out that there were many strong state self-advocacy organizations, and that they could not have a national voice unless they had a national organization that linked them all together. They said that as long as they had no national voice, other organizations, run by parents and/or professionals, would continue to speak for them nationally. They felt very strongly that as members of local and state organizations, they needed a national office to give them support, to be a kind of clearinghouse for information and news about what was happening in self-advocacy across the country. They also felt that a national office could help new groups to form, and that it could support those new groups by linking them to other groups with similar interests and needs.

These evening meetings took place two nights in a row, after long days at the convention. A tentative plan was formulated: The country would be divided into five regions, based on who was present at the conference. The people from each region would meet on the day before the conference ended. If the region's consensus was that work on something national should proceed, the people from that region would elect two people to be on a Steering Committee that would make recommendations about how a national organization could be formed. On the designated day, four of the five regions elected people for the Steering Committee. The Pacific region, which included people from California, Oregon, Washington, and Idaho, decided that they were not ready to get involved in a national organization. They felt that the next step for them was to strengthen their region.

On the last day of the conference, after more heated debate over the issue during a final plenary session, a motion was passed that read, "We authorize the Steering Committee to work out the details of a national organization within the next year, and come back with a report and recommendations at the 1991 conference in Nashville, Tennessee."

NANCY:

The thing that I remember most of all is how much it [the idea of forming a national organization] meant to everybody, and how difficult it was for everybody to understand. Because it's been drummed into our heads for our whole lives that you can't do anything until you have the money. And how you have to have an organization first before you can start something. And so, working through that with everybody made us stronger in our beliefs, because we really had to say how we felt, and really explain it and know what we were talking about. There were a lot of people who didn't understand that you don't need the money first. With People First of Nebraska, we did it before we had the money. I don't have an office, I work out of my home. And I tried to explain that to the others, that you can decide first and look for the money later.

I was excited and honored to be elected to the Steering Committee, because I really believed in it and thought we could do it. Even though some of the advisors and some of the other people thought we were having "pie in the sky," and that we weren't going to be able to do it, that's all the more reason for me to want to do it. It's real difficult when people tell you you can't do something and it's something that you believe in. That just makes you want to do it all the more. But I knew it was possible, because I had experience in it. Whereas maybe a lot of other people didn't have the same experience that I had, because we *were* running a state organization through my apartment, with very little support, compared to what they have in some of the other states.

The Steering Committee Meets in Chicago

With financial and logistical support from three* universities, plans were made for a Steering Committee meeting in a suburb of Chicago, Illinois, in May 1991. All the elected Steering Committee members and many of their advisors had talked via several conference calls to make these plans and to develop an agenda. The meeting was scheduled for a three day weekend and was hosted by People First of Illinois. Much of the funding for the Steering Committee representatives' travel was contributed by the two universities, but many of the advisors paid their own way to attend, or obtained funding from the organizations in their states.

The people present for that meeting included:

Southwest Region: Ben Borroel, from Speaking for Ourselves of Colorado; Bob Reed, from People First of New Mexico; and advisors Debbie Pierson and Patti Lampe

Midwest Region: Nancy Ward, from People First of Nebraska; Gloria Steinbring, from Advocating Change Together in Minnesota; and advisors Shirley Dean and Mary Hayden

Southeast Region: Rick Betts, from People First of Tennessee; and advisor Cindy Goodwin

Northeast Region: Roland Johnson, from Speaking for Ourselves of Pennsylvania; Elyse Collioud, from People First/Bancroft; and advisors Pat Gerke, Mark Friedman, and Bonnie Shoultz

---

* Along with the two previously mentioned, the Institute on Disability and Human Development at the University of Illinois at Chicago (UAP) provided logistical and financial support for this meeting. All three, and other organizations too numerous to mention, have supported Self-Advocates Becoming Empowered since that formative time.

Also present were several observers, including Tia Nelis and Kelly Nevins from People First of Illinois and advisor Leigh Ann Rusche, as well as Daphne Kruithof from People First of Washington and advisor Bob Furman. Even though the Pacific region had opted not to participate, People First of Washington paid the expenses of Daphne Kruithof and Bob Furman. The elected representatives invited all observers to participate but not to vote on issues.

Questions on the agenda included:

- What should the mission of a national organization be?
- What should the goals be?
- What is the best structure for the national organization?
- What are some options for funding?
- How can we communicate with self-advocates across the country?

Each representative brought information on one of these questions, and led that section of the agenda. For example, Nancy Ward and Shirley Dean from Nebraska researched the typical ways that national organizations are structured, and found that organizations can operate as loosely linked networks, as coalitions with formal agreements between member organizations, or as formal organizations that have boards of directors. They presented these options during their portion of the agenda.

The elected representatives and their advisors discussed these and other questions for a day and a half, and then the representatives asked the advisors to leave the room. They felt that things were getting too confusing, and that they would be able to make decisions if the advisors were not present. Mary Hayden, from the University of Minnesota's Research and Training Center on Community Living, was asked to stay and help them with the mechanics of the decision-making process. The group met together for an entire afternoon, and came out with the following recommendations to be presented to the conference in Nashville:

Recommendation # 1: Definition of Self-Advocacy*

Self-advocacy is teaching people with a disability how to advocate for themselves and to learn how to speak out for what they believe in. It teaches us how to make decisions and choices that affect our lives so that we can become more independent. It also teaches us about our rights, but along with learning our rights we learn our responsibilities.

Recommendation # 2: Organization Belief Statement*

We believe that people with disabilities should be treated as equals. That means that people should be given the same decisions, choices, rights, responsibilities,

---

* Some changes were made in the definition and belief statement later, to include the concept that self-advocacy is about "independent groups of people with disabilities working together for justice by helping each other take charge of our lives and fight discrimination."

chance to speak up to empower themselves, and to make new friendships and renew old friendships. Just like everyone else. They should also be able to learn from their mistakes. Like everyone else.

Recommendation # 3: Issues the Organization Should Address

Every organization has ideas and issues that are important to members. The Committee suggested five issues for the national organization to work on. They were:
- To support community living
- To make changes in the guardianship laws
- To use people-first language in legislative language
- To work for fair wages
- To make changes in the Medicaid and SSI programs

Recommendation # 4: The Goals of the Organization
- To promote legislation at the state and national levels
- To realize self-advocacy is hard work and we need to support one another and to celebrate victories
- To build coalitions
- To provide public education and awareness
- To support existing state and local organizations, to help start new organizations, and to link all self-advocacy organizations
- To provide resources and training for people with disabilities, advisors, and other people
- To share ideas and information among groups to learn from one another
- To identify funding sources and to get money to fund the national organization

Recommendation # 5: The Goals to Work on First

The Committee recognized that the national organization cannot work on everything at once. They recommended that the organization work on the following goals first because they seemed the most important:

- To promote legislation at the state and national levels
- To support existing state and local organizations, to help start new organizations, and to link all self-advocacy organizations
- To share ideas and information among groups to learn from one another
- To identify funding sources and to get money to fund the national organization

Recommendation # 6: The Structure of the Organization

The Committee recommended that the organization be a coalition of state and local organizations that vote for regional representatives to be on a Steering Committee that would guide the coalition. These representatives would work to network the state and local organizations with one another. This structure was chosen because it would keep the national organization at a grass-roots level. It would make it easier for state and local organizations to share information, ideas, and concerns with representatives.

Recommendation # 7: The National Organization Regions

The Committee recommended dividing the United States into eight regions*, with representatives from each region to serve on a Steering Committee. This plan would include every state, and make sure that every region has at least one strong chapter. The eight regions were:

- **Region 1:** Washington, Oregon, Idaho, Montana, Alaska
- **Region 2:** California, Nevada, Arizona, Hawaii
- **Region 3:** Wyoming, Utah, Colorado, New Mexico
- **Region 4:** North Dakota, South Dakota, Nebraska, Kansas, Texas, Oklahoma, Missouri, Arkansas, Louisiana
- **Region 5:** Minnesota, Iowa, Wisconsin, Illinois, Michigan, Indiana, Ohio
- **Region 6:** Kentucky, Tennessee, North Carolina, South Carolina, Mississippi, Alabama, Georgia, Florida
- **Region 7:** Pennsylvania, New Jersey, Delaware, Maryland, Virginia, West Virginia, District of Columbia
- **Region 8:** New York, Vermont, New Hampshire, Maine, Connecticut, Massachusetts, Rhode Island

Recommendation # 8: The Number of Representatives from Each Region

The Committee recommended that two people should be elected from each region as representatives to the Steering Committee. They felt that the regions were big areas, and that two people could represent state and local organizations better than one person.

Recommendation # 9: Tenure of Present Representatives

The Committee recommended that people who were currently the regional representatives to the Steering Committee should remain on the Committee for the next year. They felt that this way the Committee would not have to start all over again, and that the old representatives could share their experience with the new representatives.

---

* A ninth region was created later.

Recommendation # 10: Responsibilities of Regions

The Committee recommended that the representatives from each region should have a responsibility, and made the following assignments:

- **Region 1:** Help write grants and identify funding.
- **Regions 2 and 3:** Develop and coordinate a master list of training materials and a resource library.
- **Regions 4 and 5:** Define self-advocacy, the national organization's purpose, and the national organization's mission statement.
- **Regions 3 and 6:** Develop current mailing lists, a newsletter, and regional updates.
- **Regions 7 and 8:** Identify legislation and develop a method to notify state and local self-advocacy organizations about legislation.

Recommendation # 11: Sharing Information Between Organizations

The Committee recommended that the organization do the following:

- Add inserts into the newsletters that already exist (this would save money and get the word out to more people than developing a new mailing list and sending out a separate newsletter).
- Later, develop a newsletter for the organization.
- In 3 or 4 years, look at getting computers that would link state and local organizations together.
- Look into fax machines and a telephone tree.

Recommendation # 12: Participant Label

The Committee recommended that the people involved in the national organization should be called "members" rather than "consumers."

Recommendation # 13: Types of Members

The Committee recommended that the national organization have voting members and nonvoting members. A voting member is a person who identifies him/ herself as a person with a disability. Any person with a disability can be a voting member of the national organization. Nonvoting members are people without disabilities, and other groups or businesses that want to support the national organization.

All of these recommendations, along with a sample ballot, were put together by the University of Minnesota in a booklet called *Self Advocacy by Persons with Disabilities: Ideas for Creating a National Organization*. The booklet was widely disseminated before the Nashville conference, and was put into each registrant's conference packet, so that everyone possible would know about the Steering Committee's work.

NANCY:

Before the Chicago meeting, we had conference calls, and we found out those don't work very well. But we did decide on an agenda for the meeting. I thought the meeting was good, but it was real hard, because a lot of the advisors would interject things, and not leave room for us to make our own decisions for ourselves. I think they did that because they really do believe in us and they wanted to help us out, and also because everyone was so excited about it, they wanted the end result there right away. So we asked the advisors to leave, and then things went much better, because we were able to do things for ourselves, and take the time that we needed to take to understand what it was that we wanted.

Then we came up with recommendations on structure and on the regions, and on what each representative's tasks would be. We also came up with the mission and the belief statement and the goals for the organization. We decided which states would be in which regions. We felt great afterwards, like we had really accomplished something. The advisors told us we had done a great job, and they couldn't believe we had accomplished that much! It was great!

The Nashville Conference: A New Organization is Born!

Nashville, Tennessee was the site for a 1991 conference, open to anyone, hosted by People First of Tennessee. It was a four-day extravaganza that included country music bands, bagpipe players, and many, many serious sessions on various aspects of self-advocacy. At this conference the issue of the national organization was on the program. There was time for Steering Committee members to report in plenary sessions and in workshops. Regional meetings were held so that elections could be conducted.

The Steering Committee met before the conference began and decided how to handle many of the details so that all conference participants would have opportunities to hear about their proposals and a chance to vote on them. They decided that the vote on whether or not to accept the proposals could be held before and during the Saturday night dance. That way, if participants voted to adopt the recommendations the elections for Steering Committee members could be held on Sunday during the regional meetings that were already on the program. Advisors volunteered to help with the voting. The Steering Committee also decided to propose a ninth region, in order to break up the vast territory formerly covered by Region 4.

Each of the recommendations listed above, with the change from eight to nine regions, was approved during the Saturday evening dance. A number of advisors set up voting tables out in the hall and encouraged and/or assisted people to vote during the dance. By the end of the evening it was clear that most of the conference participants approved of the recommendations and wanted the Steering Committee to move ahead with plans for the new organization. The next day, the balloting results were announced at breakfast, and the regions met in the morning to elect Steering Committee representatives. Many regions elected alternates as well, in case the representatives could not attend meetings or serve on the committee.

During the Nashville conference, participants had the opportunity to hear from Pat Worth and other leaders in People First of Canada, who cautioned them to move slowly. They explained that People First of Canada had taken its time in forming and setting up their national organization, and said they needed the time because there was so much to understand and to accomplish. Also, it took time to raise the money for them to get together to move ahead with their ideas for their national organization. They said they felt very good about it because they felt that they had done it well rather than quickly.

The new Steering Committee met briefly at the end of the conference, before people began to leave. They shared addresses and phone numbers and agreed that they would each try to raise money in their own states for travel and other expenses for the national organization. They agreed that the University of Minnesota could open a special bank account for any funds raised for the national organization, and that Region 1 would submit a grant to get computers to link everyone together, and would apply for other grants as opportunities arose. One reason they selected the University to receive the organization's money was that the University is a non-profit, tax-exempt organization. They knew they wanted the national organization to become nonprofit and tax-exempt, but realized that could take a long time. Thinking about it all, they felt good about what they had achieved but also became aware of how much work remained to be done. There was no time to elect officers or set up a structure for the Steering Committee.

NANCY:

The best thing about Nashville was the voting part. It was neat watching people being able to vote and do that themselves, because they had pictures to go with the ideas. They still had to have people read things for them, but at least people felt like they had accomplished something and had done it for themselves. One of my friends told me he had gained a lot of confidence in himself by voting. So that was one thing that I really liked.

I also liked that it opened Justin Dart's* eyes. He saw us doing things that he didn't think we were capable of doing. We gave presentations throughout the conference about the ideas, so everyone knew what we were talking about by the time we voted.

On the last day we had elections at the regional meetings. They had voted the night before that the original Steering Committee members would stay on, but we

---

* Justin Dart, Chairperson of the President's Committee on Employment of People with Disabilities, was a keynote speaker for the conference.

had also added some regions and wanted to have two people for each region, so we had to have elections for that. At my region meeting, we didn't elect anyone else because there weren't very many people there, but I think we did a lot anyway. It was great seeing people wanting to be the representative, and going through the voting process. People learned to deal with it whether they won or lost. I think people originally thought it would be a glamorous thing to do, going off to all these meetings, but it's actually hard work!

I was worried that we left Nashville without having a structure or officers, because it made it harder to believe in it. We didn't know what was going to happen, and it's hard to believe in something that isn't there yet. You know you believe in it, but it's not there yet.

A Waiting Time

During the next year and three months, Steering Committee members and their helpers worked on getting the committee back together for a meeting. They had to identify and obtain funding, decide on what needed to be done first, and find ways to keep the communication flowing until they could meet and make assignments for all the tasks that needed to be done. Several advisors got to work right away. One advisor, Bob Furman from Washington, developed a newsletter that described the idea of a national organization, listed the resolutions that had been adopted in Nashville, and had a map showing the regional structure. He also developed a letter that each member could modify and submit with the newsletter to funding sources in their states, such as the Developmental Disabilities Planning Councils and others. He also submitted two grants, one for funds and one for computers, but neither was funded.

Another advisor, Mary Hayden from the University of Minnesota, wrote a proposal to Wingspread, a conference facility in Racine, Wisconsin that supports meetings of people who wish to address topics of national importance or interest. The two university centers also committed some funds to get the members together for a meeting, and small amounts came in from other sources, including two Developmental Disabilities Planning Councils. Two conference calls of all the members and many advisors were held in 1992, one in March and one in August, to discuss the proposals and the funding issues. This was a difficult time because no member had the authority to initiate and carry through with decisions. Thus, whenever anyone (advisor or member) wanted to get approval for anything, they had to figure out how to communicate with everyone to explain the issue and get their vote.

In the August phone call, People First of Tennessee invited everyone to come to Nashville for a meeting at a local conference facility. The Steering Committee decided to meet there in December, and to worry about the money later. They felt it was vitally important that they get together soon, because so much time had already passed. Most of the members did not even know each other, and without an officer structure the communication was breaking down. They designated Nancy Ward to work with People First of Tennessee to develop an agenda for the meeting. Fortunately, this call had been set up for a week when an airfare price war was raging. While some members had their own funding for the meeting, many did not, but there was enough by then in the treasury to cover the tickets, lodging, and food for everyone who did not have funds. After a flurry of ticket-buying, 15 members and 9 advisors (who found their own funding or paid their own ways) were set to attend.

In some ways, this waiting time was harder than anything else. People became frustrated and felt cut off from each other. No one knew how the decisions would get made, where the money would come from, or what other members were doing. But this was a valuable time, too. It taught the Steering Committee that they needed to be able to meet more frequently, that they needed officers to carry on their work more effectively, and that sometimes it is best to make a decision and figure out later how to carry it out. They also learned that conference calls involving up to 25 people are not pleasant. The waiting period also gave time for the groundwork to be laid for activity in the future. Grants were written, funding was obtained by individuals and by the organization, and some communication did occur despite the difficulties.

NANCY:

That time was real frustrating and hard. I didn't want to make a mistake, but I felt like someone had to take a leadership role, and like I got pushed into that role. I was scared about it and frustrated, too, because I wanted it to be everybody's. I didn't want it just to be seen as me doing it. And that's when we really learned how conference calls don't work. We had more than 20 people, 16 Steering Committee members and the advisors, on the calls. It doesn't work because you can't take the time that you need. Plus people were talking about personal things on a conference call, and that took time. Sometimes it was really hard to get people back on task. I guess I took a leadership role on the calls, too, because somebody had to do it.

On the last call, we did decide to meet in Nashville, even though we didn't know where the money was coming from. We had raised some money by then, and we hoped that some people could pay their own way. People First of Tennessee invited us to come, and they said they had a conference center that would be inexpensive, so we voted to do it. The members asked me to develop the agenda, with Ruthie Beckwith and Mark Friedman and Pat Gerke. People still didn't feel like it was real, because they had never met before.

What I want to say about doing the agenda is that Speaking for Ourselves paid my way to come to Pennsylvania to work on it, and both Mark and Pat were good at pulling things out of me. I knew what I wanted to do, but I just didn't know how to say it. So that worked out good, that they helped me do that. We got everybody's ideas about what should be on the agenda, and I thought we got them all on it. I liked the experience because I didn't feel like it was just me doing it.

The First Meeting of Self-Advocates Becoming Empowered

The first face-to-face meeting of the expanded Steering Committee took place in Nashville, Tennessee on December 4, 5, and 6, 1992. One of the first things the group did after dinner was to get together without the advisors. While the advisors met in another room and talked about how they could support the Committee and each other, they elected officers and decided on a structure for the Committee. They announced their decisions the next day, as follows: Nancy Ward, Chairperson; Tia Nelis, Co-Chairperson; Roland Johnson, Vice-president; Reggie Jamarillo, Treasurer; and Kammie Barfield, Secretary. The national advisors were presented: Mark Friedman, Leigh Ann Rusche, and Bonnie Shoultz. Nancy explained that they had designated roles for every advisor, whether or not they were seen as a national advisor. Committees were set up to do the work, with at least one advisor helping each committee, as follows:

Legislation:	Rick Betts, Perry Whittico, T.J. Monroe, Roland Johnson, and Liz Obermayer, with Jean Bowen and Bill Autrey to advise
Fundraising:	Joe Pichler and Keith Desrossier, with Bob Furman and Mary Hayden to advise
Newsletter:	Ron Smith, Reggie Jamarillo, and Gloria Steinbring, with Pat Gerke to advise
Officers' Committee:	Donna Lowary, with Ruthie Beckwith to advise
Membership:	Daphne Kruithof, Terry Ingram and Garry Hayhurst, with Michelle Hoffman to advise

This meeting, chaired by Nancy Ward and Tia Nelis, was difficult in some ways because the members were just getting to know each other. It was an exciting, forward-looking event also, where many important decisions were made. For example, the group adopted a name, Self-Advocates Becoming Empowered, for the national organization. A very important decision, arrived at after much discussion, was that they must develop a common mission that would guide their decisions about what they wanted to do, and that all of that must happen before they would worry about whether the money is there to accomplish their mission. They broke into committee meetings and took action on issues. The Legislation Committee wrote letters to the Administration on Developmental Disabilities and to President Clinton's Transition Team. The Membership Committee developed ideas for a membership structure. The Newsletter Committee developed a news insert that could be placed in self-advocacy group newsletters around the country. The Fundraising Committee presented their ideas, and asked for guidance from the Steering Committee, which decided that all proposals should flow from the organization's priorities and should be written with input from the Steering Committee members.

Because the Steering Committee had no operating procedures, they decided to begin work on bylaws, and to work toward incorporating as a tax-exempt, non-profit organization. This work was completed in April 1994. People First of Louisiana and of Connecticut offered to pay for the incorporation process, and the Steering Committee accepted their offers. On the last day of the meeting, they agreed to meet again in April of 1993 at the Wingspread Conference Center in Racine, Wisconsin.

NANCY:

This meeting blew my mind, especially that I was elected Chairperson. It was scary, running against strong people who would do a good job also. It took me a long time to believe it, but I had to jump right in and start running the meeting. That's what made it difficult, but it helped that I had the support of the other officers and the advisors. That support was also what caused problems, because we made some mistakes. At one point, I asked the officers and the national advisors to leave the meeting and discuss something with me, and everyone else thought that we were making decisions without them. So I learned that that isn't a good way to deal with a problem.

I'd asked the officers and advisors to leave the meeting because I didn't know how to handle it when people kept making motions about things, and I didn't think we had discussed the issues enough. What was frustrating me was that I didn't know how to make people understand that you don't have to have bylaws, and you don't have to have an office, and you don't have to have money, to do an organization, and people were making motions about getting all these things in place before we went forward. And that's what I was talking to the officers and advisors about, not changing a decision that we had all made. I would never do that, anyway, but they didn't know that. So someone suggested that I ask Tia, the co-chairperson, to handle the motions, and that's worked a lot better. Also, I think people are developing some patience about getting everything in place right away. It's not as big an issue now.

The other hard thing we had to work through at that meeting was that we had elected officers on the first night, before three of the Steering Committee members had a chance to get there. That caused a lot of hard feelings, and we had to work through the conflicts that caused. I feel like it was a mistake, voting that early, but we did it and we had to deal with it afterwards. But we had felt that we needed some kind of structure, so we knew what we were going by, and at the time it didn't seem like we could hold off until everyone got there, because we had a really full agenda. I guess we also didn't realize, when we made up the agenda, that people from the West Coast might get there late at night, or that someone might not get there until noon of the next day because of his job. I'm not trying to justify it, just explain how we made that mistake.

By doing our elections that night, we had a structure in place for the next day. We had committees, with members and advisors assigned to each, and we were ready to go, except that we didn't realize that people would be upset. Finally, the group voted that the officers would keep their offices until we had bylaws. When the bylaws were done, we would hold elections according to the bylaws.

I think that working through those two issues brought us a lot closer together. Also, at the end of that meeting I felt like we had accomplished a lot, a whole lot. I was still on Cloud Nine, so to speak, for the next several days, because I couldn't believe what we had just done.

A Great Meeting at Wingspread: Forward Movement for the Organization

In April, the Steering Committee and advisors came together again for a second meeting. Wingspread, a national conference center operated by the Johnson Foundation in Racine, Wisconsin, is a home designed by the famous architect Frank Lloyd Wright. The foundation brings people together, typically scientists or policymakers, to discuss issues of national importance; it pays the travel and hotel expenses of many of the participants and provides meeting space, meals, and ground transportation for all who participate in a meeting. Tia Nelis and Leigh Ann Rusche from People First of Illinois had visited Wingspread in January and negotiated with the staff about the details of how the meeting would be conducted.

An Executive Committee conference call was held in February to decide on the agenda, after soliciting all members' ideas for what should be addressed. Several important items were selected for the agenda. First, they decided to ask Justin Dart to attend on the first afternoon, to give them ideas about starting a national organization. Second, they saved a large block of time for team-building exercises, hoping that these would give people the opportunity to work together and get to know each other better. They also saved time to discuss fundraising and where the next national convention should be held. Two state self-advocacy organizations had asked for the Steering Committee's blessing for holding a national convention in their state in 1994, and were waiting for their decision.

Because of all the preparation, the Steering Committee members were very pleased with how they were treated by the Wingspread staff and with how well the meeting went. Justin Dart inspired the Committee with his vision of the Clinton Administration's work for people with disabilities and invited them to nominate a member for the President's Committee on Employment for People with Disabilities. After he left, the Steering Committee selected Liz Obermayer as its nominee for the President's Committee. They also selected Gloria Steinbring and Roland Johnson as nominees for the National Council on Disability, another organization Dart had encouraged them to consider.

The team-building exercises the next morning, led by Mark Friedman and Pat Gerke, had the desired results. The rest of the day was spent in committee work, with each committee developing more ideas for fundraising, legislation, communication, etc. A new Bylaws Committee began to work on bylaws. People First of Louisiana advisor Bill Autrey volunteered to develop articles of incorporation for incorporation in Louisiana, a state that does not require bylaws. He also offered to begin working on federal tax-exempt status for the organization. In the evening, the group discussed whether to apply for funding through a foundation which had invited them to do so, with the stipulation that their activities must deal with the issue of community living. Like many of the issues, this was difficult, because people were not sure they wanted to divert their energies into just one issue. Finally they decided that community living is a broad concept that could encompass almost everything they want to do for the next year or more. They appointed a small group to develop the proposal concept and report back on Sunday morning before everyone left.

On Sunday morning, they decided to hold the 1994 national conference in conjunction with People First of Northern Virginia and People First of Virginia. They also approved the proposal concept that had been developed the night before, and they decided to meet for one day at the International People First conference in Toronto in June, 1993. They left the meeting at Wingspread feeling as though they had accomplished a great deal. They knew each other better and were more comfortable with their decision-making process. They had a clearer sense of where they were headed, and they had impressed the staff at Wingspread with their seriousness of purpose and the support they had shown for each other. Each officer and each member had a better sense of his or her role within the Steering Committee. Self-Advocates Becoming Empowered was finally real.

NANCY:

One of the most meaningful things about Justin Dart's being at Wingspread was the award he presented to us. In 1992, he had accepted on our behalf the Distinguished Service Award that was awarded to the pioneers of the self-advocacy movement by President Bush. Justin brought that and presented it so all of us could be involved. He also congratulated us on behalf of President Clinton for the work we have done. That meant a whole lot to us, to be able to get that award and have it come from the President. That was pretty awesome! And then to have him tell us what I was saying, that you could operate an organization on a shoestring, meant a lot to us.

I also thought the team-building helped a whole lot. It showed us that we were using it, we were starting to work together. For example, we came up with some guidelines about what we want for the organization, and they are something we can use forever. When we divided into groups (as one of the exercises) and came up with our five most important things that a team needs to work well together, each group came up with basically the same things. That showed us that we were working together already.

Also, for me, it was important to have put that on the agenda, because Mark [one of the national advisors] had originally wanted to do it differently. He didn't want to do it as team-building, he wanted to do it through committees, which is basically the same thing, but I think this worked a lot better. Just having to work through that with him and tell him how I felt about it was real hard, because I have a lot of respect for Mark and I don't want to hurt his feelings. We both had a hard time dealing with it, but we worked it through. So I felt we accomplished a lot, not just in the work we did but also in our relationships with each other. We all believe in our organization now. We are alive and growing!

Epilogue

Three years have passed since we wrote the body of this chapter. During that time, the remarkable growth and movement forward of Self-Advocates Becoming Empowered has confirmed our optimistic words. We wish here to mention a few of their accomplishments. First, the organization has been able to meet four times a year. Most of the members have obtained funding for their travel through organizations in their own states, and Self-Advocates Becoming Empowered has paid for the others through grant money. They have successfully applied for funding, three years in a row, from the Joseph P. Kennedy Jr. Foundation, and have produced a booklet and a training package on community living in fulfillment of the grant requirements. The booklet, *Taking Place*, has been widely distributed and is available through People First of Oklahoma.

In 1994, a national conference cosponsored by People First of Northern Virginia and Self-Advocates Becoming Empowered was held in Alexandria, VA. In preparation for the conference, the Steering Committee developed bylaws that included the procedure for holding an election for regional representatives. Early in the conference, eight regions held elections for one of the two representatives' positions, and elections were held for officers the following day. Nancy Ward was re-elected as Chairperson, Tia Nelis (Illinois) as Co-Chairperson, Liz Obermayer (New Jersey) as Vice President, James Meadours (Oklahoma) as Treasurer, and Kammie Barfield (Louisiana) as Secretary.

After the conference, at a meeting in Danbury, CT, the new steering committee chose goals for the next two years. The goals, in their words, are to:

a) make self-advocacy available in every state including institutions, high schools, rural areas, people living with families, with local supports and advisors to help;

b) work with the criminal justice system and people with disabilities about their rights within the criminal justice system;

c) close institutions for people with developmental disabilities labels nationwide and building community supports.

In fulfillment of these goals, the organization has developed a plan for Operation Close the Doors, an initiative calling for the closing of institutions everywhere, and has worked with the Public Interest Law Center of Philadelphia to apply for funding through the Administration on Developmental Disabilities for a project that would address the problems of people with developmental disabilities in the criminal justice system. They have also promoted self-advocacy throughout the country and developed materials that have been published through the newsletters of other organizations.

Finally, the organization has become increasingly visible within the national disability rights movement. Steering committee members are frequently invited to sit on national organizations' boards, to attend national meetings, and to speak at major conferences. They have had so many requests to join in on grant proposals (at one point, three different groups competing for the same funding asked them to join their team!) that they had to develop a one-page response that lays out their priorities and requests written information on whether and how the proposed projects would fulfill their own goals.

The year ahead will be very challenging, as federal money is cut and millions of people with disabilities find their services diminished or eliminated. However, Self-Advocates Becoming Empowered intends to stay together and continue to develop in strength and influence.

References

Hayden, M., & Shoultz, B. (Eds.) (1991). *Self-advocacy by persons with disabilities.* Minneapolis, MN: Institute on Community Integration.

O'Brien, J. (Ed.) (1990). *Effective self-advocacy.* Minneapolis, MN: Institute on Community Integration.

Section V

Critical Views of Self-Advocacy

50 Years of No Special Reason

The day and hour had finally arrived.

This was to be the day
the consulting speech pathologist
was going to let us know when
Vi was finally going to get
her augmentative communication system.

Anticipation
loomed like the hot sticky July air,
which pervaded her unit cubicle,
where we all had gathered to hear the news.

Five minutes
into his polite but rambling recitation, though,
it became apparent that the only news
he had for us that day was no news at all:

A glitch had developed here or there,
a microswitch had failed,
a proverbial monkey wrench had been
thrown into the works again.

Nothing new
Proverbial monkey wrenches
always had a strange magnetic attraction
to Vi.

They seek her out
and then boomerang
in God only knows
how many directions.

So, it must have come as quite a surprise to him
when I asked how much longer it'd take
to get back on track this time.

"Why," he quizzically replied, "is there any
special reason for all the rush???"

"No, no special reason," I said,
in a mute sigh
only Vi could understand.

"no, no special reason at all..."

"Except that she has had
50 years of no special reasons."

— *Bob Williams* (see p. xii)

18

Self-Advocacy at the Crossroads

Bernard J. Carabello & Joanne F. Siegel, M.S.W.

BERNARD CARABELLO grew up in the disgraceful conditions at Willowbrook, the New York institution that was exposed by Geraldo Rivera in the early 1970s. In 1972, writing about the pressures to close Willowbrook, Rivera said: "If Willowbrook is ever closed... it will be more because of Bernard Carabello than anyone else." Today, Willowbrook is closed, and Bernard lives in Manhattan and works for the New York State Office of Developmental Disabilities. JOANNE F. SIEGEL is on the staff of the Rose Kennedy Center of the Albert Einstein College of Medicine, at Yeshiva University in New York. She works closely with Mr. Carabello on self-advocacy issues.

Since the self-advocacy movement began in 1972 with the development of the People First movement in Oregon, much progress has been made in changing the attitudes of both persons with developmental disabilities as well as those persons providing services to them. Society as a whole has become much more aware of the needs of persons with disabilities, and legislation such as the Americans with Disabilities Act (ADA) has given advocates the legal foundation and support to obtain equality and accessibility in all areas of life. We have gone from the closing of massive custodial institutions like Willowbrook to the opening of small apartments which are fully integrated into the community. The variety of day, work, and educational programs has increased over the years as a result of providers and governmental bureaucracies listening to the voices of people with developmental disabilities and their advocates.

However, there is still much work that has to be done before people with developmental disabilities are truly seen as capable human beings. Much more federal and state legislation is needed to ensure that the gains made thus far will not be eroded or erased by political or economic pressures. And *within the field of self-advocacy*, many questions remain unanswered. Until these questions are resolved, the movement will remain in its infancy and will not be able to proceed. Some of these questions are:

- Who are the leaders in the self-advocacy movement, and whom do they represent?
- Are they people with disabilities?
- Are the self-advocates really making the decisions for their groups, or are advisors — inadvertently or consciously — influencing the decisions of the group members?
- How much are self-advocates used for agency needs — that is, groups being formed only to meet federal requirements for consumer participation, and never given any real voice in influencing agency policy or direction?
- How many self-advocates sit as members on agency Boards of Directors, or are in actual paid positions such as executive directors of self-advocacy organizations?
- Where and how do advisors use the self-advocacy movement for agency gains at the expense of the self-advocates' individual work and ideas?
- Are people with disabilities only allowed to be "self-advocates," or can they be "advocates" as well?

Advisors must be extremely careful to make sure that what is advocated for, is what the self-advocates want and not merely window dressing for an agency's need. Bringing self-advocates to meetings without explaining to them the full concept and the innuendos and nuances that are and will be occurring during the meeting causes the self-advocates to make decisions without proper preparation. The self-advocates should be able to question staff about the particular activity in which they will be involved, without being intimidated. Self-advocates should have the right and the ability to question and possibly refuse to take part in an activity. If the self-advocate does not necessarily agree, he or she must not suffer any repercussions like being eliminated from future planning activities or, worse yet, being ostracized and ignored.

Advisors need to continually be aware of the power and influence that they have over self-advocates. Advisors need to realize that a self-advocate might not challenge the advisor because the self-advocate is too close to that individual. Until recently, persons with disabilities had few peer role models they could look up to, so they naturally looked toward advisors as their role models. Self-advocates are at a beginning stage of recognizing that they, themselves, will have to develop leadership from within their own peer group in order for self-advocacy to truly take hold and succeed.

The self-advocacy movement needs to go beyond the showcasing of individual self-advocates. Yearly meetings and conventions that provide no means of follow-up and problem solving ultimately will not provide enough substance and impact to sustain the movement. Clearly, individual self-advocates gain self-esteem from attending these meetings, but the movement has got to go beyond this forum in order to ensure its survival. The development of viable organizations of self-advocates will depend on independent funding that is not linked to any service system. Once an agency service delivery system is involved, then conflict of interest issues emerge., thus diluting the power structure of the self-advocacy program. However, the difficulty of obtaining adequate independent funding through private grants and foundations remains a major obstacle for the self-advocacy movement, since self-advocacy has a relatively low priority status for funding. Left with primarily agency-sponsored self-advocacy groups, the movement is much more subject to the limitations of a narrowly focused agenda which once again can easily be influenced or shaped by the particular service provider.

In summary, the gains made by self-advocates have just begun to take hold with new federal legislative mandates and incentives, but the future of this movement as a viable, independent and separate entity has not yet been determined. Surely, self-advocates and their advisors will need to work closely in order to ensure that agency conflict of interest remains at a minimum and that alternate sources of funding are constantly explored. Lastly, self-advocates and leaders in the field of developmental disabilities will need to work together as equals to combat any general political tides and policies that may endanger the gains of inclusion and program choice that have been made during the last twenty years.

19

"The Bruises Are On the Inside"

An Advisor's Perspective

Ruthie-Mae Beckwith, Ph.D.

RUTHIE-MAE BECKWITH is the advisor to People First of Tennessee and has helped self-advocates in Tennessee to develop one of the most successful organizations in the U.S. She holds a Ph.D., but knows that the real lessons are learned on the road and in meeting rooms across the countryside.

We drive across the state trying to find a radio station we all can agree on. Some like Christian rock, some like country, and some like heavy metal. The ashtray is overflowing with ashes and butts. The people in the back have piled in on top of a week's worth of fast-food wrappers and my sons' collection of lethal weapons and teddy bears. We drive on while I wonder how it was possible that my car got 115,000 miles on it in just two short years. I adjust the rear view mirror one more time to cut down on the glare from the headlights of other cars passing us on the interstate. We are tired from our long trip and looking forward to being home.

We travel the state of Tennessee to visit self-advocacy chapters in very out-of-the-way places. People with disabilities run these chapters as part of our statewide self-advocacy organization. We stop on the way there and pick people up for meetings. We stop on the way back to take them home. At the meetings, members talk about their feelings and problems. They talk about how to make their chapters stronger. They talk about their dream of a new system of services. What they say they want is a system that is very different from the one in which they are currently imprisoned.

Lots of dreams, ideas, pain and fear are discussed in these meetings. I sit back and focus on the details of what people are sharing. I wonder how the members of these chapters are going to survive until this new system comes about. I forget that survival is one of the things our members do best. Even so, I cannot begin to grasp how they survive the daily oppression, lack of control, and loss of dignity occurring in their lives. I sit back and reflect on the details of what many of our members have shared and confided in just over the past two months.

Talk about blatant abuse, like someone slapping them or throwing them down a flight of stairs, is rare in these meetings. Instead, members describe their problems in ways that are deceptively simple and matter-of-fact. Members don't minimize their experiences. They just tell their stories in a way that lets you know they're the ones being blamed for the loss of their freedom, the loss of their rights, the loss of their respect.

At today's meeting, a woman describes a recent experience where she received a written behavioral reprimand at the sheltered workshop for having a piece of candy in her purse. She is in tears as she shares this latest humiliation. She expresses her feeling that additional pressure is being put on her because she helped organize the self-advocacy chapter at this workshop.

I think back to another chapter's meeting a month ago, when another woman told us her housemanager had refused to let her go to church as punishment for expressing her opinion. Her opinion was a prediction that someday all of the group homes in our state would be closed and people would live in homes of their own. Her opinion is a desire echoed by the vast majority of the other members of her group.

Last week in another town, one of our members had been removed from her agency-sponsored apartment. Our member had broken an agency policy and let her boyfriend spend the night with her. Her punishment was the loss of her freedom. The news of this event was murmured softly among all the persons getting services there. They got the message; they, too, will be less likely to break this rule.

One of our members recently helped me understand why self-advocacy is such a "danger zone." He calls me from a pay phone on our toll-free number to explain why we haven't heard from him in a while. He has a phone at the agency-run house he shares with three other roommates — but he can't use it anymore for personal business. He can't call us and we can't call him. He tells me he will have to move out of his house if he breaks this rule. He doesn't want to move back to the boarding home where he never knew if he would get fed. He doesn't want to go back to panhandling and begging on the streets. Instead, he begs me not to call his social worker to express my indignation at this latest violation of his rights. He promises to call back next time he goes uptown.

In my mind these stories have entwined and merged to form a picture of a service system that has slowly come to hinder rather than help. One of our members called us for help. She gets frustrated and upset at having to live in an institution. That morning she had gotten upset again and been physically restrained and placed in her room. Another member went to check on her and see how she was doing. This member asked her if she had any marks or bruises from being physically restrained. She paused as she was crying long enough to say, "No, the bruises are on the inside."

Back in the car, we drop off the last person at her group home just in time for dinner. I head back to the office the next day still wondering what's wrong with this picture. I read my professional flyers about a conference coming up on empowerment. The theme of the conference is "Going from Rights to Responsibility." The professionals planning this event think their "clients" need to learn more about responsibility along with their rights. All I know is that our members have never let us down. They have risen to every occasion when we have asked them to call, write, organize and attend meetings that are important to them. I find myself wondering why we are the only ones who consider our members responsible.

I find it harder and harder to go to meetings where other professionals and service providers will be present. I find it hard to face many of the directors of the agencies where our members get services. Don't they know the damage their "policies" inflict on the people they *serve*? Are they simply not aware of the daily injustices their "clients" are experiencing where they live and work? As the odometer continues to rack up more miles, I find it harder to believe that there could be so many "misunderstandings" across our state.

Self-advocacy is about empowering people to speak for themselves and to believe in themselves. For ten years, our members have worked together to try to fight the fires of rights violations. Lately, it seems like we are fighting these fires while the whole forest is burning down around our heads. So, at our personnel and policies committee meetings, we talk about the increase in problems people appear to be having. We ask for ideas and a policy to help us address the problem of rights violations.

The members of this committee all receive services themselves. They know what the problems are and how they affect everyone who has a disability. The committee becomes weighted down, however, by their anger, their pain, and the sheer pervasiveness of what is happening all across the state. So, they vote to ask our board of directors for help.

At our office the walls are covered with disability rights posters. Slogans like DON'T THINK THAT WE DON'T THINK and OUR VOICE IS NEW abound. A friend from Georgia dropped us a postcard with a quote from Margaret Mead which we also put on the wall. It reads:

> *Never doubt that a small group of thoughtful, committed citizens can change the world; indeed, it's the only thing that ever has.*

Section VI

"The Past is Prologue"

WHEN NO ONE ANSWERS

A child sees me.
Naturally curious,
he looks to his
mother,
"Why?"
"Shhh!" is her
answer.
Time passes;
we meet again,
the child and I,
I smile recalling
his curiosity.
This time he
isn't curious though
He picks up a
stone, throwing
it in my direction
he yells,
"Get ya mental"
Where did he learn
that?
Surely not his mother,
her only answer was
"Shhh!"

— *Bob Williams*
(see p. xii)

20

The Legacy of Self-Advocacy

People with Cognitive Disabilities as Leaders in their Community

Michael Wehmeyer, Ph.D., & Richard Berkobien, M.S.W.

MICHAEL WEHMEYER and RICK BERKOBIEN operate the Self-Determination project for the national headquarters of The Arc. Together they work to support the participation of self-advocates on national and local boards of directors. The Arc has a longstanding commitment to supporting individual self-advocates, as well as the self-advocacy movement.

Introduction

How we view ourselves, and are viewed by others, influences much of how we conduct our lives: the activities we attempt, who we approach or avoid, which situations we enter into, how we feel about ourselves and what we expect from ourselves. We may see ourselves either as *actors* in our day-to-day lives, in control and active participants, or as *acted upon*, dependent upon the actions and decisions of others, fate or circumstances beyond our control. Historically, people with cognitive disabilities have had the latter experience. They have been deprived of opportunities for choice and control in their lives and thus view themselves as *acted upon*. Adults with cognitive disabilities have been denied the chance to live adult lives, at least partially because they have not been perceived as assuming adult roles. Conse-

* Funding for this chapter was provided in part by Grant #H158K00046 awarded to The Arc (formerly Association for Retarded Citizens of the United States) by the U.S. Department of Education Office of Special Education Programs. However, the opinions expressed here do not necessarily reflect the position or policy of the U.S. Department of Education and no official endorsement by the Department should be inferred.

quently, they may not visualize themselves in those roles, and thus may never act to achieve adult status.

Society has held multiple perceptions of people with cognitive disabilities over the years, all of which have contributed to a conception of dissimilarity (National Institute on Mental Retardation, 1976). In the latter part of the nineteenth and beginning of the twentieth centuries, people with disabilities were viewed as menaces, contributing to the decline and decay of society. Even less charitable were later portrayals of people with disabilities as objects of fear, ridicule or pity. Other misperceptions persist today. People with cognitive disabilities are seen as "holy innocents" and "perpetual children." Adults with disabilities are continually placed in the role of *student* or *learner*, a role in our society that limits one's autonomy and self-determination. The accomplishments of people with disabilities that exceed stereotyped expectations are often depicted as heroic and courageous; thus, their success is labeled as an aberration.

The status quo is changing, however, due in large part to the self-advocacy movement, which has pushed to foster the perception that people with disabilities are valued members of society. One visible outcome of these changes is that most professionals in the field and many employers today accept people with cognitive disabilities as viable members of the workforce, acceptable co-workers and colleagues. Other positive perceptions are more difficult to create, but no less important. Adults with cognitive disabilities are now being accepted as friends, not just clients. Despite the overwhelming handicap of poverty and low wages, there is an emerging recognition of people with disabilities as true contributors. As people with cognitive disabilities have broader access to the community, they take on roles as neighbors, renters, home owners. As prohibitions to emotional and sexual relationships for people with cognitive disabilities erode, they become free to assume roles of spouse and parent. Certainly, many people in the self-advocacy movement have assumed the roles of advocate, benefactor, and supporter.

The self-advocacy movement has proven to be an important agent for changing perceptions about people with disabilities, as well as providing the vehicle by which people achieve empowerment and self-determination (Wehmeyer, 1992; Wehmeyer & Berkobien, 1991). If people with cognitive disabilities are to become self-determined and empowered, much of the effort must go toward changing the beliefs and attitudes of not only the general public but also those who work in the disability field.

One important perception that has emerged because of these efforts is that of *leader*. People with cognitive disabilities have, time and again, assumed and excelled in roles of leadership. While it may be premature to talk about the heritage of the movement, it is our contention that the development of leaders may be the most important legacy the self-advocacy movement has to leave.

As agencies and systems that attempt to support people with disabilities in their quest to achieve full inclusion recognize that they must involve people with cognitive disabilities in the decisions that shape and drive the system, they turn to self-advocacy groups to provide leaders. This chapter discusses how to move toward the eventuality that people with cognitive disabilities can, if they so choose, assume roles of leadership — not only in self-advocacy groups, but at work, in church, at the local YMCA, and in the neighborhood homeowners' association.

Much of the following emerged from a forum held in Portland, Oregon, at the 1991 National Convention of The Arc (formerly Association for Retarded Citizens of the United States). This was a significant event for this organization. Due primarily to the efforts of self-advocates nationwide, the delegate body voted to change the name of the organization to The Arc, leaving behind the stigma and stereotypes brought about by the name "Association for Retarded Citizens" and recognizing that people with disabilities are people first. In this atmosphere, leaders in self-advocacy and state and local chapters of The Arc met to prepare an agenda to assist chapters to empower people with cognitive disabilities to assume roles of leadership in this organization across the country.

A New Voice

Just as the need exists to change perceptions about people with disabilities, so is there a similar need to change our conception of leadership. Too often, the term *leader* conjures stereotyped images of military generals, government heads and statesmen, wealthy magnates and industrialists, or other such powerful figures. With the advent of the civil rights movement in the 1960s, the face of leadership began to change, assuming the characteristics of people who had previously been excluded from boardrooms and congressional chambers.

Ward (1988) and Driedger (1989) recount the emergence of the disability rights movement on the heels of the social upheaval of the sixties. People with disabilities asserted their rights to self-determination and participation in the mainstream. According to Driedger (1989), the disability rights movement was viewed by its progenitors as the "last civil rights movement," following similar movements by laborers, women, people of color, colonized peoples, and poor people. The independent living movement provided the initial foray into mainstream life for Americans with disabilities.

The organization of Independent Living Centers was based on these basic principles: "Those who best know the needs of [people with disabilities] and how to meet those needs are [people with disabilities] themselves; the needs of [people with disabilities] can be met most effectively by comprehensive programs which provide a variety of services, and [people with disabilities] should be integrated as fully as possible into their community" (Driedger, 1989, pp. 22-23).

The independent living movement proved that people with disabilities could, and should, take the leading role in describing services which best fit their needs, determining where and how these supports should occur, and evaluating the effectiveness of these efforts. Leadership took many forms, from committee participa-

A DISSENTING OPINION

The perception that people with cognitive disabilities are incapable of assuming adult roles, and perhaps consequently should just be satisfied with what is given to them, was illustrated in Texas recently. After over a decade of acrimonious and heated litigation, the state of Texas finally settled a class-action lawsuit which resulted in the proposed closure of two of its thirteen state schools. Doyle Willis, a Texas state representative whose constituency included one of the two schools, announced that he would sponsor a bill to prevent the closing of any state school. While delivering his announcement and talking with newspaper reporters, this representative was confronted by a man, James Templeton, who manipulated his wheelchair to within inches of Willis and said, "I disagree with what you're saying." Mr. Templeton knew intimately what he was talking about. He had lived for thirty years at the Austin State School, in Austin, Texas, the second school slated for closure. He also had lived for the past five years in a group home in the Austin area. To reporters he later described how living in the group home had afforded him the opportunity to experience freedom, indeed even the freedom to advocate for political change. "I disagree with you about the 13 state schools. I think they should all close," reiterated Mr. Templeton. The newspaper account of the representative's reaction indicates that "Mr. Willis looked at the man in the wheelchair and said he didn't understand. Another person standing nearby told the state representative that Mr. Templeton disagreed with his philosophy on state schools." Rep. Willis' reply? "You talk to him then," and he left. Mr. Templeton, angry and belittled, said he would stay to testify before Representative Willis' committee. After waiting seven hours, he was forced to leave to catch a bus. As he left, he found that the House chambers were not physically accessible, and he was forced to wait for help and then continue home.

Mr. Templeton does not need instruction on being a leader or an advocate. He needs to live in a society that recognizes basic human rights independent of disability status. What needs to change are the attitudes and expectations of others.

(Excerpts from the *Dallas Morning News*, Tuesday, August 4, 1992)

tion to lobbying, from protest action to behind-the-scenes planning.

The disability rights movement demonstrated that a service delivery system consisting of actions of people without disabilities on behalf of people with disabilities, where there is no reciprocity, is a model that must be abandoned. Gunnar Dybwad said it most succinctly in a 1980 address to the International League of Societies for the Mentally Handicapped (Williams & Shoultz, 1982):

> A new voice can be heard in our movement. As yet it is hesitant, unsure, but it is steadily gaining in strength. It is the voice of those we once thought incapable of speaking, hence our battle cry used to be: "We speak for them." It is the voice of those once considered ineducable, who are now attending schools. It is the voice of those once deemed unemployable, indeed deemed "incapable of sustained effort," who now bring a pay check for a full work week. Let us not argue how soon or how many of our young people will be able to express themselves. Let us instead ask ourselves: Are we ready to listen to their new voice? (p. 5)

Assuming the Mantle of Leadership

There are a number of compelling reasons why people with cognitive disabilities must assume active roles of leadership in their community and in the organizations that support their inclusion. These individuals often bring with them a passion and vision created by the experience of living with a disability. This passion and vision is as important, if not more important, than the procedural and structural processes associated with leadership — which frequently become barriers to the attainment of these roles. The benefit is reciprocal, especially for disability- and advocacy-related organizations. By incorporating people with disabilities into leadership positions, organizations can avoid becoming too distant from the field and insensitive to individual needs. Alternatively, people using support services are more likely to utilize and benefit from such activities if they have a sense of ownership and a commitment to the goals of the organization.

People with cognitive disabilities in leadership roles can both assist and serve as role models for other people with disabilities "coming up through the ranks;" they can serve as teachers to their peers striving toward empowerment and self-determination. Their presence serves as a model to people without disabilities, changing attitudes, perceptions, and expectations.

In essence, however, the attainment of leadership roles by people with cognitive disabilities is a recognition of the inherent right of human beings to become self-determining, and of an individual's right to participate in decisions affecting his or her life. It is both right and beneficial that individuals with cognitive disabilities assume roles of leadership, both within disability organizations and in other parts of the community. As such, the question which merits further consideration is not

A NEW VOICE

[Excerpts from an interview with Bob Kafka, ADAPT]

Disabled people are not going to go away.

We didn't come to Orlando for Disneyland rides or fancy negotiations, nothing like that.

We're here to show the world that you nursing home operators have one and a half million of our people locked away.

We will not stand for it any longer.

Let our people go.

You operators want to pretend it's complicated. You raise a lot of pseudo-issues to disguise the fact that it's all about your money and your power.

You want to pretend you're trapped in this business, that union contracts prevent such and such... that legal liability prevents so on and so forth....

We don't want to hear any of that.

It's not complicated. It's very simple. You will let our people go.

We were arrested the first day, lots of us.

They never expected us to come close to their hotel, the place where the members of the American Health Care Association were staying while they held their convention across the street.

Yes, they knew we were coming to Orlando. They briefed the locals, had the police waiting.

So it was all set up in advance, cops on the rooftops, a police booking operation in the basement of the convention center. They were all set to cage us up for daring to interfere.

They thought they had it covered. They were smugly going about their business, expecting only a minimum of trouble for a couple of hours.

The intensity there — anyone driving by could feel it. The tons of security, the A.C.H.A. people retreating inside the hotel, aghast. It was like, "How dare they spoil our party!"

The first day, they thought they'd arrested all the 'leaders.' But with ADAPT, when folks get arrested, other folks fill in and we just keep going.

We will not be moved.

It was our intent to send the message that nursing homes have one and a half million Americans locked up. We want the nursing home operators to be publicly accountable for that.

Here we are, people who look like the folks the operators lock up at their home facilities. They're on vacation, but they can't escape. We are people with disabilities. We are everywhere.

The operators were inside having seminars on how to manage the disruptive patient. We were outside holding a seminar with the press on the economics of managing people in nursing homes.

They can talk all they want about how homelike it is. We know better, firsthand.

This will be a long struggle; we're prepared for that. Five or ten years, a long struggle.

Unless people like ADAPT are willing to stay focused and targeted, people in nursing homes and state schools are going to be forgotten all over again.

We may not win at every action, but we will win the cumulative victory. We make people think about nursing homes. They don't want to think about that. Put them away, put it out of mind, put it somewhere else.

I want to say to people who say they don't like ADAPT tactics: Do you really want our people out? Or are you sitting home saying "Oh, those nursing homes shouldn't do that!"

How many people are going to get free because you hold that opinion? What are you doing about it?

People are turned off by the arrests, by our confrontational style. 'I'm not going to do ADAPT-style confrontations' — we hear that a lot.

If you don't want to be on the front lines but you do want to help, there's plenty to do: raising dollars so we can get to our actions, working with people in your community to make these issues known, forming your own group, bringing some attention to the issues in your home town.

We sure would welcome your help.

We will not be moved.

(Reprinted from *The Mouth*)

"Can people with cognitive disabilities become leaders?" but "How can people with cognitive disabilities assume leadership roles?"

Barriers to Leadership

Becoming a leader is not typically an overnight process, and leadership is not an attribute acquired — or necessarily desired — by everyone. However, the rapid growth of the national self-advocacy movement demonstrates that, with adequate support and opportunity, people with cognitive disabilities can become effective leaders.

Barriers to leadership do exist, including a self-fulfilling prophecy based on the inaccurate belief that people with mental retardation cannot be leaders. There is frequently a double standard in the expectations for people with cognitive disabilities in leadership positions. Inadequacy and incompetence are frequently tolerated in leaders without disabilities for political or other reasons, yet people with cognitive disabilities are frequently excluded for shortcomings which may represent inadequacies in the system as much as incompetence of the person. An example of one such system inadequacy is the lack of accommodation provided to people with intellectual disabilities to enable them to participate fully in the leadership process. These accomodations can range from adaptation of materials to providing transportation to meetings.

Yet another barrier to the attainment of leadership roles by people with disabilities is that there are frequently conflicts of interest between organizations which provide services and the individuals who might serve in a leadership capacity. Consequently, people with disabilities are provided nothing more than token roles and given limited choices.

There are barriers within individuals, also, to the immediate assumption of leadership roles. Leadership results from a lifelong education in — and expectations of — self-determination, efficacy, control and participation in the full spectrum of one's life. To the extent that people with cognitive disabilities have not had such experiences, they are limited in their access to leadership roles. Certainly the formal structures of governance and responsibility, including parliamentary procedure, are merely temporary hurdles, not insurmountable.

Finally, one of the primary vehicles of leadership in our society is verbal communication. To further complicate matters, the language of human services is frequently complicated and jargon-laden. There is often no one available or willing to take the time to explain issues, situations, and events when a person with a cognitive disability says he or she does not understand.

Supporting Leadership

There is much to be done before people with cognitive disabilities are enabled to serve in leadership roles in their communities. Certainly, underlying issues of economic and social empowerment need to be addressed. Too many people with cognitive disabilities are limited in their access to volunteer and service organizations because they do not receive vacation time from their jobs, or because work hours conflict with such activities. Other people are prohibited from participation by inadequate transportation or because others (residential staff, family members) wield excessive control over their lives. Some, frankly, cannot afford the incidental costs of volunteering.

People currently in leadership roles must make the adequate representation of people with cognitive disabilities — in all levels of leadership and involvement — a priority. Physical presence alone does not ensure effective participation, but ab-

CLIFFORD

Clifford is your neighbor. His house is brightly painted and his yard neatly trimmed. He pays taxes, votes in every election and writes to his congressman. He works hard at his job, but still finds time for community organizations. He loves his family. He stays fit and is an avid baseball fan. He is fun-loving and affable.

Clifford Foster, 38, was born in Little Rock, Arkansas. He and his three brothers and four sisters grew up in St. Joseph's Orphanage in North Little Rock. When he was 16, Clifford was institutionalized for several years at the Conway Human Development Center. His reflection on those dim years are typically soft spoken. "For me," he says, "it wasn't so bad, really.... But there are a lot of people in there that should be out on their own."

Clifford knows about life on his own. He and two other housemates with cognitive disabilities have lived on their own since 1987, when they moved into their red and blue bungalow. Cliff had lived alone in an apartment for a year before that, but "I got lonely," he says. Now these men assist one another, distributing household responsibilities, sharing expenses and giving one another the support they need to cope with life in the real world.

Clifford has worked as a janitor at Arkansas Uniform and Linen Supply Company since 1982. His employer has said that living independently has made a tremendous difference for Clifford. Cliff and his roommates do most things on their own. That is the only way they will have it. "They have a true citizen support network of church members, neighbors, and friends," says Marie Pierce, an advisor for the local People First group. As president of People First for the past two years, Clifford is a strong advocate of independence and self-improvement. "I tell other people with disabilities not to put themselves down, or let other people call you 'retard' any more. Disabled people should be treated the same as all others because we all have to live together on this earth."

Being involved has always been Clifford's way. "While I was in Conway, some of the other people didn't want to try to help themselves. But I told myself I wanted to work in the community, so I delivered mail to all the offices and did grounds work cutting grass so I would have job skills." Being an advocate for himself and others has also been his way. "We [Clifford and his roommates] lived in a boarding house for 17 years after I left Conway," he says. "When the owner passed away, her sister took

(continued from previous page)

over and she took advantage of us by raising the rent too high. I told the other tenants, 'Someone has to stand up to her.' So I told her, 'You're not going to take advantage of these men anymore. You call them boys, but I call them men, and that's how they should be treated.' So we moved out."

Clifford has taken his leadership to levels beyond his local community. He has served as president of People First in Arkansas, and Vice-President of the Association for Retarded Citizens/Arkansas. Clifford was elected to the national board of The Arc in 1990 and has served on the national Self-Advocacy Committee.

Asked to sum up his active life, he answers simply, "I'm a busy man."

(Reprinted with permission from *The Possible Dream*, a pamphlet printed by the Arkansas Coalition for the Handicapped.)

sence from these situations guarantees that people with cognitive disabilities will neither learn, nor be allowed, to take on leadership roles!

When moving to include people with cognitive disabilities in leadership roles, it is important to provide experiences conducive to success. Leadership begins with committee experiences and progresses, *over time,* to roles such as board member or officer. Placing people in leadership roles for which they are unprepared may spell failure. This cannot, however, be construed as a reason to exclude self-advocates from the opportunity to serve.

Supporting effective leadership may involve providing adequate instruction in parliamentary procedures and other formal structures of leadership. Training of this nature will undoubtedly benefit all people new to leadership roles and should be implemented as policy for all leaders, not just leaders with cognitive disabilities.

In addition, there is a need to foster the development of leadership and self-advocacy skills. While in school, students with cognitive disabilities need to receive instruction which leads them to be self-determining and self-advocating. This involves a two-pronged effort: *curricular* emphasis on problem-solving, decision-making, and other skills leading to self-determination, and *non-curricular* strategies which create opportunities for learners to take responsibility for their own learning and provide them with experiences of choice and control (Wehmeyer, 1992).

Students need to have the opportunity to play a significant role in the planning of their educational programs. Public Law 101-476, the Individuals with Disabilities Education Act, requires that student preferences and interests be included when transition planning occurs. Martin and Marshall (1992) have developed instructional programs which teach students to chair their own Individualized Education/Transition Planning meeting. This includes such activities as the identification of relevant interests and abilities, skill development in goal planning, identification of necessary supports and possible resources, and instruction in the IEP procedure.

Students can take active roles in selecting the goals toward which they will be working. Teachers can identify priority areas for instruction and allow students to select from several objectives which reach this end. Students with even the most severe disability can be involved in learning to problem-solve through such procedures as self-management.

Supported Leadership

There are numerous adaptations and supports that would enable adults with cognitive disabilities to serve more effectively as leaders. These are as variable as the individual characteristics of each human being, but some examples of "Supported Leadership" (from *The Arc*, 1992) include:

- Pair board or committee members with and without disabilities, so that the person with the disability has a partner he or she can access if necessary. Make sure the individual knows how to contact that person — and, just as importantly, has the opportunity to do so.
- Allow people with cognitive disabilities to select a support person to assist them in leadership. The person selected should be someone who the individual feels will best represent his or her viewpoints and attitudes. Choices should always be available. The individual should be given the opportunity to choose the level of help or support he or she needs. It should never be assumed the person needs or requires a certain degree of assistance.
- Prior to board or committee meetings provide tutorials on issues/procedures to be discussed during the meeting.
- Provide cognitively accessible materials. Minimize the use of written materials when possible. Present written materials orally during the meeting or beforehand. Provide tape-recorded copies of all written materials. Picture-code the agenda and other handouts.
- Send out materials early. A person with a cognitive disability who cannot read requires extra time to go over the materials with a support person.
- Set up co-leadership situations where two people (with or without disabilities) assume the responsibilities normally contained in a single position. This might enable more folks with disabilities to participate in a meaningful way.
- Tape meetings, so that the person can replay the meeting to refresh his or her memory or to listen to discussions which he or she did not completely understand.

Resa

Resa Hayes lives in Spokane, Washington and is the president of People
First of Washington. She was interviewed during her trip to the Second
Annual North American People First Conference in Nashville, Tennes-
see in June of 1991.

"Being active and speaking out seems to come naturally to me, but I did
find out along the way that if I wanted people to listen to me, I needed to
develop some skills."

"There were no leadership-skill classes taught in any of the schools I
attended, but as I moved through school, I learned that if I wanted to go
to things like basketball games or Camp Fire meetings, I would have to
make arrangements myself when my folks couldn't take me. I learned that
I had to take charge when I needed to make things go."

"I had good role models. My parents, brothers, and sister were all active members of many clubs, farm organizations and school activities. They
also held offices, so I heard a lot of talk about the correct way to lead a
meeting and how to get things done."

"There needs to be more stress placed on the fact that people with
disabilities have the talent and ability to be leaders. They need to be worked
with. I think schools and self-advocacy organizations like People First could
really help out with this."

"I think training for leadership should start early — say in grade school.
If students with disabilities had the opportunity to belong to clubs that
they could manage — and if they had the opportunity to make things go
themselves — I believe it would give them the self-confidence to be good
leaders. They would get the idea that they could do what everyone else is
doing. They would have the feeling of belonging."

"Belonging to People First has given me the chance to learn what it
means to be a good leader. You have to be organized, you have to have
your information at hand, and you have to present it in a way that is easily
understood by your audience. A good leader must also work to develop
harmony within their organization so that everyone can work together."

"That way, everyone can learn to be a leader."

(Reprinted from *Habilitation*)

- Assign committee and board responsibilities according to individual skills, not simply on a blanket basis. Identify what the person with mental retardation can contribute, then match him or her with that activity.
- Finally, commit to working diligently to empower people with cognitive disabilities to assume roles of leadership even in the face of doubt, discomfort or dire predictions.

Conclusions

Napoleon Bonaparte said, "Ability is of little account without opportunity." William Shakespeare wrote, "Action is eloquence."

The time has come for both opportunity and action: Opportunities for people with cognitive disabilities to act to assume control in their lives and to take leading roles in defining the direction of services meant to support them. Opportunities for people without disabilities to learn that people with disabilities can be good neighbors, effective coworkers and friends.

It is incumbent upon those persons involved in education, social work, rehabilitation, psychology and other professions first to change our perceptions of people with disabilities, and then to work with people with disabilities to change others' perceptions of them. We must work *with* people with disabilities in this effort, allowing them to take their rightful position in this movement... in the lead.

References

The Arc (1992). *The roles of people with mental retardation in leadership.* Arlington, TX: The Arc National Headquarters.

Driedger, D. (1989). *The last civil rights movement.* New York: St. Martin's Press.

Martin, J.E., & Marshall, L.H. (1992). *Colorado self-determination transition checklist and curriculum guide.* Colorado Springs: Center for Educational Research.

National Institute on Mental Retardation (1976). *Your Citizen Advocacy Program.* Toronto: Author.

Ward, M. (1988). The many facets of self-determination. *NICHCY Transition Summary, 5,*

Wehmeyer, M.L. (1992). Self-determination and the education of students with mental retardation. *Education and Training in Mental Retardation, 27,* 302-314.

Wehmeyer, M.L., & Berkobien, R. (1991). Self-determination and self-advocacy: A case of mistaken identity. *TASH Newsletter, 17*(7), 4.

Williams, P., & Shoultz, B. (1982). *We can speak for ourselves.* Bloomington: Indiana University Press.

21

Leadership in Developmental Disabilities

Where We've Been, Where We Are, and Where We're Going

Hank Bersani Jr., Ph.D.

What is past is prologue. — SHAKESPEARE, *THE TEMPEST* (II, i, 261)

This book has focused on the past: not only to record the events of the past, but because — as the above quote from the entrance of the National Archives building states — all that has happened to this point, is only the prologue to the future. As I read the chapters that preceded this, I was struck by many questions about the nature of self-advocacy, leadership, and the making of a social movement. What does it take to be a leader? What makes a movement? Is there a developmental disabilities movement, and if so, who are the leaders? What will come next? In the past, these were relatively straightforward questions with fairly clear, direct answers. Today, however, the responses are more complex because so many more voices are being heard. Most significant is the addition of the loud, clear voices of self-advocates.

In the past their voices were silent, disenfranchised, or ignored. Today, they form a chorus commanding our attention. Leadership in the developmental disabilities movement has emerged where we never expected it a few decades ago: from

* Production of this chapter was supported in part by Grant #90DD0380 from the U.S. Administration on Developmental Disability. The opinions represented in this chapter are those of the author, and do not necessarily represent the views of the Administration on Developmental Disabilities.

people with developmental disabilities. This fact represents the latest of three stages or "waves" in the evolution of the movement to date.

The First Wave: Professionalism

Not all that long ago, the field of developmental disabilities was more of an academic discipline than the rights movement we know today. Professionals were in fact not interested in the rights of the people they called *clients, retardates* and *mentally deficient*. Among these professionals, leaders were people with academic credentials who held positions in the related fields of medicine, psychology, education, special education and social work. From as early as 1850 to as recently as 1950, the list of leaders in the field we now call "developmental disability" were professionals who had developed test procedures, reached clinical insights, identified new disabilities, described various impairments, and started new programs. Any book on what they called "Mental Deficiency" featured information on the "early leaders" such as Jean Marc Gespard Itard, Edouard Seguin and Samuel Gridley Howe, physicians and humanitarians in the 1800s.

Leaders in an academic field often function within professional organizations. The oldest, largest professional organization in the field was founded as the Association of Medical Officers of American Institutions for Idiotic and Feeble-Minded Persons. Later, it was renamed the American Association on Mental Deficiency (AAMD). For over 100 years, AAMD was an association of professionals, by professionals, for professionals, and the assumptions of the time were clear: *People with disabilities are defined by their disabilities* (mental deficiency), *and skilled researchers and scientists will lead the way.* A few reformers lead the way to some types of reform, but the overwhelming focus of "leadership" was on prevention, eugenics, confinement, segregation, and control. I have called this stage of leadership development the First Wave.

In those days, at the height of the First Wave, professionals defined the issues and created the new discipline of mental retardation separate from the fields of medicine, psychology, and education. They made decisions on their own, or in consultation with each other. Parents, physicians, and the general public assumed that the professionals, based on their professional training, knew what was best.

The professional activities of leaders were to form state and national organizations, convene national conferences, publish in research journals and books on disability, and consult to programs locally, nationally and even internationally.

Professionals spoke in their own language, and put forth new position statements. They identified themselves as having created something new — the field that they came to call "mental retardation." As professionals, they examined and diagnosed. They gave out labels and offered sweeping prognoses. They decided on who got therapy, what therapy they got, and when such therapy was pointless. They determined who went to school and who could not benefit from school. They said who could learn to work and who was "non-feasible" for rehabilitation. They set the criteria to evaluate who was ready for the community and who would never be ready to live in the community.

During the First Wave, the people in these programs were often seen as less than human. To most professionals, they were "subjects" in experiments, and the objects of studies. In fact, one ethicist, Joseph Fletcher (1972), actually put forth an ethical argument that individuals with tested IQ scores below 40 might not be human, and that those with IQ's below 20 were in fact not human, and did not need to be treated as such.

Much of the social context of the time was the growing role of science in our lives. Therefore the goal of the field at the time was to apply science to better understand the causes and possible cures of the "deficiency" — so people themselves (often described as "mentally defective") really had nothing to contribute to the field. In fact, as the science around disabilities was developing, it focused on prevention — immunizations, testing for problems like PKU, etc. In an era that focuses on the science of prevention, it is hard to find a use for people whom we see as the product of our failure to prevent their existence. At the same time, the parents of people with disabilities were seen as *victims* or *clients* as well. When textbooks discussed parents at all, the parents (usually the mothers) were described as needing counseling to work through stages of denial and guilt.

The Second Wave: Parents as Partners

The late 1940s and early 1950s brought a dramatic development. After World War II, there was a new prosperity; people had more leisure time and more income. This meant that they were able to turn their attention to issues other than basic economic survival. Concurrently, the "baby boom" was taking place. The dramatic increase in the U.S. birth rate meant not only that more babies were being born, but also that more children with developmental disabilities were being born. As a result of this combination of factors, parents of children with disabilities, especially mental retardation and cerebral palsy, formed their own groups. At first, the goal of these organizations was simply for members to support each other. Later, as the organizations matured, parents began to advocate for themselves, for their children, and each other. This was the beginning of the Second Wave.

In order to win the respect of the professionals in the field and to be more effective, parent groups began to organize. Today, we call it the "Parent Movement," but at the time, no one called it a *movement*. As parents of children with disabilities sought each other out, they formed local, state, national, and finally international organizations. In the U.S., the organization was known at first as the National Association for Retarded Children (NARC).

Not all professionals of the day saw individuals as research subjects and parents as clients. One by one, professionals joined in the parent rebellion. By the late

1950s and early '60s, writings by Gunnar Dybwad, Burton Blatt, and Wolf Wolfensberger began to point out the humanity and importance of people with disabilities and their families. Their work stood out as support for parents in the Second Wave.

The parent movement had a profound effect on the field. Parents acknowledged that there was a role for professional expertise, but they pointed out that they knew their family members better than any professional ever would. As parents, they had a lot to say about their family members, especially their young children. They demanded that parents be included in the room when professionals met to discuss the needs of children with disabilities. Many parents joined the American Association on Mental Deficiency (AAMD) and other professional organizations. At one point, there was a suggestion to have the emerging parent organization NARC become a part of AAMD. Mildred Thompson, then-president of AAMD, had the good sense to say that the best way that AAMD could support the parent movement was by assisting them to develop their own organization. At the height of the Second Wave, the membership of the National Association for Retarded Children (NARC) grew to far exceed that of AAMD. Several other parent organizations formed concurrently as well, most notably the United Cerebral Palsy Association of America

Parents said, *We are the consumers, we use your services, and we speak for our disabled children. It is our families that are getting help, it's us who are getting the services,* and for a while the consumer movement in this country in fact meant dealing with the parents of people with different kinds of disabilities. The Parent Movement grew slowly in size and power; it attained more and more respect as people became more and more competent. They learned the jargon and technical terms, or they got brave enough to say "I don't understand what you mean by that — explain it to me."

Parents established themselves as leaders. They joined professional organizations, formed their own organizations, established their own newsletters and journals that focused on parent issues, and even published articles in professional journals and chapters in professional texts. The Parent Movement was well established, and parents were clearly seen as leaders in the field. They — in conjunction with growing numbers of like-minded professionals — shaped the language of the field, redirected the emphasis at conferences, and even affected the content of the professional journals. In fact, the leaders of two parent organizations, Elsie Helsel of the United Cerebral Palsy Association (UCPA) and Elizabeth Boggs of the National Association for Retarded Children (NARC), are credited for formulating the concept of "developmental disabilities" and for writing the Developmental Disabilities Act of 1970.

There is no doubt that the parent movement — the Second Wave of leadership — is responsible for the proliferation of services. Models of service grew out of the needs and experiences of families, not out of the research of professionals. Parent associations — assisted by professional allies — pioneered new service concepts, piloted them, and then did the necessary political work to have them funded.

The Third Wave: Self-Advocacy

In the early 1970s, something remarkable happened in the field of developmental disabilities. In the U.S., the 1960s had been a time of new "advocacy" groups forming. From Ralph Nader advocating for all consumers, to Rosa Parks and Martin Luther King in the civil rights movement, to Gloria Steinem in the women's movement, people were claiming greater power, control, rights and freedom for themselves and others. People with developmental disabilities — the same people who the professionals and even the parents had called *mentally deficient, clients,* and *retardates* — began to organize themselves, often helped by staff, parents, and other allies. What emerged as the Third Wave of the developmental disabilities movement became known as the Self-Advocacy Movement.

In the past 20 years, self-advocates have formed their own organizations at the local, state and national levels. These state and local organizations were formed partly in reaction to the attitudes promoted by parent and professional associations, but also in an effort to emulate the effective advocacy approaches of these groups. From the humble beginnings in Washington and Oregon described in this volume by Shoultz, Ward, Furman, and Schaff, over 600 self-advocacy groups across the country are listed today in a national directory.

For many of these organizations, it is a measure of success to take on the same structures as the professional and parent organizations. They organized their own conferences to discuss the issues that are most important to them. Many have also joined professional and parent organizations like AAMD and ARC. They came up with their own name for their organizations and for their movement: "People First" and the "Self-Advocacy Movement. As with the parents and professionals before them, their organizations have run their own meetings and held elections, formulated their own issues, and changed the language of the field. Under pressure from self-advocates, the Association for Retarded Citizens (ARC) became The Arc, and the American Association on Mental Deficiency (AAMD) changed its name to the American Association on Mental Retardation (AAMR). Although the self-advocates were not totally pleased with the new names, all of them — and most professionals and parents — were pleased to see the "R" word dropped from The Arc, which is now a formal name, not an acronym, and the word "deficiency" dropped altogether.

Today, People First organizations exist all over the U.S., and similar groups have sprung up in over a dozen other nations. For several state groups, the annual convention is the highlight of the year. Just like the professionals and the parents, many self-advocates look forward to their annual convention. It provides the opportunity to get away from home, to meet and discuss important issues, and of course, to socialize with people with similar interests. The national organization, Self-Advocates Becoming Empowered, organizes national conferences of, by, and for self-advocates. To the leaders in the movement, the formation of a national organization was a major step so that they could have a national presence, organize a national conference, hold national elections, and establish national officers. Self-advocates have published articles in their own newsletters, as well as in the journals and newsletters of the parent and professional organizations. Self-advocates have given major addresses at AAMR and Arc conferences, and served on the President's Committee on Mental Retardation. They have published chapters in books; most recently, *The National Reform Agenda and People with Mental Retardation*, a book published by the President's Committee on Mental Retardation (1994), features a section with chapters by several self-advocates.

Measures of Success

Many self-advocates have their own favorite signs of success. For Valerie Schaaf, it was the Oregon group's formal incorporation as "People First International" over 20 years ago. For Barbara Goode, a self-advocacy leader from Canada, it was being chosen to give a speech to the United Nations. For Nancy Ward, it was the formation of a national organization. Self-advocates working in Tennessee with advisor Ruthie-Mae Beckwith are proud of the fact that they have brought a lawsuit against the state. Self-advocates in Colorado fought to have people with disabilities included on the boards of directors of service agencies. To other self-advocates like T.J. Monroe and Bernard Carabello, an indicator of success is that they have become sought-after speakers and consultants who build on their institutional background and vision of the future. To others, like Victor Ramirez, a measure of success was the fact that shortly before he died, he met personally with several U.S. senators and told them he was advocating not for himself, but for his friends who still lived in the institution. For Michael Kennedy, it is escaping the institution, advocating successfully against the Medicaid system, helping others across the nation become self-advocates, developing his literacy skills, and buying a home with his wife Lori. For Peter DeNegris, success is making it "on the outside" after two decades of growing up in New York state institutions.

For most self-advocates (and for me), the real measure of their success is how they have affected the rest of us — the professionals' and the parents' movements. They have changed our organizations, our attitudes, our language, and our practices. Most of all, they have changed our communities and even our government. In the Third Wave, self-advocates have given us several slogans to guide our policies and actions, such as "People First language" and "Nothing about me without me." They have caused us to redefine our issues, and to rethink all our old assumptions. And, they have made us nervous.

A CONTINUING STRUGGLE

The development of a national self-advocacy movement has not been an easy one. Professionals were reluctant to give up any of their power to parents. Some of them still resist.

In turn, many parents and parent organizations have been reluctant to give up any of their power and influence to self-advocates. Nationally, there is still a parent organization called The Voice of The Retarded. If a group already exists to be *The* Voice for a group (unfortunately still called "The Retarded"), then why would they support self-advocates? This organization and others like it claim to be about promoting good institutions for those who need them. In fact, they are about denying the ability of people to speak for themselves. They oppose self determination. They fight progress. They deny the obvious. They are stuck in the Second Wave.

As a young advocate-in-training, I learned from my mentor Burton Blatt that making people nervous is a measure of success. If a would-be social movement has only a few members and no power, they do not make us nervous. We become concerned when the group becomes big enough and organized enough to become an effective movement. That causes a reaction from those who want things to remain unchanged. They wonder, "Will this go too far?" "What will be our role as parents or professionals if they become leaders?" "What part of our professional expertise is still wanted or useful?" These are questions that we still struggle to answer. They are questions that parents and professionals must struggle with personally.

Today, some parents and parent organizations — in addition to some professionals and their organizations — are reluctant to give up any of their power and influence to self-advocates. *But there is no changing the inevitable.* Today, we cannot discuss policies for services to people with intellectual impairments without the presence and participation of people with disabilities themselves. This is as it should be. Today, no list of leaders in the movement is complete without including the names of several self-advocates who are clearly today's leaders and are leading us into the next century.

POWER GENERATES CONFLICT

One of the things that happens when a group becomes empowered is that those previously in power do not always see things the same way. As people develop self-advocacy skills, they will ask for things the rest of us don't approve of. That comes with empowerment. It's a time-honored problem: The more people advocate for themselves, the more likely they will be to advocate things that professionals and parents (even their allies) don't approve of. That realization, however, is not justification to block empowerment.

If we listen to people with disabilities, three messages become clear in the Third Wave.

First: *"We have different values and different concerns than you professionals and even our parents have."* Years of growing up with a disability means that many self-advocates have different priorities. Professionals and parents must stop and listen to the unique concerns raised by people whose lives have often been determined by the services they receive.

Second: *"We value choice, independence and risk; we know that we're going to make mistakes, and we're willing to accept those mistakes, to accept the penalties and risks of those mistakes."* The rest of us do lots of things that are not good for us against the advice of people who know better than us, and we say "It's our choice." We all value choice, independence and risk — as do self-advocates. In 1985 Michael Kennedy said in an address to the U.S. Senate Finance Committee, "We would not be here today if we did not take risks. We take risks every time we get up in the morning."

Third: *"We have dreams for our futures."* As we listen to self-advocates, they are telling us they have their own dreams for the future, and they want room to pursue those dreams. Many of the dreams are modest — to have a job, a home, a spouse. Other dreams are a bit more challenging — to be a U.S. senator, to be President of the United States, to be a millionaire. The test of these dreams is not the likelihood of their success, but rather the direction they lend to the dreamer's life — and to the field. As Rowitz (1991) indicated, "...leaders with mental retardation must be a part of the 1990s. They need to have a vision for the future, or the future will blur" (p. iv).

IS SELF-ADVOCACY A NEW SOCIAL MOVEMENT?

What makes a social movement? A recent article in a British journal (Shakespeare, 1993) asks whether the self-organization of people with disabilities represents the emergence of a new social movement. Although his examples are drawn from the self-help groups of people with physical disabilities, he offers a clear vision of self-help as a social movement. In 1976 (as People First International was forming in Oregon), Safilios-Rothschild suggested:

> The time may be ripe for the disabled to generate a social movement patterned after the at least partially successful examples of the Black Movement and the Women's Movement. (p. 45)

These social movements and others seem to have several features in common — features that may help us determine that self-advocacy is in fact a social movement.

Johnson, Laraña and Gusfield (1994), writing about what they call "New Social Movements," give some insight into what makes a social movement today.

- First, in a social movement, *members go beyond their typical social roles.* Surely the consumers of human services standing up, organizing, and saying that they want control over their lives is a departure from former social roles.

- Second, a social movement *usually represents a strong ideological change.* Certainly the self-advocacy movement represents a profound ideological change — seeing people with intellectual disabilities as leaders rather than as mere consumers, or less.
- Third, social movements *involve the emergence of a new dimension of identity, often drawing upon a characteristic formerly seen as a weakness.* For example, in the early Black Pride movement, having kinky hair (an Afro) became something to be proud of — even though "good hair" had previously been defined as smooth and more like white Europeans' hair. Today, self-advocates are proud of who they are, and use a variety of bumper stickers, posters and slogans to say so: "Disabled and proud," "Don't think that we don't think," and even the more blunt "Piss on pity."
- Fourth, in a social movement, *the relationship between the individual and the movement is blurred.* Thus, self-advocates no longer advocate just for themselves. They advocate for others; they advocate for the movement; and a few, such as Bernard Carabello and Michael J. Kennedy, now hold paid advocacy positions — so *they* are, in that sense, "professionals." In this sense, the movement has begun to outgrow its name. Too many rigid professionals want to limit self-advocates by applying the name too literally. When Colorado self-advocates demanded voting positions on the county service agency boards of directors, they were told that as self-advocates they could participate in their own service plan meetings (be *self*-advocates), but not have decision-making authority that would affect other people with intellectual impairments.

Successful social movements seem to have several commonalities:

- *Redefining the problem.* The early civil rights movement redefined "The Negro problem" as a problem of prejudice. Similarly, the self-advocacy movement has redefined the "disability problem" as being less about rehabilitation and more about equality.
- *Isolating one or several targets.* The civil rights movement targeted Jim Crow laws — being seated at the back of the bus, and the lack of access to public accommodations. Now decades later, the disability rights movement has also targeted segregated transportation, and a lack of access to public places and accommodations.
- *Landmark events.* In the Civil Rights movement, landmark events included breaking the "color barrier" in professional baseball and in our public schools and universities, a march across an Alabama bridge led by Martin Luther King, and the beating of four black men for sitting at a lunch counter in Greensboro, North Carolina. Self-advocates' landmarks are their first conference, the first meeting of the national organization, and the

first lawsuit brought by a self-advocacy group on behalf of others with disabilities.

- *An agenda.* Critics speak harshly of "the black agenda" or "the women's agenda." What they seem to mean is that the movement has a new world view. Social movements strive for change: not merely small refinements to discrete aspects of the broader culture, but dramatic changes to the status quo. The self-advocacy movement agenda ranges from individual acceptance and freedom to dramatic social reform in housing, employment, and legal rights.
- *Self-naming.* In the civil rights movement, blacks rejected the terms *Negro* and *colored* in favor of *Afro-American, black,* and more recently, *Afrcan-American.* The women's movement worked hard to get us to refer to *women* rather than *girls,* and created alternatives to old sexist language. Today, the disability movement offers non-handicapist and people-first language as preferred alternatives to old formulations. They have called for changes in agency names, and the language used in legislation. By changing what they are called, and by asserting the right to determine what they are called, people with intellectual impairments are asserting a number of changes. They are changing how they see themselves as individuals, and how others see them as a group and as individuals. Finally, they challenge the old assumptions made by professionals and parents.
- *Indicators of success.* The women's movement charts the relative income earned by men vs. women. The civil rights movement keeps track of the number of blacks in positions of authority. The self-advocacy movement records the closures of institutions, membership on boards of directors, and recognition as serious advocates.

Ed Roberts, the founder of the World Institute on Disability (WID), said, "I am convinced that we are making the most profound social change that our society has ever seen" (World Institute on Disability, 1990). Ed was a man of great vision; it is clear to me that he was not just talking about WID, nor were his comments limited to the physical disabilities movement. Rather, he was referring most broadly to people with disabilities and their allies, who together are making the most profound changes that our society has ever seen.

Future Controversies:
Disability Culture? Disability-First Language?

Longmore (1995) states that the movement of Americans with disabilities (actually, he uses the non-people-first formulation "disabled Americans") is moving into a new phase. He states that the previous phase was one of establishing civil rights, equal access, equal opportunity, and inclusion. Although these battles are by no means over, Longmore suggests that efforts are shifting to the development of *"disability culture."* He points out that the *disability rights* approach is still in some sense rooted in the assumption that disability is less desirable. By contrast, the *disability culture* movement states that disability is not to be hidden, healed or even overcome. It is a culture to be honored and practiced.

The vision of disability as culture is not in competition with disability rights and self-advocacy. Rather, they complement each other. To those trained in rehabilitation and prevention of disabilities, disability culture is a challenging concept, but that does not make it any less valid. One of the most obvious implications of the disability culture movement is the fact that many disability activists, especially people with physical disabilities, are rejecting "people first" language in favor of older formulations. They call themselves "disabled people" to point out that they are *proud* of their disability and that it need not be hidden. They seem to be advocating what I call "disability first" language, although they have not used the term yet. Cynics may say that the impending split between "people first" and "disability first" language is indicative of a deep rift in the movement. On the contrary, I would argue that this discussion, and differences of opinion show a greater unity — unity in *the assertion of the right of self-naming.* People with disabilities, or disabled people, will be the ones to decide how they shall be called.

FINAL WORDS TO SELF-ADVOCATES

Whether one's focus is on civil rights or disability culture, advocacy will remain a constant theme in the foreseeable future. In 1971, Charlotte DesJardins wrote an organizing manual specifically for the emerging parent movement. She offers this advice on "How to move the bureaucracy":

> *You must stop feeling guilty and insignificant.*
> *You must stop apologizing for asking a bureaucrat to do a job you are paying him to do.*
> *You must stop begging for what you are entitled to by law.*
> *You must not accept these old excuses: "There isn't any money"; "We need more time."*
> *You must stop whispering while everyone else is shouting.*
> *Do not be afraid to complain.*
> *You must use mass action.*

These words were written 25 years ago, and directed at parents, but today they are as relevant as ever to self-advocates and self-advocacy organizations. These days, I put my own positive spin on DesJardins' thoughts:

> *You should feel proud.*
> *Let the system know what you need and what you want.*

Know your rights, and use them.

*Make sure the world knows about your successes. You have proven what can
be done.*

Stand up and speak out for yourself.

Work together as a group, not just alone as individuals.

References

DesJardins, C. (1971) *How to organize an effective parent group and move bureaucracies.* Chicago: Coordinating Council for Handicapped Children.

Fletcher, J. (1972). Indicators of humanhood: A tentative profile of man. *The Hastings Center Report,* Vol. 2 (November).

Johnson, H., Laraña, E., & Gusfield, J.R. (1994). *New social movements: From ideology to identity.* Philadelphia: Temple University Press.

Longmore, P.K. (1995) The second phase: From disability rights to disability culture. *The Disability Rag,* Sept./Oct. Syracuse, NY: Avocado Press.

President's Committee on Mental Retardation (1994) *The national reform agenda and people with mental retardation.* Washington, DC: U.S. Department of Health and Human Services.

Rowitz, L. (1991). Leadership in mental retardation. *Mental Retardation.*

Safilios-Rothschild, C. (1976). Disabled persons' self-definitions and their implications for rehabilitation. In G.L. Albrecht, *The sociology of physical disability and rehabilitation* (p. 45). Pittsburgh, PA: University of Pittsburgh Press.

Shakespeare, T. (1993). Disabled people's self-organization: A new social movement? *Disability, Handicap and Society, 8*(3).

World Institute on Disability (1990). *World Institute on Disability Seven Year Report, 1983-90.* Oakland, CA: Author.

Wolfensberger, W. (1977). *A multi-component advocacy and protection schema.* Toronto: Canadian Association on Mental Retardation.

Epilogue

Thoughts on the Death of a Valiant Self-Advocate

Bern Graney, Ph.D.

BERNARD GRANEY, PH.D., *a former student of Dr. Gunnar Dybwad, has worked closely with self-advocates in Massachusetts for many years.*

John Patrick is a man who gave us all two elements that are all too lacking in today's world — courage and inspiration. In most ways, John was a very quiet and serene man. He was always quite at peace with himself. And now, after much suffering with his body, we pray he is at peace with his Maker. If anyone might have raged about injustice or unfair treatment, it could have been John. For many years, he was institutionalized and treated very badly. His own high sense of justice and fair play may have been born from the unfairness, discrimination, and dehumanizing atmosphere of the former state school where he was kept against his indomitable will.

But John did not rail on about *his* past treatment excessively. He worked incessantly and with great perseverance to develop the notion of *self-advocacy*. He developed and showed leadership in instituting a program of former residents talking with people left in the state schools so they would not fear leaving the familiarity of the grounds or have fears about their new lives in the community.

Quietly, with a sense of purpose and dignity, John Patrick carried on. His frequent appearances at public hearings and firm advocacy on behalf of others was always basic — *simple, direct, and very inspiring to observe.* For after all, John was teaching the most important lesson to us all — that persons labeled as "mentally retarded" (a label he despised and worked to overcome) could speak for themselves, have an articulate view and were, above all, the real experts in this battle over the question of institutionalization and segregation. John taught us that we needed to listen very carefully to the people we serve — a lesson that is unfortunately forgotten by some — even today!

John was a very articulate and purposeful advocate against injustice, discrimination, and unequal treatment of others. *We shall all miss him greatly. But we should not forget his legacy.*

John's legacy is self-advocacy. John's legacy is his quiet, always polite, and very kind and caring manner... mostly his kindness and caring for *others*, not himself. This man devoted himself in a voluntary capacity to *building*: building a consensus and a force of will that state quite forcefully, "NEVER AGAIN" should we fall into the practice of neglecting others... "NEVER AGAIN" should we tolerate injustice toward others without speaking out... "NEVER AGAIN" should we fail to listen to the people we serve. His spirit will live on in all whose lives he touched. He probably did not realize what a profound and important influence he had on us all. His spirit will live on every time we perform an act of advocacy or defend another human being. John Patrick will live on, even though his body is leaving us. For he was truly a courageous and inspiring person.

I hope these words give you comfort! They do for me.

About the Editors

Gunnar Dybwad was born in Germany in 1909, and received a Doctor of Laws degree in 1934. He also has a degree from the New York School of Social Work. He has been awarded the status of Fellow by the American Association on Mental Retardation, the American Sociological Association, the American Orthopsychiatric Association, and the American Public Health Association. He is also an honorary fellow in the American Academy of Pediatrics.

He has published several books on the issue of mental retardation and has also been published in over 20 journals, including: *Journal of Rehabilitation, CHILDREN, International Rehabilitation Review, Policy Studies Review, Journal of Rehabilitation in Asia,* and the *International Journal of Religious Education.*

He was Executive Director of the National ARC, served as a consultant to President Kennedy's Special Assistant on Mental Retardation, and has been an expert witness in several of the landmark cases on the right to education and on institutional abuse.

Considered by many to be the grandfather of the self-advocacy movement, probably no one alive today has had a wider influence on the lives of people with developmental disabilities than Professor Dybwad.

Hank Bersani Jr., Ph.D., is a graduate of St. Michael's College and Syracuse University, and a former student of Professor Dybwad. Dr. Bersani is currently on the faculty of Oregon Health Sciences University, with an appointment in the Department of Public Health and Preventive Medicine.

Dr. Bersani has worked as a special class teacher, a work-study coordinator, and an institutional employee. He has taught special education at Syracuse University, Miami University, Portland State University, Lewis & Clark College, and Nova Scotia's Acadia University.

He has served as a consultant to the President's Committee on Mental Retardation, the U.S. Department of Justice, the Canadian National Institute on Mental Retardation, and the Swedish Institute on Integration.

Dr. Bersani has received several national honors, including The Arc of the U.S. Franklin Smith Award for National Service, the Joseph P. Kennedy Jr. Foundation National Fellowship in Public Policy and Mental Retardation, and the Distinguished Researcher Fellowship of the National Institute on Disability and Rehabilitation Research.

He has traveled to 49 states, 9 Canadian provinces, Australia, Norway, and Sweden, meeting with thousands of self-advocates over the past 20 years.